WALTHER HEISSIG

A Lost Civilization

THE MONGOLS REDISCOVERED

BASIC BOOKS, INC., *Publishers*
NEW YORK

TRANSLATED FROM THE GERMAN BY D. J. S. THOMSON

This edition © Thames and Hudson 1966
© 1964 Econ-Verlag GmbH, Düsseldorf and Vienna
Library of Congress Catalog Card Number: 66–18156
Printed in Great Britain

A Lost Civilization
THE MONGOLS REDISCOVERED

CONTENTS

LIST OF ILLUSTRATIONS

I · VOICES FROM THE PAST

THE MONGOLS AND THEIR 'SECRET HISTORY'

What images are conjured up in our minds by the word 'Mongols'? We think of the invasion of Russia, Hungary and Silesia by swift-moving armies of wild horsemen, of the bloody battle of Liegnitz in 1241. We remember the name Jenghiz Khan and with it the legend of terror with which he was associated. The fear aroused in our forefathers seven hundred years ago and more by the stocky horsemen on their small, shaggy horses, horsemen who, they thought, came straight 'ex tartaro' or 'out of hell' – for that is why they changed the name Tatar to Tartar – that same fear still lingers on in our subconscious minds. The chroniclers who wrote in the period following Jenghiz Khan, those who witnessed his warlike exploits, and the medieval historians have all gone out of their way to present him as a cruel conqueror. When the Mongols approached the capital of Northern China in 1214, sixty thousand Chinese maidens flung themselves down from the city walls, according to a Persian source, rather than fall into the hands of the Mongol soldiery. 'The bones of the slaughtered rose mountain-high, the earth was fat with human fat and the rotting corpses gave rise to a plague,' ran one report from Jenghiz Khan's head-quarters in Khwarizm in 1215 following the conquest of North China. Flushed with victory, Jenghiz Khan is said to have exclaimed: 'A man's greatest joy is to conquer his enemies, to drive them before him, to rob them of their possessions, to see their loved ones in tears, to ride their horses and to sleep on the white bellies of their wives and daughters.' The authority for this is again

9

an historian from Asia Minor, one of the conquered, not one of the conquerors. Mohammedan writers, describing the Mongol invasion of Asia Minor, claimed that 'in many places not even dogs and cats survived the invasion of Mongol horsemen'. Subsequent campaigns after Jenghiz Khan's death are described in similar terms.

According to one Russian account of the capture of Ryazan on 21st December 1237, there was 'not a single eye open to weep for the dead'. And another chronicler writes of the fall of Moscow: 'There was nothing to be seen but earth and dust, sand, ashes, many dead bodies lying around and the sacred churches, devastated, orphaned, widowed. The churches mourned for their brethren, most of whom were slain, as a mother mourns for her children.'

The annihilation in 1241 at Liegnitz of the army of German and Polish knights led by the Silesian Duke Heinrich intensified Europe's fear of the Mongols. Canon Roger of Varazdin in Hungary, who managed to escape death at the hands of the Mongols advancing into Hungary, wrote these tragic words in his Carmen Miserabile: 'We found nothing but human corpses and Christian bloodstains on the palace walls and the walls of the churches.' Matthew of Paris echoed the feelings of his European contemporaries when he wrote of the Mongols: 'Swarming like locusts over the face of the earth, they have brought terrible devastation to the eastern countries and have destroyed them with fire and massacre. They are bestial and inhuman, more monsters, who thirst for blood and drink it, than human beings. They know no human laws, no decency, they are wilder than bears' – again the testimony of fugitives who feared further invasions.

Virtually all the sources of information on Jenghiz Khan and his successors are subsequent accounts by Near Eastern, Mohammedan historians. Even the great Chinese history of the Mongol Yüan dynasty, which ruled over China until 1368, was only written after the dynasty had been overthrown by a Chinese national movement. The eighteen Chinese authors, who began their task in 1369, were not exactly friendly disposed towards the Mongols.

WHAT IS KNOWN OF JENGHIZ KHAN?

One wonders what kind of man this really was, who within a few decades forged an empire which stretched from North China to the Volga. There is only one portrait of him extant, which goes back to a fairly early date. It is one of the portraits of Yüan emperors in the Historical Museum in Peking. One must assume that these likenesses of the Mongol emperors and their wives have some historical foundation. Jenghiz Khan is portrayed as an old man with a sparse, white beard. Eye-witness accounts of the campaign in 1222 against Khwarizm in Western Mongolia, the modern Turkestan, describe him as tall and broad-shouldered with thin grey hair and eyes like a cat. This tells us little of his personality. Is there no other memorial to this great man? Here again the answer is in the negative. All attempts to trace his place of burial have been in vain. In the dry and almost barren Ordos region which lies in a great bend of the Hwang Ho (Yellow River), there is a monument and place of sacrifice, the 'Eight White Tents', which for centuries has been dedicated to Jenghiz Khan and which was, in fact, erected around the time of his death in 1227, when four imperial tents were set up at four different places as catafalques in his honour. Since the fifteenth century, when the Ordos tribe settled in the bend of the Hwang Ho, these eight white tents have been places of worship. Four times a year great ceremonial offerings were and still are made. The white double-tent called the 'Palace of Jenghiz' contained a coffin with the alleged mortal remains and relics of Jenghiz Khan. Whatever may have been in that coffin went up in flames during the revolt of Chinese Mohammedans from 1862 to 1877. A historical document called the *Red Chronicle*, which was said to be very old, was also destroyed.

WORSHIP OF RELICS WITHOUT RELICS

In 1939, when there seemed a danger that Japanese troops might cross the Hwang Ho into the Ordos province and capture the

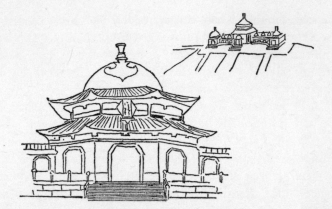

Main entrance of the museum at Echen Horo. Above: Japanese design for Wang-yeh-miao

sacred tents of Jenghiz Khan, the Chiang Kai-shek government moved the tents to safety in an underground temple at Lanchow. This prize having eluded them, the Japanese tried during the Second World War to win the sympathy of the Mongols by exploiting their reverence for the relics in the 'Eight White Tents'. They planned to build a Jenghiz Khan temple in a mixed Sino-Japanese style at Wang-yeh-miao, which was then the administrative capital of the occupied Hsingan provinces in Eastern Mongolia. A propaganda placard at that time ran as follows: 'We wish to build a great temple at a selected spot in Wang-yeh-miao before the Khan mountains, where the guardian spirit of the holy founder of the Mongol dynasty will be deeply revered, so that it may become a shining example for the creation of a united Greater Asia and an enduring bulwark in the north-west of Greater Asia . . .' At that time the Japanese were hoping to combine something of the ancient Mongol Jenghiz Khan cult with a new cult based on the Japanese Bushido. Japan's defeat brought to an end these plans and the construction of a Jenghiz Khan temple at Wang-yeh-miao in Eastern Mongolia.

Following the Communist victory in China, the Red Chinese were faced with the problem, what to do with the relics and tents from the old Jenghiz Khan shrine, which had been moved to Lanchow. The Chinese Communist government was well aware that camp-fire dreams of a great Mongol empire under a new Jenghiz were still very much alive among the Mongols, even if their camp-fires were now burning in co-operatives.

So in 1955 at Echen Horo in the Ordos region, where the Mongols had traditionally worshipped Jenghiz Khan and where the 'Eight White Tents' had stood until 1939, the foundations of a new shrine were laid. The 'Museum House', as it is officially called, covers an area of 2,400 square metres. It bears a striking resemblance to the design publicized by the Japanese for Wang-yeh-miao. Over the gateway leading into the dome-shaped main building is the inscription 'Jenghiz Khan's Palace', to right and left are flat-roofed chambers leading to further domed buildings. In the connecting chambers are the old tents with the Jenghiz Khan relics, while the lateral buildings with their fifty-foot high domes contain the banners, the 'black' and the 'spotted' standard. On 8th April 1956, in the presence of high Mongol and Chinese Communist dignitaries, the memorial-museum was officially opened in a ceremony of dedication to Jenghiz Khan, which was entirely in accordance with ancient ritual. Four times a year since then the traditional site of Echen Horo has been the scene of solemn sacrificial rites in honour of Jenghiz Khan. Unlike the Mongolian People's Republic, which for years has lain under the Russian yoke, Red China has not anathematized Jenghiz Khan as a feudal oppressor of the Mongols but has accepted the prevailing Mongol view and taken account of Mongol national pride.

RECORDS OF THE PAST

If the historian is to find out what the past was really like, if he is to write its history, then he must have sources. Contemporary observers of the Mongol invasion of eastern Europe wrote their accounts of it in Latin or in Russian, while the subject peoples, such as the Persians, Armenians and Georgians, wrote in their respective languages. China, the country which had the closest and longest experience of the Mongols, has many works on them in Chinese: official histories, chronicles and personal accounts.

And what of the Mongols themselves?

For many years it was generally held that the Mongols had no historical records and no literature of their own. Throughout the last century there was only one known Mongol history: the chronicle which the Ordos prince Saghang Sechen had written in 1662. But during the past sixty years the picture has changed. More and more Mongol manuscripts containing historical data have been discovered.

During periods of unrest and war it is always difficult to preserve records of the past. The history of the Mongols is a particularly warlike one. Nevertheless it is becoming increasingly clear that the Mongols produced more historical works than any other Central Asian people.

Much, of course, has disappeared, has been forgotten, burnt or wantonly destroyed or simply found its way into ignorant hands.

In 1742 the Manchu Emperor, Chien Lung, decreed that all books in the possession of Mongol families should be collected and brought to Peking. The decree was primarily intended to cover religious books, but a great many Mongol historical works must also have disappeared into the palace archives in Peking.

An eye-witness account of the Boxer Rebellion in 1900 gives some idea of the large number of forgotten literary and historical works and treasures in the temples and summer palaces which were destroyed through ignorance or vindictiveness. Riding northward towards the Great Wall, he and his horsemen finally came upon one of the 'little mountain burgs, with great thick outer walls and tall watch-towers, where, in olden days, the marauders from the Mongolian plains were held in check until help could be summoned from the country below'.

The report continues:

'At the very top of one tower we discovered a locked door, and beating it in amidst showers of dust we penetrated a room such as a witch of medieval Europe would dearly have loved. Nothing but cobwebs, dust, flapping grey-yellow paper and decay. It was immensely old.

'And yct we found something. For there were some chests hidden away, and prizing these open we discovered great books of yellow parchment, so old and so sodden, that they fell to pieces as soon as one touched them. They were in some Mongol or Manchu script. They, too, were centuries old. But there was something else; a great discovery. Beneath the books we found helmets, inlaid with silver and gold, and embellished with black velvet trappings studded with little iron knobs. There were also complete suits of chain armour. It seemed to us, in that early morning, that we were suddenly discovering the Middle Ages, perhaps even the Dark Ages. For these things were not even early Manchu; they were Mongol . . .'

He does not mention, however, what became of the decayed historical documents. It seemed at the time much more important to transport the ancient armour to Europe, where it would grace the walls of some country house.

In 1870 the Chinese Mohammedans in the north-west provinces of China, the Tungans, rebelled. Plundering and looting, they also invaded the Mongol area, Ordos. They attacked Echen Horo, the shrine of the Jenghiz Khan cult, burning a chest which contained not only some strands of Jenghiz Khan's hair and his stockings but also two ancient chronicles in the old Mongol script. A Buryat scholar, who went to the Ordos province in 1910 to search for old Mongol historical scripts, was told of the incident by the Darchats, the guardians of the Jenghiz Khan shrine.

In 1927 Mongol scholars had learned that a copy of one of the historical works which had been destroyed, the *Red Chronicle*, was in existence in the Ala Shan mountains and was in the possession of the native Urat Mongols. They searched and actually found a manuscript. But on the return journey they ran into a group of Chinese soldiers near the town of Paotow, led by General Feng Yu-hsiang who bore the self-adopted and sadly misplaced title of 'the Christian general'. The Chinese soldiers burned the irreplaceable historical work together with another very old work, which was written in almost indecipherable Uigur-Mongolian script and was called *The golden riddles of Jenghiz Khan*.

This list of works which were lost could be prolonged almost indefinitely. The Mongols today are taking a lively interest in their national literature. Fresh treasures are still being unearthed in the ruins of old monasteries, in chests buried in sand-dunes. During the short summer months scholars and book-lovers in the Mongolian People's Republic wander through the thinly-populated steppes looking for manuscripts. One Mongol scholar alone during a brief summer expedition in 1960 brought three and a half truck-loads of old manuscripts back to the capital, Ulan Bator. F. Bischoff, whose father had been for many years Austrian Minister in Moscow until his death in 1960 and who travelled through the Mongolian People's Republic in 1957, describes how Mongol scholars spend their annual holidays searching for old literary documents. In the course of his journey he spent a few days on the Three Lakes 'Gurban Nor', 'at a place in north-eastern Mongolia, traditionally regarded as Jenghiz Khan's birthplace, where the Mongolian government has built a picturesque rest-house for its officials. Mr Delig,' reports Bischoff, 'a publicist in Ulan Bator and a bibliophile, was our next-door neighbour. He was spending his leave buying books from livestock-breeders and former Buddhist monks. He washed the pieces of cloth, in which the books were wrapped, and hung them to dry on the line next to our hut. This was how we became aware that he was a collector. Our curiosity gave us no peace. But, by the time we felt bold enough to ask Mr Delig if we might see his treasures, he was already preparing to leave and had packed his books. In face of our obvious disappointment, however, Mr Delig was kind enough to unpack a few of his acquisitions. . . .'

There is no sign as yet that this store of hidden treasure is nearing exhaustion. Mongolia is passing through the same phase in the discovery of its ancient literary and historical records as Germany passed through in the lifetime of the Brothers Grimm: the collectors' period.

Voices from the Past

THE GOLDEN BOOK

When the learned Jew, Rashid-ad-Din, Vizir of the Mongol ruler of Persia Gazan (1295–1304), was ordered to write the history of the ruler's Mongol forefathers, he was not allowed to draw upon the official chronicles of the Persian ruling house. These were regarded as secret and were only accessible to members of the ruling house. They were written in the Mongol script and consisted, so Rashid-ad-Din assures us, of a great many single, unrelated fragments. The *Altan debter* or *Book of the golden (family)* was kept so secret, that not even the historian commissioned by the ruler himself was allowed to see it. No one, apart from the members of a Mongol tribe, which was charged with the protection of the *Golden Book*, and apart from members of the royal family, has ever seen this ancient historical work.

That was true in 1310 and it is still true, for the manuscript of the *Altan debter* has never been found to this day.

Another family chronicle in the Mongol script, which was also kept hidden from the eyes of the profane, was nevertheless consulted by a commission of Chinese scholars, which compiled an official history of the Mongol dynasty after its fall in the fourteenth century. This we know, because the work is referred to in the Chinese history. But again no copy of the chronicle appears to have survived. Thus there were Mongol records dating back to the time of Jenghiz Khan and his sons, but they seem to have been lost.

Five hundred years passed before anything new became known of the Secret Chronicle of Jenghiz Khan's family. During the last century, when the Russian Orthodox Church made a deliberate effort to convert the Chinese to its form of Christianity, a 'religious mission' was set up in Peking. Some of its members had specialized in the languages of the Chinese Empire and they carried out valuable research and produced highly competent translations of Chinese historical works. One of the learned priests who lived just over a century ago in the great court quarter in the north-east of

Peking, where the Russian religious mission was situated near the great Buddhist temple of Yung-Ho-Kung, was the Archimandrite Palladius. He was a scholar with a penchant for old Chinese books. One day a Chinese work fell into his hands, which contained a detailed history of Jenghiz Khan. Palladius translated it in 1866. Another six years passed and fate again placed a manuscript in the hands of the Russian Orthodox dignitary, which was to throw an entirely new light on Jenghiz Khan and his exploits. In 1872 Palladius bought a manuscript which contained, transcribed into Chinese characters, the text of the early Mongol chronicle, to which Rashid-ad-Din had tried in vain to gain access. As we are told at the end of the chronicle, it was 'concluded when we camped with the palace . . . in the seventh month of the Year of the Rat (1240) for the meeting of the great Imperial Diet'.

Palladius had acquired the manuscript from the library of a Chinese bibliophile. He soon realized what priceless historical material it was, but he was also under no illusion as to the difficulties involved in recovering this treasure from the obscurity of early Mongol history. For this history of the Mongols was not written in Mongolian; Chinese characters gave a phonetic rendering of the original.

Chinese characters can be employed to reproduce any language in the world. Thus Jenghiz was translated as follows:

成 = Ch'eng

吉 = Chi

思 = Ssu

and in the same way every word in the original Mongolian text was translated into Chinese symbols. Palladius set to work to reproduce the original but he was unable to complete the task. In

1878 he returned to Europe and he died in Marseilles. His work found its way into the hands of the Russian Mongolist A. Pozdneev, who published the first chapter of the reconstruction. Only one copy of this ever reached a western country. Then the curtain dropped on the history of Jenghiz Khan. For years rumour had it that Palladius's reconstruction of the Mongolian text had been stolen by a student and disappeared. But when Pozdneev died Palladius's reconstruction was found in a corner of his desk in Leningrad. To this day, however, it has not been published. To satisfy his own ambition, Pozdneev imposed a personal ban on any further research for several decades.

VINDICATION OF THE MING DYNASTY

One sometimes has the impression that historical discoveries and revelations have to mature slowly before they burst upon an astonished world. Once the point of maturity has been reached, nothing can be done to prevent the news breaking. It breaks of itself, regardless of whether the world is ready for it or not.

Palladius had barely brought that chronicle from the early Mongol period into the light of day, when the Japanese historian Naito had the good fortune in 1899 to discover another manuscript of the same work, yet another rendering of the original Mongolian in Chinese characters. And before long, in 1907, the text appeared in print.

The title of it was *Monghol-un niguca tobciyan* – The *Secret History of the Mongols*. When one compared the information it contained with that given by Rashid-ad-Din and other Mohammedan historians of the fourteenth century, whose chief source was the *Golden Book*, the two were found to be identical. So the *Secret History*, the chronicle of the deeds of Jenghiz Khan and his sons which had been kept secret from the people, had been found.

But how had the most important work by the Mongols on their own history come to be written in Chinese characters?

Contrary to the general belief that the Chinese rebels, after driving the Mongols out of China in 1368, destroyed everything they could find in Mongolian script, the Chinese in fact cultivated and developed Mongol traditions. After 1368 thousands of Mongol soldiers went over to the Ming, the new rulers on China's throne. The remainder of Asia right across to the borders of Europe had become as accustomed to using the Mongolian language as we have become today to the use of English as a language at international congresses, conferences and meetings.

The Mongolian language thus gained rather than lost ground with the advent of the Ming dynasty. In 1407 the Ming Emperor in Peking set up an Institute for Foreign Languages, which specialized in Mongolian and encouraged it. In 1452 Chinese diplomatic notes to the West were still being written in Mongolian.

It was during this period that the *Secret History of the Mongols*, the early history of Jenghiz Khan and his son Ogotai, was transcribed from the Mongolian into Chinese characters and was included in the great collection of classical literature of the Ming Emperor Yung Lo. At that time the Chinese were a tolerant people.

COMPETITION AMONG SCHOLARS

The new edition of the Chinese version of the *Secret History*, which the Chinese scholar Ye Te-Hui had produced in 1907 and which was based on the early-fifteenth-century script, would in turn have attracted no attention, if the French scholar Paul Pelliot had not commented on it. Only then did scholars begin to compete for the honour of producing the original, which had been written in 1240 in the reign of Jenghiz Khan's son Ogotai. For a time it was assumed that Pelliot would bring out his version of the original Mongolian text with a translation, but years passed and nothing appeared.

Finally the German scholar Erich Haenisch, who was then Professor of Sinology at the University of Berlin, set to work and in 1940, after he had published his version of the original text, his translation of the ancient chronicle appeared. As a result, much more is known today of Jenghiz Khan and his life. The *Secret History*, which is half chronicle, half epic, records the exploits of the man who transformed the Mongols from a tribe into a world power and who subdued half the known universe. Since then the German has been followed by Russian, Japanese, Turkish and English translations.

WHAT BECAME OF THE ORIGINAL?

The raw material on which Haenisch, Pelliot and a number of scholars since then have worked was a phonetic rendering of a Mongolian text, which had been put together some time before 1407. But the existence of the original remained a mystery which haunted Mongolists in the 'twenties and 'thirties. Was there, in fact, such a thing as an original in Mongolian script? Or had the text been put together in Chinese characters in the first instance, simply reproducing the individual syllables of Mongolian words?

In 1929 the Mongols on the Scientific Committee of the Mongolian People's Republic discovered a manuscript, which bore the title *Golden Short History*. A close study of this manuscript showed that more than two-thirds of it was a literal reproduction of large parts of the *Secret History*. Its author was a Buddhist monk, who around 1655 had compiled this work from various old chronicles.

The Mongols sent a photostatic copy of the new text to Paul Pelliot in Paris. Pelliot mentioned it in subsequent publications of his own but he never published it.

In 1936 Erich Haenisch made a special journey to Mongolia to look for the original text of the *Secret History*. He spoke to Buddhist priests and shepherds, penetrating to the most desolate parts of the country. 'I had pitched my tent on the wooded mountain Bogdo Ola on the south bank of the Tula, opposite the town,' he wrote. 'My boy, a Buryat and former Cossack, saw to my needs. In the mornings I fetched water from a nearby stream for washing and making tea. At night I could hear the wolves howling in the woods. But I spent the evenings in the tent of a Russian colleague talking to Mongolian lamas. Did the land of the Germani also have mountain spirits like those in Mongolia, which appeared as wild horses or wild white camels? The Bogdo Ola had such a spirit, which took the form of a wild ox. It had been seen many times . . .' What Haenisch did not find on this journey was the original manuscript of the *Secret History*. Nor was he shown the *Golden Short History*. 'In Urga' (the old name for Ulan Bator), he wrote, 'where I spent over a month in the Institute of Science, sat almost every day in the library, held every printed work and every manuscript in my hands and, above all, searched for the *Secret History*, it was thought advisable not to tell me of the recent discovery of a Mongolian manuscript; presumably out of loyalty to our colleague in Paris, to whom a photostatic copy had just been sent.'

The Mongols, however, did not keep silent very long. In 1937, a year after Haenisch's visit to Ulan Bator, they published the newly-discovered manuscript of the Altan tobchi, the *Golden Short History*. No one could foresee that, due to the outbreak of the Second World War and post-war delays, copies of this work would not reach Western scholars until about 1950. Since then it has been established that this chronicle, written in 1655, contains transcriptions of the *Secret History* which in many instances are much more comprehensive than the Chinese rendering in 1368. Thanks to the magnificent work done by Erich Haenisch, the *Secret History* is no longer a secret. But in 1655 there was an even more extensive Mongolian original, whose whereabouts today remains a mystery. All the secrets of the *Secret History* have not yet been revealed. The original manuscript may still be lying somewhere in the abandoned ruins or sand-dunes of Mongolia.

THE BLUE CHRONICLE

More than twenty years ago I arrived at the small border-town of Kailu to start on a journey through the part of Eastern Mongolia inhabited by the Naiman, Aru-Horchin, Bagharin and Djarut tribes. In one of the long streets of mud-brick houses and seemingly interminable walls I came upon the 'Eastern Mongolian Literary Society', which published Mongolian literature and was run by the Mongolian nationalist Bökekeshik.

Amongst the books, which the Mongols had printed in cheap lithograph editions in an attempt to promote their own modern literature as well as literary works from the past, I noticed a pile of twelve books, beautifully bound in violet-blue silk. It was an edition of the Inchanashi *Blue Chronicle*. The twelve volumes, which must have totalled some two thousand pages, were prefaced by an account of the origins of the work. The book, though printed on cheap newsprint and so in parts difficult to read, was fairly expensive, but I managed to buy two copies. As far as I know, these are almost the only copies of this edition to have reached the West.

Having made my purchase, I hurried back to the inn near the city gate, where I was staying. I tore open the parcel containing the two thick silk-bound volumes, pulled out the two ivory pins which, as is usual in China, held the blue silk wrapping in place, and took out the first volume. Then I began to read and compare the *Blue Chronicle*. In 1929 a Horchin-Mongol by the name of Temgetü had published twelve chapters of a *Blue Chronicle* but without giving any indication who was the author of this rather romantic account of the youth of the first Mongol ruler, Jenghiz Khan. There was also no hint as to the period in which the work had been written. Temgetü interspersed ancient Mongolian customs with creations of his own, highly colourful imagination, quoted passages from old epic poems on Jenghiz Khan from other Mongolian sources, and described the life and times of Jenghiz Khan against a nineteenth-century background. He had chosen for this Mongolian work the structure and idiom of a Chinese novel. I now discovered, on reading the *Blue Chronicle*, that this torso tallied with the first twelve chapters. But then I opened the volume containing Inchanashi's biographical notes on the history of the work.

POLAND
LITHUANIA
Novgorod
HUNGARY
MOSCOW
WALLACHIA
Kiev
Dnieper
Oka
BULGARIA
UKRAINE
Volga
Kama
Bulgar
URAL MTS.
SIBE
Istanbul
Tyumen
Tobol
BLACK SEA
Don
Rostov
Azov
Stalingrad
Ural
KAZAKHSTAN
Irtysh
Astrakhan
CAUCASUS
CASPIAN SEA
Tbilisi
Aral Sea
Kzyl-Orda
L. Balk
Tabriz
Kungrad
WEST TURKESTAN
Ili
Cairo
Jerusalem
Resht
Otrar
Syr Darya
Kash
Baghdad
Bukhara
Samarkand
TRANSOXANIA
IRAN
Karshi
Amu (OXUS)
Ghazni
boundaries of the Mong
Western   and   southern
Indus
Delhi
INDI

0   500   1000
Miles

K.P.S.

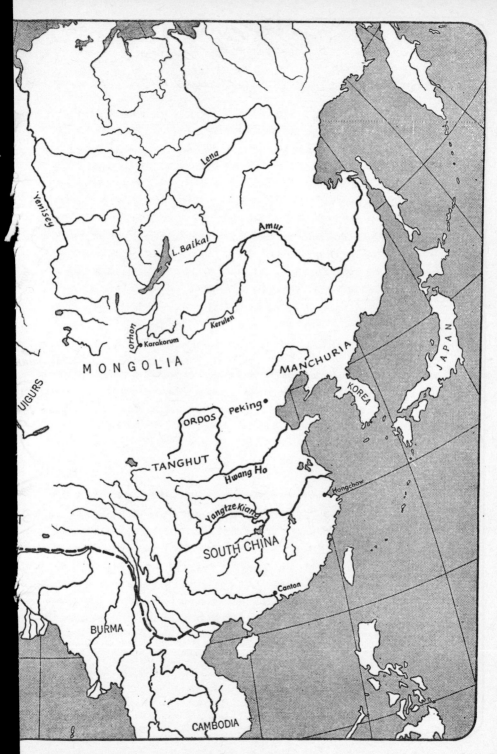

The Mongol Empire in the thirteenth century

FIVE-AND-A-HALF CART-LOADS OF OLD BOOKS

Inchanashi describes in detail how his great work was completed. Above all he admits that he had grave doubts as to the authenticity of his sources. His critical approach is not unlike that adopted by the French historians of the age of enlightenment. At the same time it is clear that, despite this critical approach, this historic work is not a work of history. What Inchanashi succeeded in writing was a historical novel, which drew upon historical sources only for background detail, sources which the author tried so hard to authenticate. For the rest he chose the literary form of the Chinese novel. At the beginning of each chapter, for example, is a poem and at the end of each chapter is a reference to the following one with a promise to the reader that he will be enlightened on any points that may still be obscure. Each chapter is prefaced by a brief résumé of its contents.

As Inchanashi himself is at pains to explain, illness, personal problems, the death of children and finally the loss of his property prevented him from pursuing his great ambition, which was to complete a history of the Mongol rule in China in the twelfth and thirteenth centuries started by his father Wangdchinbala. Only when these problems of everyday life had been overcome was he able to settle down to his great task. True to the tradition of Chinese scholarship, he retired to his study in his country estate. There he took up the *Blue Chronicle* where his father had left off, when he decided to do his duty as a soldier in the Opium War. Inchanashi describes how, despite considerable misgivings, he decided to retain the literary form employed by his father in the first eight chapters, in other words to imitate the narrative form of the Chinese novel. This means that Wangdchinbala, a Mongol nobleman and official, was, even in the first half of the last century, sufficiently familiar with this literary form that it seemed to him the only appropriate form to adopt for a comprehensive and graphic presentation of Mongol history. And indeed, as we know from other contemporary Mongolian translations of Chinese novels, the Mongol upper class had already become avid readers of the Chinese novel in translation and special editions. Around 1813, an anonymous Mongol translator assures us, almost all important Chinese novels were being read in translation by the Mongols. At that time they were prepared to concede that these Chinese products of narrative literature, and particularly their more lyrical passages, were superior to original Mongolian works. During the long winter evenings translations of Chinese novels were read aloud in the princes' palaces and in the country houses of Eastern Mongolian nobles. Wandering story-tellers included them in their repertoires; at temple festivals and markets and by the camp-fires of families they met on their way, they would retain excerpts and whole chapters from these translations night after night. As time went on, they embellished the translated material with passages from old Mongolian epics. And eventually they started involving characters from the popular Chinese novels in new Mongolian adventures. In particularly dramatic passages they made use of alliteration and the alliterative rhyme so common in the old Mongolian epic poetry. Gradually a whole new history was poured into an old epic form, till finally the Chinese novel, or rather what still remained of it, became a new Mongolian epic. And even today new epics of this kind are still being created. The work of the epic poet Padshai, a middle-aged man who lives in Inner Mongolia, is example of this development.

Inchanashi was also a connoisseur of these Mongolian translations of Chinese novels. He even played an important part in fostering the spread of the Chinese novel among the Mongols, since before he settled down to work on the *Blue Chronicle*, he himself had written two Mongolian novels. These were also adaptations of well-known Chinese novels. He took both characters and setting from the famous Chinese novel of the Ming period, *The dream of the red chamber*. Inchanashi merely drew upon his imagination to embroil them in fresh adventures. Only when he had completed *One terrace high* and *The red hall in which one weeps*, both continuations of the Chinese novel mentioned above, did he set to work on the *Blue Chronicle*. And what he did was to take the official Chinese annals of the Mongol dynasty (1260–1368) and clothe this skeleton of dry but historically accurate facts in living flesh, which derived partly from his own imagination, partly from a mass of material culled from other but primarily Mongolian historical works, collections of poems and stories. There is ample confirmation in the work itself that this was the procedure he adopted. On quite a number of occasions he actually questions the authenticity of his Mongolian historical sources.

At that time, in 1941, no other Mongolian historical work had been heard of, apart from the *Secret History of the Mongols*, an epic account of the rise and rule of Jenghiz Khan, which was written in 1240, an anonymous chronicle called the *Golden History* and the *Precious Chronicle*, written in 1662 by Saghang Sechen. This last work was translated into German in 1829 by Isaak Jakob Schmidt and since then it had been generally assumed that any further search for Mongolian historical works was fruitless. Scholars resigned themselves to the conclusion that, if any other historical works had ever existed, they had been lost. But here was Inchanashi assuring me that he had been able to draw on many other Mongolian historical works and chronicles. He quotes from and criticizes them.

The day I read Inchanashi's description of how he sorted out 'five-and-a-half cart-loads' of old Mongolian, Tibetan and Manchurian books from his late father's library with a view to continuing the work on the *Blue Chronicle*, I felt that my fondest hope and ambition might yet be fulfilled, namely to establish that a Mongolian literature of substantial proportions did exist.

SEARCH FOR THE ORIGINAL MANUSCRIPT

I was now extremely anxious, before I left Kailu to continue my journey, to find out from Bökekeshik, the President of the 'Eastern Mongolian Literary Society', where the original manuscript of the *Blue Chronicle* had come from. If it was still in Kailu, I wanted to see it. Unfortunately my conversation with this industrious and ardent champion of an independent Mongolian literature produced no positive result. While he was still a student in the early 1920s, he had started his publishing-house with a group of like-minded Mongol students at Peking University. The object was to provide the Mongols with printed literature and educational books in their own language, in order to counteract the influence of the Chinese language and culture. So he was keenly interested in my inquiry. But he was not able to tell me much that I did not already know. The original manuscript, it seemed, had been returned a long time ago to its owner, a Harachin Mongol, whose present whereabouts were unknown. The manuscript had apparently been far from complete. The printed edition merely represented what had so far come to light of the original.

I then learned that the *Blue Chronicle* had covered much more ground and that, while no one had seen the entire work, the information had been handed down among the Tumat and Harachin Mongols, that Inchanashi had written a history of the Mongols up to the beginning of the Manchu dynasty in 1644. If this information was correct, it meant that somewhere or other there must be an original manuscript of at least another two thousand pages, if not more. But Bökekeshik and his colleagues had no idea where it might be. It was not that they were not willing to tell me. They simply did not know any more. There may also have been an element of injured pride. Why should anyone be searching for an old, dilapidated original manuscript, when they had spent thousands of hours producing a beautifully-written and neatly-printed lithographic edition? It must really have been a laborious job setting up every page carefully and in beautiful Mongolian script on the lithograph stone and then pulling proofs of each page several hundred times by hand. Printing machines and Mongolian type for book-printing were still rare in Mongolia at that time and still are. Even today editions of old works are frequently written out by hand and photostatically reproduced. In Mongolia the practice of copying books by hand has continued much longer than in other countries. Hence the large number of manuscript copies of one and the same work, which can be found in a library. This is an indication of the popularity of the book. But when one finds a manuscript of a book, this does not mean that it is written in the handwriting of the author or translator. Some anonymous person has made a copy. Schoolchildren write out copies of their favourite works. So hardly any of the manuscripts are originals, and the age of the paper and the style of handwriting are the only pointers one has to the age of the manuscript. Sometimes an added clue is given by the owner's seal.

The *Blue Chronicle* was immensely popular with the Mongols. I came across it frequently and in the most unlikely places – a shepherd's tent, the miserable mud hut of a Mongol who had abandoned the nomadic life, the guest-house of a Buddhist monastery in mid-winter – where a Mongol would either be reading it alone in some corner or reading it aloud to a whole group of people. The few Mongolian newspapers that exist have all printed parts of it. But the immense popularity of the *Blue Chronicle* was only partly due to the wide circulation of Bökekeschik's printed edition. There were a great many hand-written copies of the work, which had been made shortly after the turn of the century. The work was known and loved by Mongols in the farthest corners of Inner Mongolia, in the Ordos bend of the Yellow River just as much as in Chahar or in the Soviet-dominated Mongolian People's Republic in Northern Mongolia. The political revolution in China and the Communist régime have also brought many changes in the Mongolian areas which form part of Red China. But the popularity of Inchanashi and his *Blue Chronicle* has not been affected. As recently as 1959 a beautifully printed edition appeared in China and both Inchanashi's novels have also been printed. If one is prompted to ask why this literary work has retained its appeal, the answer is that, apart from its high literary quality, Inchanashi's work satisfies, as no other work can, the desire of the Mongols for evidence of their former greatness and bolsters their self-esteem. And that was precisely Inchanashi's intention: to wean the Mongols away from their sense of bitterness, resignation and frustration and encourage them to look towards a new future. He had already overcome his father's escapism. In consequence the *Blue Chronicle* emerged as a work which during the past fifty years has fired the most diverse political groups among the Mongols with enthusiasm and given them a feeling of self-confidence.

THE GREAT DISCOVERY

At first my search for Inchanashi's original manuscript was entirely unproductive, although there were times when I seemed to be very near my goal. There was the occasion when a rumour reached me that the complete manuscript of the *Blue Chronicle* was in a monastery on the Wu-t'ai-shan, one of the sacred mountains of Buddhism. But that was during the war and the part of the holy mountain on which the monastery lay was in the hands of the 8th Communist army. It was impossible for anyone to get there from the Japanese-occupied area of China. I tried sending Mongols but they failed to get through. Then one day a Mongol came and told me of an old man in the Harachin Banner who had buried a manuscript of the *Blue Chronicle* under his front threshold. Again I sent Mongols out to investigate but again they came back empty-handed. In the meantime the old man had died and his only daughter, who was a semi-idiot and with whom he had shared the house, knew nothing.

Time passed. Then one day I met an old Mongolian bibliophile and scholar, Keshingga, a Horchin Mongol, who looked more like a Chinese scholar who led a secluded life or a government official of the old school than the general picture one has of a Mongol, whose chief occupation is cattle-breeding and who is only really at home in the saddle. Keshingga was in fact employed in some translation and publishing capacity. His sole interest in life was in old Mongolian and Manchurian books. It took me some time to win his confidence and to convince him that he would not be showing his treasures to a mere novice. We spent many hours together talking about Mongolian works and the period that had given birth to them. Naturally I brought the conversation round to the *Blue Chronicle*, in order to hear this connoisseur's views on it. Perhaps he knew something of the whereabouts of the original manuscript? Then one day Keshingga opened a cupboard, rummaged in it and brought out a large package in a blue cloth.

He opened the package. Inside was a bundle of medium-sized books, each bound in blue silk brocade. He handed the top one to me, remarking with a smile that this might interest me. I think the moments of excitement which a scholar experiences in his search for literary works can only be compared with the tension which the hunter feels when he sees something moving in the clearing before him and raises his field-glasses cautiously to ascertain what kind of wild animal is emerging from the forest. Taking great care to curb my impatience and not to arouse the almost morbid mistrust of this bibliophile by snatching the book from him, I took it from his hand and opened it. It was a very beautifully written manuscript. The title was *Blue Chronicle of the rise of the Great Yuan dynasty*.

I looked through volume after volume. There were nine of them altogether, each consisting of about 120 pages. They comprised Chapters 43–72 of the *Blue Chronicle*. Almost every volume contained notes and poems at the beginning, though in some cases they appeared on the end-papers.

MICROFILMS IN THE OPEN AIR

I asked if I might take the manuscript home with me, in order to study it more closely and compare it. Keshingga, it seemed to me, wrestled with his conscience before his natural generosity won the day. Perhaps the thought also crossed his mind that in such troubled times it was just as well to have such a rare manuscript photographed.

In short, after some hesitation he agreed that I should photograph the manuscript. But he would only trust me with one volume at a time. I did not receive the next one until I had returned the one before.

I spent weeks photographing the beautiful manuscript with a Leica. I had no flash bulbs, so all the pictures had to be taken in the open air. It was a blessing that the sky in Northern China and Manchuria is almost always blue and that the sun invariably shines. The only disturbing feature was the west wind that blows constantly from the Mongolian high plateau. The slightest puff of wind was enough to flutter the thin paper of the manuscript, although the movement was not always visible to the naked eye. But the result was that the photograph was not sharp enough and had to be taken again. But at long last the work was completed. Before me lay all nine volumes in microfilm together with enlargements. Now I could settle down to reading through the whole manuscript and comparing it with the printed *Blue Chronicle*.

The introductory remarks, written by Inchanashi himself and his contemporaries, by visitors, by the abbot of a monastery close to where Inchanashi lived, all proved beyond doubt that this was Inchanashi's original manuscript. But only a small proportion of the text of Chapters 47–72, as contained in the slender blue silk volumes of the original manuscript, tallied with the printed version, which was a paraphrase and simplification of the original. A very good adaptation but not the original. The identity of the author, whether it was Inchanashi himself between the years 1872 and 1896 when he died, is something that remains a mystery. Keshingga had acquired this particular section of the original manuscript from the West-Tumat Banner and it was doubtless returned there, after I gave it back to Keshingga.

In the troubled years after 1943 I lost touch with Keshingga and so with the manuscript. I was afraid it might be lost. Imagine my surprise, therefore, when I recently received a biography of Inchanashi, written by a young Inner Mongolian scholar and literary historian, Erdenitoghtachu, and found that it contained not only pictures of the first pages of the original manuscript but also Inchanashi's critical remarks and essays taken from his preface to the manuscript. This proved that this part of the original manuscript had survived the ravages of time and found its way into a library.

But even the young and energetic Mongolian literary explorers of Inner Mongolia have not succeeded in unearthing more of the manuscript than I had the privilege of seeing. The remainder must be found. It is still not known how extensive the first historical novel of the Mongols really was or who was responsible for the version we know today.

REPORTS FROM THE TIME OF JENGHIZ KHAN

We know from Mongol and Chinese histories that Jenghiz Khan had a record kept of his legal judgements. In 1206, after the Mongols had elected him Khan, he gave orders that Shigis Hutuktu, one of his most faithful followers, should record 'all cases of partition and litigation concerning the entire people in a blue book in writing'. It was Jenghiz Khan's wish that anything that was decided in council and 'entered into a book in blue script on white paper' should remain unchanged 'for posterity'.

But so far no trace of the Blue Book has been found. What is clear is that at Jenghiz Khan's court there were people who could write Chinese.

SUBSTITUTES FOR A SCRIPT

The simple Mongol of that period could neither read nor write. So the custom had grown up of issuing all important decrees, orders, bans and instructions in rhyming speech. The rhymes were in the first syllable and were alliterative, that is, two or four lines began with the same letters:

> Cacar mayiqan, cirig-ün Küriyen
> cigeresün ger üd-i barigad
> cirig-ün olan arad-iyan tegün-ü dotura saguljamui
> Qarag u uljitu mayiqan-i qagan-i dagari gulun bariba
> Qabcuud noyad, yekes bagatur tegün-ü dotura sag aduba . . .

'After forming a circle of felt tents
and building huts of straw,
accommodate the ordinary soldier in them.
Build tents with black ornaments at the edges for the
bowmen and great fighters to move into . . .'

This is an example of an oral instruction to soldiers on how to build a field-camp. The alliteration is designed as an aid to memory. The procedure is the same as in the many rhyming verses one learns at school as a means of memorizing important dates or grammatical rules.

Orders given by subordinate troop-leaders were not in writing but in rhyme. This also had the advantage that military information could not fall so easily into the hands of the enemy. The dead could not speak and the living, under torture, could only reproduce the oral message and sometimes not even that. Jenghiz Khan's utterances and words of counsel, which were to serve subsequent generations of rulers as guides to action, were also handed down, to begin with, by word of mouth. On the hunt or on the march they were sung as 'saddle songs', with the result that later, in the seventeenth and eighteenth centuries, they could still be recorded in writing with little or no distortion. Right up to the eighteenth century, messages, in time of war, were sent across the steppes both in writing and in rhymed speech, the latter to be passed on only in cases of emergency.

Then there were signal-arrows. As different arrows were designed to convey different meanings, there was no need to write or speak. Amongst the Mongolian epics is the Geser Khan song, which describes how Geser Khan is given the food of forgetfulness by his beautiful wife Arula. He no longer thinks of his friends and companions. In order to remind him of them, a white magic arrow of one of his companions is shot into Geser Khan's palace with a message attached. When he sees the arrow, he exclaims: 'Ah! is not this the arrow of my noble friend Dchasa?' and he remembers his warriors.

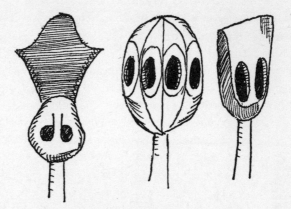

Mongol whistling arrows

Another historic legend recalls how in 1675 Ligdan Khan's grandson, Burni Wang of the Chahar tribe, who was in danger of being captured by an advancing Manchu army, dispatched an arrow to alert his vassal Garma. 'Even as he shot an arrow from his tent,' the story goes, 'so within a second the arrow dropped on the table in front of Garma, who was drinking tea. When he picked it up and looked at it, the message it conveyed to him was: "This is the Prince's arrow; the great army is coming".' Whereupon Garma called his men to arms.

A BORROWED SCRIPT

But no State can be founded and still less maintained without some use of a script. Jenghiz Khan gave instructions that the Uigur script should be used by the Mongols. The script of this Turkish people was well-suited to Mongolian words. The Uigur counsellors and scribes, who after the voluntary submission of the Uigurs in the oases of Eastern Turkestan in Western Mongolia in 1206, had served Jenghiz Khan and the Mongols, found no great difficulty in employing their ancient script, when they had to record something for the Mongols. In the first instance, however, it had not been an Uigur script at all, for the Uigurs had acquired this right-to-left manner of writing from the Soghdians, a Persian people, who in their turn had taken it from the Aramaeans. So the Mongolian script had its origins about a thousand years before Christ.

To begin with, the Mongols, or rather the Uigur scribes who were in Mongolian service, employed the Uigur script without

The Jenghiz Khan stone of 1225
in Uigur-Mongolian script

modifications. They introduced only one decisive innovation. From now on they no longer wrote horizontally from right to left but vertically from top to bottom. Probably the influence of the horizontal Chinese script was responsible for this.

Tradition has it that the first use of the Uigur alphabet was made in Mongolia in 1204 and Jenghiz Khan is said to have given instructions shortly after, that 'the heir to the throne and the princes' were to learn to write in the Uigur script. Nothing has survived of these early writing-exercises by the Mongols. At least nothing has been found up till now. The earliest known specimen of the new Uigur-Mongolian script is a stone which was found near Nerchinsk on the Russo-Mongolian border. It dates back to the year 1225. Inscribed in the elongated characters of the Uigur-Mongolian script is a tribute paid by Jenghiz Khan to one of his great bowmen Yisünke. At the time when Jenghiz Khan had mobilized his nation of warriors to fight against the Mohammedans of Turkestan, Yisünke shot an arrow a distance of 'three hundred and thirty-five paces'.

The adopted script of the Mongols continued in use for centuries. With all its shortcomings, it was nevertheless employed by all Mongols until 1649. Then Rabchamba Jaya Pandita (1599–1662),

West Mongolian script

who came of a noble family from the Koshut tribe in Western Mongolia and had become a Buddhist priest, devised a new script, which is better suited to his native dialect in Western Mongolia. He called it 'toto usüg', the 'clear script'. In this new script the Jaya Pandita proved to be a proficient and prolific translator. In the twelve years that passed between the discovery of the 'clear' script and his death, he translated 170 works from Tibetan into Western Mongolian. During the same period his closest collaborators have been credited with a further twenty-four translations.

The 'clear, lucid' script is still used by the Mongols in Tien Shan and on the Koko Nor in China. The Volga Kalmucks employed it right up to the 1930s, when, under Russian pressure, they had to adopt the Cyrillic characters of the Russian script. But the other Mongols continued to use the old Uigur-Mongolian script. There was, of course, a marked difference between the written word and its pronunciation in the various dialects, more marked than in any other language. Not even in English is the disparity between the written word and its pronunciation so great as between Mongolian written in the old script and spoken Mongolian.

This was the main reason why since 1937 a determined effort has been made in the Mongolian People's Republic to modernize the Mongolian script and to bring the spoken and the written word closer together. A decisive factor in formulating this policy was undoubtedly the desire to bind the Mongols of the Mongolian People's Republic more closely to the Russian culture. Since 1947 the Russian alphabet has been in use in the Mongolian People's Republic, supplemented by a few additional letters. The written language is the language spoken by the inhabitants of the Mongolian People's Republic.

The antiquated orthography of the old script has been officially abandoned. Anyone learning to read and write learns the 'new' script, which is similar to the Russian script. The old Uigur-Mongolian script, however, continues to be used in private life, for it is a relic of the past to which a number of people are still devoted and which has not completely died out.

 АХ ДҮҮ ГРИММ НАР

ЗОРИГТ ОЁДОЛЧИН

'The brave little tailor' of the Brothers Grimm, Ulan Bator, 1952

CULTURAL IRREDENTA IN SCRIPT

Although since 1950 there has been a strong movement in those parts of Inner Mongolia which remained in Red China to introduce, with slight modifications, the Russian Cyrillic characters as used in the Mongolian People's Republic, the old Uigur-Mongolian vertical script has nevertheless remained. The first text-books for the teaching of the new Cyrillic alphabet had already been printed and distributed, when it was unanimously decided at a conference that the old script should be retained in Inner Mongolia.

So all publications in Inner Mongolia, including ten newspapers, are printed in the old characters. Editions of works, which had previously appeared in modern Russian characters in the Mongolian People's Republic, are described as 'translations' in the Inner Mongolian Autonomous Republic.

II FROM PEKING TO MOSCOW

QUARREL OVER THE EMPEROR'S RELICS

The unveiling of a thirty-foot-high monument in Deliün boldog, reputed to be Jenghiz Khan's birthplace, on 31st May 1962 marked the climax of the eighth-centenary celebrations of Jenghiz Khan's birth in the Mongolian People's Republic.

Almost immediately after there were great celebrations in Red China in front of the 'Museum building' containing the Jenghiz Khan relics in Echen Horo. On 16th June 1962 some thirty thousand people gathered to pay tribute to the memory of the great Mongol ruler.

The Russians, who had maintained a discreet silence in face of this revival of the Jenghiz Khan cult by their satellite, the Mongolian People's Republic, felt compelled to protest against this Chinese tribute to the dead Mongol ruler. Leading Russian historians and experts on Mongolia such as Ivan Maisky and L. V. Cherepnin suddenly attacked Jenghiz Khan as a symbol of reaction and condemned his glorification.

The Mongolian People's Republic took the hint. The impressive stamps which had been printed for the eighth-centenary celebrations disappeared unobtrusively. Rather less quiet and unobtrusive was the disappearance in September 1962 of Temürochir, a member of the Mongolian Revolutionary People's Party and President of the Society for Mongolian-Soviet Friendship, from his post.

In August 1962 the leading daily newspaper of the Mongolian People's Republic *Ünen* (Truth) had already delivered the official rebuke: he had 'supported nationalist tendencies, which aimed to

glorify and idealize Jenghiz Khan and to misrepresent his reactionary role in Mongolian history. He had directed all his
energies towards arranging a massive celebration of the 800th
anniversary of Jenghiz Khan's birthday'.

For, as was decreed in this official statement by the Mongolian
People's Republic, Jenghiz Khan was a figure in reactionary history
to be utterly deplored. 'Jenghiz Khan's predatory wars,' the statement continued, 'led to a reduction of Mongolia's productive
capacity and brought untold misery to the Mongol people. Any
denial or underemphasizing of the reactionary nature of Jenghiz
Khan's deeds amounts in essence to deviation from the basic
position of the Party and to stimulating nationalism.'

The Mongolian statement carefully avoided any direct attack on
China. The Russians repaired the omission. 'Jenghiz Khan Personality Cult' was the accusation made against the Chinese by *Pravda*
on 21st July 1962. The newspaper reprimanded the Chinese and
the Inner Mongolian organizers of the celebrations at Echen Horo
for looking upon Jenghiz Khan's murderous invasions of the West
not as a great historical tragedy but as exploits which contributed
'to a mutual cultural exchange between east and west'.

Thus 756 years after his death Jenghiz Khan had again become
almost overnight a figure of prime political importance.

No evidence has come to hand so far to show what the Mongols,
who stand, and must stand, on both sides, really think. But these
incidents at least show how the Mongols are situated in the great
power-struggle between Russia and China. It is clear that the
Russians are allergic to any doctrinaire influence the Chinese might
exercise on the Mongols, although the Mongols have supported
the Soviet Union in its quarrel with China ever since it began.

OPPRESSOR OR OPPRESSED

On 25th August 1227, when Jenghiz Khan died after several bouts
of fever which began with a fall from his horse, the seventy-two-
year-old ruler held sway over the entire area from Peking in the

east to the present Soviet Union, as far as Ural'sk and even beyond
the Urals in the west. Wherever the hooves of the Mongols' horses
had left their mark, Jenghiz Khan's rule had been proclaimed. At
the same time, his conquests had been made with a brutality which
was without parallel even in an age which was not renowned for
its moderation. Resistance had been punished with death, the population of the subject cities and lands massacred in their thousands;
only artisans and artists were spared, together with people who
could contribute to the Mongols' war potential and were employed
as slaves. Only superlatives will serve here: the greatest empire in
history was built up in the most brutal and cruel way. But it is
easier to explain how it arose than why it arose.

Jenghiz Khan's father, Yesukai, belonged to a group of small
tribes and powerful families, who had adopted the name Manghol,
from which the name Mongol was derived. The Manghols and the
Tatars, another powerful tribe, fought for supremacy over the
steppe pastures and the forests of Northern Mongolia. Cattle-
breeding nomadic warriors and hunters, they were surrounded by
peoples of higher culture and civilization, some of Turkish origin,
adherents of the Nestorian creed of Christianity, and in the compact
cities the highly developed Uigurs. To the south and southeast
lay China: rich, powerful, a paradise for the nomads, who lived in
conditions of extreme hardship in the steppes and could find everything they lacked in China. From China came the products of
advanced agriculture, clothing materials, silks, brocades, articles
in iron and bronze, and extra foodstuffs such as rice and millet
which were so essential for the winter. If these things could not be
bought, they could be acquired by organizing raids across the
Chinese border. The 'northern barbarians' had descended on China
in periodic waves from the steppes, had robbed, plundered and returned to the steppes with their booty.

This tension between the dynamic of the nomadic herdsmen
and the saturated static of the Chinese with their economic self-
sufficiency also contributed to the rise of Jenghiz Khan.

Yesukai, his father, was poisoned in 1171 by the Tatars. The

MONGOLIAN TERRITORY

OIRAT

TURFAN

CHIN

Liaoyang

Peking

Ninghsia

Hwang Ho

Tanghut

Kaifeng

SUNG KINGDOM

The campaigns in North China up to 1215

future Khan of all the Mongols had a very hard upbringing. Berries and herbs were the only staple diet the widowed mother could offer the young man and his brothers. 'With a splinter of juniper in her hand,' so runs the oldest Mongol chronicle, the *Secret History*, 'she dug up roots and fed them with them.' The family had been abandoned by all its retainers and servants and was entirely without followers. In a feudal age governed solely by power and force, Jenghiz Khan's future prospects were anything but bright. But a few courageous single-handed forays soon attracted a small number of companions of the same age, with whose help he was able to begin fighting to regain his heritage. So his career began with the formation of a small band of men. There was no sign as yet of any ambitions of power. His position was strengthened by a period of service as a mercenary with the Chin dynasty of Northern China against the enemies of his family, the Tatars, who in the meantime had grown too powerful. He increased the number of his followers and defeated the Tatars. In 1206 the 'peoples who lived in felt tents' and whose allegiance he had won made him their ruler and gave him the title Jenghiz Khan.

No sooner were the reins of power firmly in his hands and the nomads, who had been so often split by internal dissension, finally united under him, than Jenghiz Khan turned eastward towards China. Like the leaders of earlier nomadic bands and like those who came after him, he too could not resist the economic challenge of China. And, as had so often been the case before, the Chinese and the frontier areas of China were no match for this invasion. Jenghiz Khan's victories came in rapid succession:

In 1207 he conquered two forest peoples, the Kirghiz and the Oirat. In 1209 he attacked the border kingdom of the Tanghuts in Northern China, conquered it and so gained an excellent supply-base for operations against China. Particularly significant was the confiscation of *all Tanghut camels,* which provided reserve forces for the Mongol cavalry.
In 1211 the former vassal of the Chin dynasty attacked Northern China. After a series of great encircling battles.
In 1214 the military power of the Chin was destroyed. The Mongol armies joined forces outside Peking.
In 1215 Peking fell. The whole of Northern China was in the hands of the Mongols.

But neither Jenghiz Khan nor the Mongols were mature or experienced enough to carry the burden of administering the conquered territory, much less of absorbing it politically. Their sole interest in China was booty. Northern China, plundered and debilitated, no longer had any appeal for the Mongols and certainly represented no threat to them. The cities were to be sacked, the arable land turned over to grass. In 1216 Jenghiz Khan moved back with the main body of his army to the Mongols' tribal lands on the Kerulen river. Only one general remained behind with the occupation force in Northern China. Up to this point even Jenghiz Khan seems to have had but one driving force: the dynamic of the steppes and their peoples. Laden with booty, the Mongols appeared to wish for nothing more than to live in peace till their booty had disappeared and they felt the lure of China again. The clearest indication that Jenghiz Khan shared this satiated desire for peace is the fact that he wanted to trade with the rich Mohammedan cities and states in the west. Everything pointed to the beginning

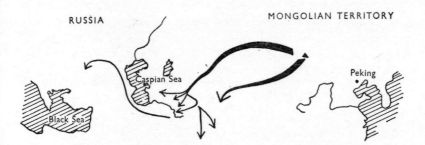

The campaign against Khwarizm and Russia, 1219–23

of an 'open door' policy. Trade caravans were sent to the west to pave the way for commercial relations. But in that same year a Mongolian trade delegation, which had been sent to the Khan of Khwarizm, was slain at Otrar. Their deaths had to be avenged. So what began as a peaceable effort to establish trade relations with Central Asia and Asia Minor ended with yet another campaign and a series of brilliant military victories; Jenghiz was compelled to move westward:

In 1219 the Mongol army with 200,000 auxiliaries began its march on Central Asia.

By 1220 it had already reached the area which is today the Russo-Afghan frontier.

In 1221 the forces of Khwarizm suffered their final defeat on the Indus.

In 1223 Mongol troops moved into Russia and defeated a Russian army in the battle of Taganrog on the Sea of Azov.

In 1224 Jenghiz Khan returned home victorious, having appointed his sons and faithful followers governors of the conquered territories. Conquest led inevitably to government and to the acquisition of political experience by the Mongols. The Mongol world-empire was the product not of one bold plan by a single individual but of various unco-ordinated campaigns of conquest and revenge.

In 1227, just when the Mongol Empire was beginning to take shape and the Mongols were maturing reluctantly and unexpectedly into a nation, Jenghiz Khan died on a punitive expedition against the Tanghuts, who had not contributed any troops to the western campaign, although since their subjection in 1209 they were under an obligation to do so.

FROM PEKING TO MOSCOW: SONS AND HEIRS

None of the sons and grandsons inherited the vitality, spontaneity and cruelty of their father and grandfather, and yet they succeeded, to begin with, in extending the frontiers of the Mongol Empire still further. Jenghiz Khan's son, Ogotai, who succeeded him, destroyed the last of the Chin dynasty only a year after ascending the throne. Both Northern and Central China were now in the hands of the Mongols. Southern China alone remained, unconquered, under the Sung dynasty. In these wars the Mongols had used gunpowder for the first time against the Chinese walled cities.

In 1235 an imperial diet was held in the heart of the Mongol territory, at which it was decided to make a fresh attack on Russia.

Under Batu, a grandson of Jenghiz Khan, the Mongol riders swept across Russia and Eastern Europe. By 1236 they had reached the Volga. The ice enabled them to cross the broad river and on 21st December 1237 they were on the farther bank. Nothing now stood between them and the Russian timber-walled towns, which fell in rapid succession. Moscow, a small trade settlement which stood where the vast complex of the Kremlin stands today, was burnt down.

In 1238, after the Mongol horsemen had acquired new energy from the rich grasslands of the Crimea, they made a fresh onslaught on the West to punish the Hungarian King Bela IV for granting asylum to his kinsmen, the Kumans, when they fled from the Volga basin before the advancing Mongols.

The Mongol horsemen invaded South-eastern Europe in three great army-groups. The northern wing entered German territory and destroyed an army of German-Polish knights at Liegnitz. It then swung southward into Hungary in order to join up with the main army. Germany with its dark forests did not appeal to the Mongol horsemen; they needed broad valleys and pasture-land, in order to deploy their forces and feed their horses. Their goal was the Theiss (Tisza) and the southern Danube. These, and not the heroism of the German knights, were the decisive factors which saved Europe from being overrun by the Mongols.

By April 1241 the flower of Hungary's chivalry had been trampled underfoot and she was entirely in the hands of the Mongols. But the victors were just beginning to settle down in Hungary, to strike the first coins, when Batu, the 'Rex Tartarorum', as his contemporaries called him, ordered a withdrawal to the Volga basin. News had come that on 11th December 1241 the Great Khan, Ogotai, had died suddenly in a drunken stupor. His dying words were: 'After I had been raised to the high throne by my imperial father and his many states had been laid upon my shoulders, I committed the error of allowing wine to conquer me!' The relays of Mongol horsemen, which formed a news-network across the entire occupied territory of the empire, were able to bring Batu the news of Ogotai's death within a matter of days. His presence was vital when the new Great Khan was chosen. Hence the abrupt withdrawal from Hungary. Central Europe breathed a sigh of relief: the Mongol threat had passed, and in its place there were diplomatic exchanges between the Mongols, the Pope and the French Kings. For the first time Europeans, monks and merchants, were able to travel right into the heart of the Mongol Empire, to Karakorum, and bring back fresh information about the Mongols. In 1298 there was even an exchange of diplomatic messages, in which a joint Franco-Mongol attack on the Mohammedan unbelievers in Egypt was mooted. Arghun, the Mongol ruler of Persia, promised the French king Jerusalem, the holy city of Christendom, if he would take part in the war against Egypt.

Mongol imperial seal

The territory Batu had conquered in Russia became the Empire of the Golden Horde, ruled over by his successors. In 1255 Hulagu, brother of the Great Khan Mangu, was entrusted with the task of consolidating Mongol rule in Central Asia. In 1258 he took Baghdad, the city of the Caliphs, which marked the beginning of Mongol rule in Persia, the Empire of the Ilkhans.

In 1260, when Mangu's brother Kublai became Great Khan, the fate of the Greater Mongol Empire was sealed. Kublai had strong

Chinese leanings and, in particular, a great admiration for Chinese culture. He transferred the capital of the Mongol Empire from Karakorum to Peking. His whole policy was directed towards Southeast Asia. Southern China was conquered and from there Mongol armies pushed on to Indochina and Burma. Japan was also a target for invasion but two attempts to land on the Japanese islands in 1274 and 1281 failed.

With Kublai's death the last bonds holding the Mongol states in Persia and Russia to the Great Khanate snapped. The forces of disruption proved too strong: the Mongol Empire collapsed by virtue of its size and the rivalries among its rulers, the descendants of Jenghiz Khan.

WHILE THE EMPEROR DANCES

Mongol rule was almost universally unpopular throughout China. It began with slaughter and looting. Very much against his wish Jenghiz Khan was dissuaded from carrying out his original plan, to raze the conquered cities to the ground, to wipe out the population and to convert the entire arable land of North China into pasture for the Mongol horses. Following the accession to the throne of Jenghiz Khan's grandson Kublai in 1260, conditions in China improved. The new ruler was interested in the arts and science and he was a shrewd judge and admirer of Chinese culture. He tried to persuade the Chinese to play a more prominent part in government, but the top dog in every instance was always a Mongol with other non-Chinese – Uigurs, Turks or Persians – also holding high positions. Even the Italian Marco Polo, son of a Venetian merchant, enjoyed the Emperor's confidence for many years and occupied senior posts. The Chinese had to be satisfied with very subordinate positions. Under subsequent Mongol emperors, who sat on the throne of China and who were less enlightened and less able, the administrative machinery ran steadily down and with it respect for the Mongols deteriorated. The Chinese population no longer bore the burden of Mongol rule in silence but grew refractory and resentful. There were conspiracies and local revolts. In 1333, when Toghon temür (1320–70), who was destined to be the last Mongol emperor in China began his reign, his throne was no longer secure.

'In the east was attack, in the west oppression, in the south reprisals and in the north war. On all sides people were joining forces secretly, for everyone hoped that a liberator would appear,' wrote a contemporary Chinese source on the situation around 1350.

The Emperor alone was unconcerned. He was entirely dominated by an Uigur adviser. Tibetan Buddhist monks had instructed Toghon temür in the secret teaching of sexual tantra. These exercises were reputed to prolong life and to transfer a woman's powers to a man. What had been a pious faith in India, where it originated, degenerated into a series of wild orgies at Toghon temür's court. Together with ten chosen friends, he abandoned himself to a life of debauchery with beautiful women, who were brought together from every corner of the empire and accommodated in the 'Palace of deep clarity' in Peking, which had been specially built for them. 'All who found most pleasure in intercourse with men were chosen and taken to the palace. After a few days they were allowed out. The families of the common people were glad to receive gold and silver. The nobles were secretly pleased and said: "How can one resist, if the ruler wishes to choose them?"' wrote a contemporary chronicler.

The 'Palace of deep clarity' had several hundred rooms, in which the girls danced. 'In the Emperor's presence,' wrote the same chronicler in 1369, 'naked men and women had intercourse. Sometimes prince and subject lay together. Sometimes they made arrangements to share the women.'

The Emperor and his ten 'friends' wore Buddhist priests' cowls with golden Buddha emblems and carried garlands of roses in their hands. Sixteen ladies of the harem danced the wild-goose dance. 'They had their hair in pigtails and wore ivory crowns. On their bodies they wore jewelled bracelets and deep-red priest's clothes sprinkled with gold.'

Warning voices could be heard, but Toghon temür would not listen to them. He abandoned himself to the secret cult to the point of exhaustion; his only other passion was building. The Chinese referred to him scornfully as the 'Carpenter-Emperor'. When the second Empress rebuked him for his loose living and told him, 'You are befuddled by the troupe of wild-goose dancers. Why do you not spare your illustrious body?', he merely replied, 'Am I the only one? There have always been emperors.' He even had the young Crown Prince, a minor, initiated into the secret Buddhist cult, in order to 'prolong his life'.

Finally the Chinese revolted against Toghon temür and the Mongols. Peking fell, the Mongol Emperor fled to Shangtu, his cool summer-residence near the Dolonor, but at the end of August 1368 this city also fell. Toghon temür just managed to make his escape with the Empress and his concubines under cover of darkness. He took refuge in Karakorum, the original Mongol capital, which had since fallen into decay and neglect. The rule of the Mongols in China was over. The national Chinese Ming dynasty assumed power. Historians of the new Ming dynasty would have us believe that all this happened quite painlessly and that there were no outbursts of popular anger against the Mongols. We are told that only those who refused to submit were executed. Otherwise, according to the Chinese chroniclers, after the fall of Peking *not a single person was put to death*. 'Storehouses and treasure-chambers were sealed up, documents, drawings and valuables taken into military custody . . .'

Mongol coin from the period of the Emperor Kaishan, *c.*1310

Chinese folk-lore has a different story to tell. In Peking each August people still exchange presents of full-moon cakes, small round cakes decorated with pictures of the moon-hare and bearing a small piece of paper in the middle. Popular legend has it that, during the last weeks and months of Mongol rule, the Mongols, who had become mistrustful and insecure, kept a very close watch on the Chinese. There was virtually a state of emergency. People were not allowed to stand about in groups talking and in almost every family there was a Mongolian spy. The Chinese were forbidden to carry arms. Only one in ten families was allowed to have a carving-knife. All this made it difficult to give the signal for an uprising against the Mongols in Peking. Finally someone had the brilliant idea of using the moon-cake, which was exchanged between one family and another on the occasion of the mid-autumn festival, by sticking a piece of paper on it, which was, in effect, the signal for revolt. So in August 1368 the Chinese population of Peking rose against the Mongols and massacred them. The moon-cakes today are a reminder of the Mongol heads which were sacrificed to the moon after the Chinese victory.

THE PENDULUM SWINGS BACK

Following the flight from Peking, Toghon temür and his successor tried to remobilize the Mongol forces from the old capital in the steppes. But the armies of the new Chinese national dynasty, the Ming, crushed the last Mongol resistance. Many of the Mongol garrisons which had been left behind in China fought on the side of the Ming against the deposed emperor. And this marked the beginning of an epoch, lasting more than two hundred years, in which the Mongols were torn by internal dissension and internecine war and exposed to frequent attacks by tribes from Western Mongolia.

Islam took over the Mongol Empire in Russia. By the beginning of the sixteenth century the Mongols had been forgotten and their power destroyed. In Persia internal struggles for power had already begun to threaten the Mongol rule in the fourteenth century, and here too conversion to Islam wrought a change in the Mongol character. By the middle of the fourteenth century Mongol rule in Persia was also in decline.

This process of dissolution into small, warring groups coupled with the Mongol retreat from China had the effect of disrupting the overland route between Europe and China, which had been kept secure by Mongol arms. Merchants now reverted to the sea-route and gradually the regions beyond the Urals lapsed into obscurity. Their sole contribution to history for some centuries was the continuation, on the old familiar pattern, of the conflict between the steppe peoples and the agrarian population of China in the form of raids across China's borders, the raiders retiring each time as soon as they had collected enough booty.

BETWEEN MOSCOW AND PEKING

In the seventeenth century a new force emerged in Northern Mongolia; the Russians. From then on they were to exercise an important influence on the fate of the Mongols.

It was during this century that a Don Cossack leader named Jermak Timofejewich made the first Russian incursion into Siberia. In 1643 the first Cossacks reached the Sea of Okhotsk. A few years later, in 1658, the Chinese, recognizing this new danger, tried to halt the Russian advance in a battle at the confluence of the Sungari and the Amur. But the Russians held their ground. They fortified Nerchinsk and established towns and trade-settlements near the Chinese border. They also began to negotiate with the Chinese over frontier demarcations. The Treaty of Nerchinsk in 1689 finally laid down the frontiers between Russia and China. Mongolia was still a part of China.

But with Russia's entry on the scene the Mongols realized that they now had a new bargaining-counter. If they did not get what they wanted from the Chinese, they could turn to the newcomers from the west. Refugees preferred life on the other side of the border to capture by Manchu officials or soldiers. It was the Western Mongols who from 1604 onwards had come into contact with the Russians. Russian arms were greatly coveted as presents. Galdan, the Western Mongolian prince, who drove the Kalka Mongols from their grazing-grounds in Northern Mongolia in 1688 because they would not support his plan to create an independent Mongolian State under Western Mongolian leadership, was the first to offer to enter an alliance with the Russians against the Manchu in China. But his envoys arrived too late. The Russians had just made peace with the Chinese at Nerchinsk. Nevertheless talks were held with the Western Mongolian envoys in Moscow, for Mongolia was already a part of the disputed area between Russia and China.

DECLINE OF THE GREAT KHAN

In 1622 almost all the tribes of Southern and Eastern Mongolia had aligned themselves with the new Manchu rulers of China. Not that they felt any spontaneous sympathy with the Manchu dynasty. Their main reason was the intolerable arrogance of the last Mongol claimant to the title of Great Khan, the Chahar prince, Ligdan Khan. Unfortunately, not all of them realized that Ligdan's extravagant claims to sole rule in the years 1604–34 represented, in fact, the last attempt to restore the khans to their former position of power and thereby to restore the unity of the Mongols. They also failed to recognize that they would have achieved more by negotiating with a weakened Ming dynasty in China than by allying themselves with the Manchu invaders. They were a people of related stock from Northeast Asia, who had close family ties with the eastern Mongols, particularly the Horchin.

Infuriated by Ligdan Khan's autocratic ways and extravagant demands, the tribes of Southern Mongolia turned to the Manchus. In 1632, when Ligdan Khan led his forces westward towards the Tibetan border, in order to prevent the Manchus from outflanking the Ming troops in northern and central China, only the people of his own tribe, the Chahar, rallied to his support. The other tribes were either fully committed to the Manchus or sympathized with them. Ligdan died in 1634 near the Koko Nor and his tribe, completely disorganized, fled eastward to their old grazing-grounds, where the Chahar also submitted to the Manchus. This marked the beginning of China's claim to the southern and eastern areas of Mongolia, which are now known as Inner Mongolia.

MONGOL REUNIFICATION

In 1691 the Chinese territorial claim was extended still further to include the Kalka area in Northern Mongolia, which is today the Mongolian People's Republic. In that year the Manchu Emperor, Kang Hsi, and the Mongol princes met in the monastery town of Dolonor in Inner Mongolia, and the princes of Northern Mongolia submitted to Chinese rule. But they did not do so voluntarily.

The Kalkas were fugitives at the time. Goldan had invaded their tribal lands from the west and driven them out, so they sought protection from Kang Hsi. In so doing the Mongols were pursuing their traditional policy of allying themselves with, and submitting to, whichever of their neighbours could offer them security. In 1691 it was the Chinese Empire to the south.

'By the absolute grace of the Emperor the Mongol slaves, who were close to death, were given new life!' said the Tüschijetü Khan Dshahundorchi of the Kalka, weeping, at the ceremony of submission.

From then until 1911 the Kalka princes and their highest lamaist dignitary, the Jebtsundampa Hutuktu, paid a yearly tribute of eight white horses and a white camel, the so-called 'Nine Whites', as nominal tribute to the Manchus. But their territory was called Outer Mongolia. Even when the proud Kalkas shook off the Chinese yoke with Russian help in 1911 and declared their country independent, China only agreed on condition that Outer Mongolia remained an 'integral' part of China. It was not until 1924, when

Outer Mongolia with the help of Soviet troops became the Mongolian People's Republic, that the term Outer Mongolia lost its meaning.

The Kuomintang government retained the term until 1945, when a referendum was held in Northern Mongolia, at which the Chinese were represented and which left no doubt that the Kalka Mongols preferred independence from China within the Mongolian People's Republic. But the Chinese continued to refer to Southern Mongolia as Inner Mongolia. Its Mongol tribes remained under Chinese sovereignty, although in 1911, with the sole exception of the Mongols in the Ordos region, they had openly supported the Kalkas' declaration of independence. At that time Chinese troops had intervened to prevent the fusion of Outer and Inner Mongolia into one nation-state, and this situation continued until fairly recently. In 1945, when the Red Army together with cavalry and tanks of the Mongolian People's Republic advanced against the Japanese in Inner Mongolia and the Mongol areas of Manchuria and drove them out, the Mongols thought the time had come to unite the various parts of Mongolia. The troops from the Mongolian People's Republic took a number of leading figures from Inner Mongolia back to the People's Republic for indoctrination, and the formation of a United Mongolia seemed imminent. But at the Yalta Conference the Great Powers decided otherwise. Chiang Kai-shek's acceptance of the *status quo* in Outer Mongolia, in other words China's recognition of the independence of the Mongolian People's Republic after a delay of some twenty-two years, dealt the final blow to Inner Mongolian hopes of joining it. Recognition of the situation obtaining in Mongolia in 1945 meant that Inner Mongolia and the Mongol areas of Western Manchuria were part of China. The soldiers of the Mongolian People's Republic, who had been hailed as liberators in Inner Mongolia, obeyed the order to withdraw behind their own frontier with unconcealed reluctance. The Soviet Union took the precaution of leaving some of its motorized units, which had advanced into Inner Mongolia with the Mongol units and had now withdrawn to the Mongolian People's Republic, on the borders of the North Mongolian State, in order to check any popular feeling on reunification. Some years passed before these guarantors of 'friendship' with China were withdrawn from the Mongolian People's Republic to the Soviet Union. For in the meantime Chiang Kai-shek and the National Kuomintang government of China had moved to Formosa and China had become a People's Republic. Peoples enjoying the same form of government should have no differences! The two neighbouring People's Democracies concluded pacts of friendship and solidarity. The Mongols of Inner Mongolia remained a part of Red China with administrative autonomy, while the Kalka Mongols had their own State between the two Communist giants, Russia and China, so that China's claim to Inner Mongolia remained precisely as it had been under the Manchu dynasty.

THE CHINESE TORRENT

In the early part of the present century the Mongols of Inner and Eastern Mongolia were made painfully aware of the expansionist claims which the Chinese had been making for centuries. Shortly after the turn of the century the first railways were built in Jehol province, the old imperial hunting-park of the Manchu imperial house, and beyond Ku-pei-kow and the Great Wall to the fertile pasture-lands of the Tumat of Kweihwa, and they brought hundreds of thousands of Chinese settlers every year. Skilled farmers with more than four thousand years of experience behind them mingled with the native Mongol population, who moved with their flocks between winter and summer quarters in the most fertile and fattest grazing-grounds. The developments of eighty and fifty years before in Eastern Mongolia began to repeat themselves in Inner Mongolia. Small market-settlements and trading stations for barter between Chinese and Mongols grew into large towns with a preponderantly Chinese merchant and artisan population. But the Chinese settlers also brought the plough into areas which had hitherto been populated solely by grazing herds of cattle, horses and sheep. The princes and landowners became indebted to the Chinese merchants and exchanged land for Chinese luxury goods and additional food supplies, which had been delivered against bills of exchange. Nomadic flocks and herds require large grazing-grounds. In a steady rhythm, which is conditioned by the size of the herd and the grazing-area required, the herds move from summer to winter pastures and back. The reduction of the grazing-grounds by the settlements of industrious Chinese peasants resulted in a numerical reduction of the herds. The brown ploughed fields of the Chinese settlers spread like some kind of skin disease over the green face of Mongolia.

The Mongol livestock-breeders felt a mounting hatred for the Chinese, who were turning their land 'yellow'. But the Chinese government did nothing to halt this infringement of the rights of the Mongols, although Sun Yat-sen, the spiritual father of the first Chinese revolution against the Manchu, had laid down three basic principles in 1911, one of which was that the equality of all five races and peoples in National China should be guaranteed. On the contrary, the Chinese government encouraged the expansion of Chinese settlements in Mongolia. The Mongols, of course, like the Tibetans, were represented in the Popular Assembly in Nanking and there was a special Tibetan-Mongolian Council to safeguard the national interests of the Mongols and other minorities, but in the period following the First World War only the Chinese received any support from the Chinese government. In self-defence the Mongols frequently resorted to force. Attacks by robbers and bandits on Chinese settlements increased, but what the Chinese condemned as acts of vandalism and countered with police-action was a form of protest by a minority, which was shabbily treated, looked down upon and constantly victimized by the Chinese. The Mongol princes, little kings by the grace of China, failed to measure up to this crisis. Slaves, as they were, to the attractions of Chinese culture, to a life of luxury and, more often than not, to opium, they tried to get as much as they possibly could for themselves out of the Chinese expansion and land-hunger. Many of them sold estates to the Chinese, in order to be able to maintain a feudal standard of living that was on the way out. But the Mongolian people grumbled in secret, suffered and hoped.

> 'If you see one with the button of rank (of a prince),
>   blue or white, of lapis lazuli or coral,
> He is one, who, full of scruple, peaceably
>   and shrewdly rules with a firm hand!
> But if you see covetousness, greed and great longing —
> He is merely one who tramps an unfriendly
>   road, after having armed himself with a straight stick.'

Such were the ironical words of the lamaist poet Ishidangchinwang-chil (1854–1907), a Chahar Mongol, who was a monk in a small Ordos monastery in Southern Mongolia and who wrote a pamphlet entitled *The Words of the Enlightened One from the Duke's Temple*, in which he criticized the princes for their remoteness from reality.

Hopes that the Mongolian People's Republic might provide the impetus to create a Greater Mongolia comprising all Mongols, free from China and Chinese influence, were dashed in the 1930s. In the People's Republic, which had gained its independence from China in 1924 with the help of the Red Army, a political pattern was imposed by the Russian protector. The second half of the 1930s brought a hardening of the Stalinist policy. Attempts to reform the outmoded economic and social structure by force led to major political purges and trials, which disposed of many of the nobles, the lamaist priests and the owners of large herds. Fugitives from Kalka Mongolia to Inner Mongolia, brought out detailed reports.

To whom should and could the Mongols of Inner Mongolia look for protection against China's colonization plans? A new force emerged to the east. In 1932, after years of preparation, Japan had occupied Manchuria and in 1934 had made it the nucleus of a new kingdom, Manchukuo, closely allied with Japan. The eastern Mongol tribes, which lived in this Japanese puppet-State, had been given self-government and an autonomous administration in the so-called four Hsingan provinces along the Hsingan range which runs to the north-east. There the Japanese encouraged Mongolian ambitions for cultural self-determination, opposed the entry of Chinese settlers and adopted an altogether anti-Chinese policy. And, something that weighed even more heavily with the Inner Mongolian nobility, the Japanese looked for their main support to the Mongol princes.

In 1936 (in 1935 Japanese troops and pro-Japanese partisans had 'adjusted' the frontier between the new State of Manchukuo and Inner Mongolia) the Japanese began to give official backing to Prince Teh of the Shilingol Federation who was striving for independence for Inner Mongolia, and the majority of the population of Inner Mongolia now looked to Japan to free their country from China. In fact, there were even Inner Mongolian princes who hoped that, with the help of the Japanese and by distributing Japanese arms among the inhabitants of the Mongolian People's Republic, whose morale had been greatly undermined by purges and witch-hunts, a wedge might be driven between the People's Republic and the Soviet Union and all Mongols would be united in a Greater Mongolia.

On 12th April 1936 the Mongolian People's Republic had concluded a Pact of Solidarity with the Soviet Union. The Japanese plans and the pan-Mongolian ambitions of the Inner Mongolian princes represented a sufficient threat to internal security for the Soviet Union to feel obliged to protect its Mongolian buffer-state, the MPR, by means of a Solidarity Pact. These Inner Mongolian and Japanese hopes of a change in the good relations between the MPR and Russia suffered a severe setback in the years 1935–37. Ably supported by political police and Russian troops, Marshal Choibalsang, who was later to become Head of State of the MPR, wiped out the groups of Kalka Mongols who believed that it was impossible to apply the Communist economic system to Mongolia and who had even said so quite openly. Amongst them was Gendun, who for many years had been Minister-President.

But this brutal counter-measure was also directed against those people in the MPR who saw in Japan's anti-Chinese policy a sound reason for ending the MPR's dependence on Russia.

MONGOLS UNDER RED CHINA

One-and-a-half million Mongols to eight-and-a-half million Chinese – that is the ratio today in the Inner Mongolian Autonomous Region of Red China. And yet it is one of the largest minority areas in China. It is said that Mao Tse-tung has himself made every major decision of a cultural nature affecting Inner Mongolia. Most of the one-and-a-half million are engaged in livestock-breeding, which is still one of the main sources of production in that area. Following the catastrophic drop in Inner Mongolia's cattle stocks after 1945, an intensive effort was made and by 1958 there were 28,167,000 head of cattle. Is it perhaps true to say that the Mongols' contribution on the economic front is the main reason why they are given special treatment?

The Communists do not like a nomadic economy. In the Communist view, the development necessary to create the ideal Communist State is only possible with the establishment of a proletariat. Workers and industrial capacity are inextricably bound up. Hence the sudden drive towards industrialization and the declaration of war on backward methods of production. One of these, in the Communist view, is the nomadic pastoral economy of the Mongols. In the Mongol-inhabited areas of the Soviet Union, among the Kalmuks and Buryats, nomadism has been abolished and the former nomads have become sedentary. But their herds and their grazing-lands have been collectivized. In the Mongolian People's Republic collectivization of herds has top priority in economic planning. The same is true of the Inner Mongolian Autonomous Region, where the Chinese Communists have also declared war on the nomadic cattle-breeder. Around 1958, according to official Chinese statistics, there were some 8,000 nomadic and 25,000 semi-nomadic herds.

By 1961 it was planned to incorporate all of these in collectives. In 1958 the plan was half-way to completion, but even by then eighty per cent of all nomads in Inner Mongolia were said to be living in permanent yurts. According to official sources, the area has 153 communes and more than fifty state-farms. A number of permanent wells were sunk, winter-quarters were built for the cattle, veterinary surgeons were drafted into the area and mobile seriological units vaccinated the cattle. Although the social structure of the Mongolian population was seriously disrupted, the collectivization policy also produced positive results. The number of cattle began to increase; 22 million head of cattle in 1957 increased to 28 million in 1959. According to the Five-Year Plan adopted in 1958, the target for 1962 was between 50 and 60 million head of cattle in Inner Mongolia. The greater part still consists of small livestock, mostly goats and sheep. The number of cows in Inner Mongolia in 1958–59 was estimated at 1.3 million. Great importance is attached to milk-products. Despite the large number of sheep, the production of wool is not satisfactory. In consequence, Chinese planners are calling for increased pig-breeding. This too points to a reduction in nomadism among the Mongols, for pig-breeding on a large scale is not possible in a nomadic or even semi-nomadic society.

Agriculture as such has remained in the hands of the Chinese population, and all the good soil is under cultivation. In spite of all the talk about unity and cultural autonomy, the fact is that the south-eastern part of the region is primarily agricultural and predominantly Chinese. This rough division in terms of population coincides with the dividing-line between good agricultural land – which was originally good pasture-land – and sandy or hilly pasture-land, into which the Mongol herds have now beaten a retreat. Apart from millet (kaoliang), maize and wheat, the main crops are sugar-beet and pumpkins. Particular attention has been given to the cultivation of sugar-beet, which until recently was unknown in the Mongolian border area. In Kükehot, Paotow, Ulanhot, Linho, Tungliao and Chifeng large sugar-refineries have been built, partly by Russian technicians. At the same time great importance is attached to the cultivation of wheat. At the end of 1959 there were some 1,700,000 acres of wheat. Out of the entire 290,000,000 acres of land in Inner Mongolia, about 14,000,000 acres are under cultivation and about 200,000,000 acres are pasture, in other words land that is less well suited to agriculture. But the Chinese planners are tackling the problem. A major irrigation campaign was launched, which was to bring 7,500,000 acres under irrigation by 1962. By 1957 about 2,000,000 acres were already being supplied with water. Large numbers of workers were mobilized from every town and village to build canals in the Ordos region and on the Liao-ho, the Shara mören in Eastern Mongolia, where dams and reservoirs were also built to provide even more extensive irrigation. All this is part of a strict anti-nomadic policy.

A communications network has also been created in Inner Mongolia during the past ten years. The railway-line from Ulan Bator across the Gobi Desert and through Inner Mongolia to Peking has been in operation since 1957. As far as Tsining it has the Russian gauge. In the Hsingan mountains several short-distance railways were also built, which are used for transporting timber. The railway connection between Lanchow and Paotow was also completed in 1958. But one of the major achievements in the field of communications has been the construction of more than 250 miles of desert roads, which are specially protected against the common hazard of any desert road, drifting sand. They form part of the thousand-mile road to Shensi.

There are ample indications, not only in official propaganda but also in use of the vernacular and in publications, that the Mongol minority are being given particularly friendly treatment and considerable encouragement by the 600 million inhabitants of the Chinese People's Republic. Plague and syphilis, the two traditional enemies of the Mongols, have been largely brought under control. Great importance is attached to hygiene in Inner Mongolia today. As a result the population is rapidly increasing. But the special treatment given to the Mongols is particularly apparent in the field of education, as, indeed, in other cultural activities as well. Does this mean cultural autonomy?

The battle against illiteracy amongst the Mongol minority has been so successful since 1949 that 1,290,000 Mongols can now read. Only ten per cent are illiterate. 15,000 elementary schools have been built in the Inner Mongolian Autonomous Region. Most of the pupils, on the other hand, are Chinese. In 1959 there were 42,000 Mongol children attending school, and out of a total of 140,000 secondary schoolchildren 21,436 were Mongols. Educational facilities are the same for Mongols as for Chinese. But since 1939 at all elementary schools – including the Mongolian schools – Chinese has been compulsory from the third year onwards, whereas previously it had only been compulsory from the fifth. The Mongolian language is only obligatory at six Mongolian secondary schools. Of the students at the seventeen colleges and technical schools in the region and at Kükehot University only about 100 are Mongols; all the others are Chinese. While one might detect signs here of a long-term policy of sinocization, it is only fair to point out that all Chinese officials are instructed to learn Mongolian.

Many Mongolian publications appear and a Mongolian literature is emerging in print. Since 1947 the Institute of Minorities in Peking, the Mongolian Publishing House, which has branches in Kükehot, Kalgan and Mukden, and the Minorities' Printing House in Sinkiang have together published 104,131,000 works. Even allowing for the fact that many of these are pamphlets, this is nevertheless a large figure for a mere one-and-a-half million Mongols in Inner Mongolia. Besides the Party publications and translations of standard Communist works by Marx, Engels, Stalin and Mao Tse-tung, old Mongolian works also appear. Much that was only available in manuscript in private collections has now appeared in print and has been widely read. Special commissions are working on Chinese-Mongolian and Mongolian-Chinese dictionaries, with a view to fostering closer understanding between the Mongol and Chinese populations of Red China. New words are being coined to replace Chinese words of the same meaning.

Already 10,775 new words have been adopted in the fields of law, politics, industry and education. Does this suggest that this modernization process is designed to lead eventually to a sinocization of the Mongols?

It is difficult, in examining the policy adopted on instructions from official quarters in Peking, to ascertain how much of it has been due to the obstinacy with which the Mongols have clung to their culture and to their claim for cultural autonomy. The ancient literary milestones of the Mongols are being systematically collected and equally systematically made public. In the libraries of the Institute of Minorities in Peking, in Kükehot and in Ulanhot, formerly Wang-yeh-miao, hundreds of old prints and manuscripts from the fifteenth to nineteenth centuries have been collected. An effort is being made to provide evidence of a specifically Mongolian literary tradition. Just as special commissions were set up in Red China to collect and inscribe Chinese folk-songs and folk-poems, so the folk-lore of Inner Mongolia, which had hitherto been handed down by word of mouth, is now being committed to paper and published. Editions of Mongolian literary works, which had already appeared in the Mongolian People's Republic, are being reprinted in Inner Mongolia, and the same is true of works by literary historians from the University of Ulan-Bator, the State University of the Mongolian People's Republic. Ancient Mongolian literary works such as the *Blue Chronicle* (Kök sudur) of the Mongolian writer Inchanashi, his other novels in the Chinese style and, above all, such epic works as Geser Khan, the Jangar epic, the collection of fairy-tales called *Stories of the 32 wooden men*, and other works of this kind were printed and given wide circulation. It is striking, in this respect, that during the early years when Communist China was making its influence felt in Inner Mongolia, most of the works in circulation were translations of Chinese authors. Today, however, a marked emphasis is being laid on Mongolian literature, and amongst the works and authors published, are some which show unmistakable anti-Chinese tendencies, although criticism is confined to the bourgeois society and gentry of the Manchu dynasty in the late nineteenth century and early twentieth. This is true, for example, of the works of Inchanashi, a fervent Mongolian nationalist and who writes with bitterness and scorn of the exploitation of the Mongols by the Chinese.

Even printed editions of folk-literature such as the anecdotes of the *Mad Monk Shagdar*, which were first published as recently as 1959 in Kalgan – the first impression ran to 3,500 copies – make no bones about reproducing anti-Chinese passages, although they are always clothed in the mantle of history, and criticism and contempt is directed mainly against the landowners, the rich princes, the corrupt officials and the decadent and immoral lama monks. Thus the following story is told of Shagdar, the rascally monk, a character based on a former wandering monk, who lived between 1869 and the 1930s:

'The annual festival organized at the monastery by the Bogharin has always been well attended by traders from the interior of China.

'Shagdar went up close to the side of the tent occupied by these traders, set up three stones to form a fireplace, produced a Tibetan cooking-pot, helped himself to water from the Chinese traders' earthenware water-container and, using some of their firewood, lit a fire under the pot. When thereupon the eldest of the traders cursed him and called him a madman, Shagdar replied:

' "I, Shagdar, have only drunk the water from my native soil, heated with nothing more than the brushwood from my mountains. I used none of the water or firewood that you brought with you from Shantung.

'You, who have gnawed much meat from the bone, you children of unmarried mothers (bastards), you belong there.'

'Shagdar abused them thus in Mongolian and in Chinese.'

Why is all this happening? Why was the old Mongolian script preserved, while there are still Mongols in the Mongolian People's Republic who mourn its passing? There are several answers to the question why the Mongol minority in Red China has been given special treatment.

The Chinese Communists still have to reckon with a Mongolian nationalism, which became stronger during the Japanese occupation and which resists any form of sinocization. In May 1958 the Mongols of Inner Mongolia even formed a Communist party of their own, because they were not satisfied with the Chinese Communist Party. The policy which has been adopted in the field of culture and literature is designed to satisfy or at least blunt this nationalist urge.

But there is another and even more important explanation. The Inner Mongolian Autonomous Region, which is the Mongolian minority area in the Chinese People's Republic, lives cheek by jowl with the Mongolian People's Republic, which, within the framework of the Soviet satellite states, enjoys a high degree of autonomy and which, with the powerful Soviet brother behind it, feels itself to be on almost equal terms with the Chinese People's Republic. If the Mongols of the Mongolian People's Republic are not to remain indefinitely anti-Chinese, if the Mongol minority inside Red China is to be prevented from looking constantly and longingly towards the Mongolian nation-state in the north, and if, at the same time, the Inner Mongolian Autonomous Region is to be presented to the Mongols under Russian influence as a shining example of Red China's socialist policy on minorities, then the Chinese Communists have no alternative but to choose the way they have chosen; to highlight the special character of Mongolian literature, while at the same time pursuing a policy of sinocization by economic and social means.

The special cultural position accorded to the Mongol minority in Red China is, therefore, a concession made in view of the existence to the north of China of a Mongolian State. How else is one to explain the publication of so many old works, the emphasis placed upon and encouragement given to Mongolian literature? The subtlety of this literary policy and the element of cultural irredentism implicit in it can be illustrated by one small example. During recent years both the Chinese and the Inner Mongolians have been stressing the fact that almost all the famous Chinese novels were translated into Mongolian in the nineteenth century and that they inspired itinerant Mongolian singers and Mongolian writers, who drew upon Chinese themes, to create a new form of Mongolian tale in the Mongolian-Chinese borderland, which had then spread throughout Mongolia and become very popular.

A not unimportant feature of this cultural irredentist window-dressing for the benefit of the Mongolian People's Republic and its Russian friends was the retention of the 'old' Mongolian script. So long as there is some good reason for this policy of cultural irredentism, the Mongol minority in China, one-and-a-half millions in the ocean of 600 million Chinese, will continue to enjoy a close season, their culture and literature will be fostered and explored, and the 'old' script will be cherished and used.

III REMAINS OF THE PAST

MONGOLS ON THE VOLGA

Since 1630, when a horde of Western Mongols appeared on the banks of the Volga, the Europeans have remained aware of and interested in the Kalmucks. Tired of the endless quarrels between the various Zungarian princes, sections of the Western Mongolian tribes – the Torgut, Dörbet, Hoshuit, Khoit and Zungar – left their old grazing-grounds between Altan and Tien Shan. There was no outlet for them to the east. They had been driven out of the Kalka territory in 1468 by Dayan Khan, after they had tried to conquer it. So they moved westward. After long and adventurous marches, they reached the Volga and took possession of the broad steppes on the lower reaches of the river. It was some time before they realized that they had penetrated into Russian territory. The towns in the Volga basin offered rich booty, so they overran them as well. The Russians for their part did not proceed to deal with these unexpected intruders as forcefully as they might have done, for they were anxious not to lose these new subjects. Gradually the Russians and the Kalmucks found ways of living with each other. The Kalmuck herds grazed and their camp-fires glowed on the banks of the Volga, while the Russian czar and his officials tried to gain an influence over these new subjects. But, as a Russian historian has put it, the Kalmucks, 'in their relations with the Russian government, clung to the policy of the nomads – opportunism – and accordingly were servile one moment and the next moment were raiding Russian caravans and towns or even establishing relations with the court in Peking and expressing their resentment against the Russian authorities'. Throughout all this, however, they remained in active contact with their fellow-tribesmen, the Zungarians, supported them in war and had no qualms about fighting against either Russia or China, depending upon the circumstances.

The close relations between them and their fellow-tribesmen in Western Mongolia explain the cultural and literary affinity between the manuscripts collected by Zwick (see below) and the literature and customs of the remaining Mongols. The Volga Mongols worshipped the same gods, used the same words to invoke the fire-goddesses and called upon the Tsaghan Ebügen, the 'white old man', to bless their herds.

For more than a hundred years the Russian government endeavoured to rule the Torguts on the Volga with a not too heavy hand. And when, between 1725 and 1770, the Russian authorities dealt more harshly with the all-too-independent Volga Torguts, they became increasingly discontented. The Russians now claimed the right to appoint the khan of the Torguts, a claim which was resisted by the Mongols. In 1771 they decided to leave Russia and return to their former homeland between Altai and Tien Shan. There were rumours that Russia proposed to force them to adopt the Christian faith and to appoint the Dondukow princes, who were Christian Dörbet princes and had become completely Europeanized residents of St Petersburg, rulers of the Volga Torguts. The plan to leave Russia and return to the old Zungarian grazing-grounds on China's northwest border was kept completely secret from the Russians. When an enemy of the Torgut Khan, Ubashi, warned the Governor of Astrakhan, Beketow, that unrest was brewing among the Torguts, the latter did not take the report seriously. But on 4th January 1711 it happened. The Torgut Khan, Ubashi, assembled his troops and told them, 'with tears in his eyes', that the Russian Empress had ordered him 'to send his son together with the children of five high nobles to St Petersburg and furthermore to pick out ten thousand recruits from the Kalmuck people and send them to join the Russian army'. The only way he could see of evading this order was to flee from Russia's tutelage.

The Cossack troops which barred the way to the east were scattered. All the Torguts and Hoshuts, who had been living as nomads on the left bank of the Volga, started off eastward *en masse* in the direction of Lake Balkhash. The Dörbet tribe, who lived on the right bank of the Volga, were unable to follow. The frozen Volga, which they had hoped to cross quite easily with all their goods and chattels, horses and baggage, thawed overnight, rendering the right bank of the river impassable. So 11,000 families remained in Russia and became known as the Kalmucks from the Mongolian word 'chalmagh', which means 'those who remained behind'. These are the Kalmucks whom H. A. Zwick and other Moravian missionaries from Saratov tried to convert and from whom they obtained manuscripts.

The Russian government took immediate steps to frustrate any attempt by this group to escape eastward. The Kalmucks have a song in which they immortalized the ill-fated march of their brethren and criticised Ubashi Khan. What else could they do, since the road to their fellow tribes to the east was barred for all time?

The main body, however, moved quickly eastward. The Cossacks who were sent out after them engaged them in a few skirmishes but then abandoned the chase, as they were numerically inferior. The Russian government therefore called upon the Kazakhs and Kirghizes, through whose territory the fugitives had to pass on their way to the Chinese border, to lend support. Raids by both Kazakhs and Kirghizes decimated the fleeing tribesmen, disease and thirst wrought further havoc. Forced by the Kazakhs to take to the desert, the Torguts are alleged to have lost 300,000 men before they reached the Chinese border. This figure is an exaggeration, for only 33,000 yurt families altogether had succeeded, under Ubashi's leadership, in fleeing from the Volga. Nevertheless, when the Torguts finally crossed the Chinese border and reached the Ili region, their future home, there were only some 85,000 survivors. All the others had died of hunger or thirst or had been killed. And with them perished irreplaceable treasures of their culture and literature.

The Chinese gave the repatriates a friendly welcome, not out of sympathy for the poor, homeless refugees, but because the return of the Torguts fitted in with Chinese plans to resettle their most westerly province, Sinkiang. Not long before, the last of the other Western Mongolians, who under Amursana and Dawachi had rebelled against the Chinese yoke, had been wiped out in a series of bloody battles. The country was empty. The Manchu troops had virtually annihilated the other Western Mongolians. There was no one to take over the dying herds. So the arrival of some 85,000 nomadic herdsmen on the Ili border came as a godsend to the Chinese economy in that area. The Emperor Chien Lung had every reason to issue instructions that the refugees should be treated 'with exemplary humanity'.

The broad green pastures were given to them, on which, a century before, the yurts of their dead kinsmen had stood. But for them too the dream of Western Mongolian independence remained a dream. Their princes were drawn into the hierarchy of rank and tribute, which the Manchus had devised; instead of being subjects of His Imperial Majesty the Czar, they were now subjects of His Imperial Majesty the Chinese Emperor.

China's attitude to the fugitives from Russia soon found an echo in Europe through enthusiastic reports by Jesuit missionaries such as Joseph Amiot in his 'Monument de la transmigration des Tourghouths des bords de la mer Caspienne dans l'Empire de la Chine', which appeared in 1776. In 1837 De Quincey wrote a highly romanticized account of the flight and of the paternal welcome given to the Torgut fugitives by the Chinese Emperor, Chien Lung, an account which again stirred the hearts of the Europeans and won renewed sympathy for the kindly Manchu Emperor.

The Torguts themselves, however, were bemoaning the loss of their freedom. The bitter words were passed from mouth to mouth: 'We had bonds of cord; now we have bonds of iron,' and the legend of Djawa Batur was told and retold. He was revered as one of the heroes of the flight from Russia. The common people believed that, but for his acts of heroism and those of Djingin Batur, they would never have survived that hellish march across the barren steppes and the constant attacks by the Kirghizes. For that reason Khan Ubashi had forgiven Djawa Batur twelve offences which he had committed during the march to Lake Balkhash. But no sooner had the Torguts reached the Ili region and the Manchu had heaped rank and honours upon Ubashi, than he had but one ambition: to show his gratitude to Peking. He forgot to show his gratitude to Djawa Batur. Instead he threw this undesirable witness of the past into prison, where the latter was guilty of yet another minor offence. The Khan then gave secret orders for Djawa Batur to be handed over to the Chinese as a dangerous criminal. But Djawa Batur succeeded in escaping from prison. He entered the Khan's house late at night, stepped up to the bed in which the Khan was sleeping with his wife and lifting the curtain, said to the terrified Khan: 'Turn your face towards me! I have come to look upon you for the last time! I go now, because you are repugnant to me. You have forgotten how I saved you from the Kirghizes and now you will hand me over to the Chinese? Just as you have betrayed me, so you will betray the whole people!'

Khan Ubashi pretended to be asleep and said nothing. Djawa Batur took the Khan's musket down from the wall. It had the longest range of any known to the Mongols. It was known as the 'Gun of the Volga'. He left the Khan his short-barrelled gun with gold-chased stock and went out, never to return. The police who were sent after him by the furious and deeply-insulted Khan and still more police who were put on his trail by the Manchu Resident at Ubashi's request were unable to find him.

Popular legend has it that, in farewell, he uttered the ironical words:

'There are two things, for the sake of which we left the Volga: feathers and buttons. [A reference to the Chinese officials' hats.]

'Two things we desired passionately: a coat and a stove-bed. [The heated clay bench of the Chinese.]

'What we came to find are: rocks and stones.' [A reference to infertile land which the Chinese had allotted to the Torguts.]

Remains of the Past

CHARRED REMAINS OF THE PAST

Among the many Mongolian and Kalmuck manuscripts, which were left in 1887 by the Mongolist B. Jülg (1825–86) to what was then the Royal Library in Berlin and later became the Prussian State Library are a strikingly large number of fragments in Kalmuck and Mongolian script, charred scraps of paper which are very soiled and usually lack both beginning and end. Bernhard Jülg was particularly interested in the Kalmuck fragments. As a result of his research into this West Mongolian period, he was able to unearth and translate priceless examples of the literary tradition of the Mongols, such as the Ardshi-Bordshi tales and the tales of the magic corpse.

But where did the large number of charred, dirt-encrusted, torn fragments come from? While these fragments were being studied with a view to including them in the large German catalogue of manuscripts, the contents of most of them were deciphered and it became clear that they represented an interesting cross-section of the enormously varied narrative literature of the Mongols as well as of their religious writings. Both the Kalmuck and the Mongolian scripts are employed. This suggests that they originated in the Oirat region on China's northwestern border, where both scripts were used concurrently. Many of the manuscript-fragments in Kalmuck and in West Mongolian script go back to the seventeenth century. The fact that so many old manuscript-fragments, most of which have neither beginning nor end and all of which were damaged by water or fire, were discovered in one and the same place, suggests that they came originally from one of the small chapels that served at one time as storehouses for manuscripts in every lamaist monastery. The entrance was walled-up, leaving only a small aperture through which the remains of sacred, incomplete and therefore dispensable works were thrown. Anything written was sacred; there was a certain element of magic in the written word. To those who believed that a few chosen words written on a piece of paper would protect the bearer against all dangers and threats it seemed natural that nothing written should be destroyed. So a place was set aside for storing manuscripts which had ceased to have any practical value – a custom which enabled later historians and scholars, thanks to the dry desert climate of Central Asia, to make many important discoveries.

About the middle of the last century a traveller in the Northern Mongolian-Oirat border area must have come upon one or more of these manuscript-cemeteries and given their contents to Jülg. Who the travelling scholar was, to whom we owe these remains of Oirat literary works from the seventeenth century, is not known, but there is reason to believe that it was M. A. Castren, the great Finnish philologist, who travelled between 1845 and 1849 from the Chinese border to Siberia, where he studied the dialects of Siberian tribes. After Castren's death in 1852, Anton Schiefner, Professor of Indology, at Berlin, published the results of Castren's research. Jülg was a close friend of Schiefner's. It is on the evidence of this friendship alone that the supposition regarding Castren is based.

That the charred, soiled and torn manuscripts recovered from these Oirat 'graveyards' date back largely to the seventeenth century is clear from their contents. But they also explain the condition in which these manuscripts were found, dirty, tattered and burnt. They are relics of the last, bloodstained chapter in the struggle for power, in which the Manchu emperors were engaged at that time against the Oirats of Western Mongolia and the Zungars and which ended in 1760 with the virtual annihilation of the Oirats.

ADVERSARIES OF THE SUN KING

Europe in the late seventeenth and the eighteenth centuries was a fascinated spectator. In 1697 a broadsheet, a forerunner of our modern newspaper, was sold in France which reported on the 'Great struggle and victory by the army of the Emperor of China over Caldan, King of the Elutes'. The reporters were mostly French Jesuit monks, who were advisers, astronomers, mathematicians or geographers at the Chinese court. They maintained that the Manchu Emperor, Kang Hsi (1662–1722), was as illustrious a prince in China as King Louis XIV (1660–1715) in France. So anyone who dared oppose the Chinese Sun King was certain to arouse lively interest in the land of the French Sun King. And the Jesuits saw to it that there was no shortage of news from China. Another factor was the close similarity in the political situations. The Western Mongols, who were constantly threatening the Chinese border, were compared with the Turks. (In 1660–63 the Turks advanced as far as Vienna and threatened the capital of the Holy Roman Empire. In 1683 they were defeated near Vienna by Sobieski. Hence the keen interest in news from China, which brought reports of a similar threat by wild horsemen.)

What had really happened in China? Galdan, son of the Zungar king, had gradually taken all power into his own hands. As a young man he had been trained for the priesthood and had taken his first theological training and vows in Lhasa, the seat of the Dalai Lama, spiritual head of the lamaist Buddhists.

On his return from Lhasa, the ex-monk had quickly realized that the independence of the Mongols was seriously threatened by the expansion of Chinese power towards Central Asia, a policy which the Manchu emperors had been systematically pursuing since 1634. He tried to win over the Kalka Mongols to his side but they fled and turned to Kang Hsi for help.

Russia's penetration into Transbaikalia, which had led to the Treaty of Nerchinsk in 1689 and to the demarcation of the borders between Northeast China or Manchuria and Russia, had made the Emperor Kang Hsi particularly sensitive to anything affecting the northern and western borders. He recognized the importance of Northern Mongolia as a buffer-zone against any Russian drive towards China, but, apart from that, Galdan's idea of a new Mongol state on China's north-western border was not likely to appeal to any Chinese emperor.

A strong Chinese force was sent out against Galdan and the Elute prince's army was defeated in 1697. His beautiful wife

Le grand Combat & la Victoire remporté ʃur l'Armée de l'Empereur de la Chine ʃur Caldan Roy d'Elouth.

ON a' reçu des Letres de Pexin Capitale da la Chine dr 8. Octobre mil ʃix cent nonante ʃix qui contiennent les nouvelles ʃuivantes. l'Empereur de la Chine fut occupé pendant cette annee à faire la guerre u Roy d'Elouth, pays ʃitué dans la Tartarie, à trois cent lieuës de Pexin du coʃté du Nordoüeʃt. Ce Prince Tartar nommé Caldan avoit eʃté le plus conʃiderable diʃciple du Grand Lama de Barantola, que tous les peuples idolâtres de la tartarie reconnoiʃʃent pour Chef de leur Religion, mais le Roy d'Elouth ʃon frere eʃtant venu, à mourir, il quitta le ʃervice des idoles, pour luy ʃucceder. Comme il eʃtoit entreprenant, il vinquit le Roy d'Ircan, Subjuga les pays de Camul & de Turfan, ʃituez à l'Oüeʃt de la Province de Chenʃi, par leʃquels paʃʃent les marchands de Simarcand qui vont negocier à la Chine. Son ambition augmentant, il s'approcha en 1695, de la Tartarie ʃujette à l'Empereur de la Chine, qui y eʃtoit allé chaʃʃer ʃuivant ʃa coûtume, & qui fut bien-toʃt averty qu'il ʃollicitoit d'autres Princes Tartares de ʃe joindre à luy, pour attaquer la Chine, ainʃi l'Empereur reʃolut de le prevenir. Il employa quatres mois à faire ʃes preparatifs, faiʃant ʃondre trois cent petites pieces de campagne ou pierriers, & faire des juʃte-aucorps de ʃoye de quatre-vingt doubles à l'epreuve du mouʃquet pour les Officiers & d'autres de cotton à l'epreuve des fleches pour les ʃoldats. Il partit au mois d'Avril 1696. à la teʃte de 3. cens mil hommes, avec cinq de ʃes fils, laiʃʃant le Prince heritier Hoan-tay-tʃé, pour gouverner en ʃon abʃence, menant avec luy les Peres Gerbillon, Pereira & Tomas Jeʃuites, il ʃit partir

Paris broadsheet on Galdan Khan, 1697

Anudara, who fought like an amazon in copper armour at the head of one battalion, was slain in the battle. Galdan managed to escape but died soon afterwards, presumably of poison.

Thousands of warriors had fallen. For a time there was peace in Central Asia. The land-route from Russia to China seemed safe again. In 1703 Leibnitz, the German philosopher, who since 1697 had taken an active interest in China, wrote to his French colleague Fontaney: 'Someone has told me that, since the King of Elute was vanquished, one can travel to China both by way of Persia through the land of the Uzbeks and across the country of the Mongols. And indeed, if one could be sure of travelling there just as well as by sea, this route would be preferable to any other.'

But Leibnitz had been too optimistic. Galdan's nephew Tsewangrabdan and, after him, Galdan Tsering, carried on the war against the Manchu emperors and successors to Kang Hsi, against his son Yung Cheng and his grandson Chien Lung, with only the occasional truce or enforced submission. The fighting became more and more bloody. Galdan Tsering died in 1745, after he had made peace with China. But his sons quarrelled over the succession. The Emperor Chien Lung realized that the pacification of Central Asia, which had been so hard to achieve, was again in jeopardy and he decided to silence the Zungars once and for all. In 1754 he attacked the Zungar grazing-grounds in the Ili and Altai regions with a large army. The new Zungar ruler Dawachi resisted as best he could, then fled to Turkestan, where a Mohammedan prince, Hojis Beg, took him prisoner and handed him over to the Chinese. Chien Lung generously forgave the rebellious Zungar prince and allowed him to live in style in Peking, where he died in 1759.

There were few Western Mongols left in the Ili region after the Manchu troops had passed through. Chien Lung chose Amursana, another Zungar prince, to rule over them, but he had barely returned to Ili when he too rebelled and demanded independence for the Western Mongols. The Manchu Emperor's patience was at an end. Another Manchu army marched into the Ili region. Amursana escaped to Russia, but only to return and incite the

Mongols to fresh revolt against the Manchus. The Chinese showed the Zungars no mercy. By 1757 the war was officially over. When Amursana died of smallpox in Russia, the Russians sent his corpse to the Manchus, who had it burnt. His child died in prison. During the next few years many surviving Zungars were executed by the Chinese. The name Zungar was banned and such members of the tribe as had survived were obliged to call themselves Elutes. China had pushed her border forward as far as the Altai. Something that did survive from the Zungar yurts, which were burnt by the Manchu soldiery, was the charred fragments of paper now in the Marburg Library.

MAGIC LONG-DISTANCE WEAPONS

Amongst the names of those who are known to have contributed to the collections of Mongolian manuscripts in Germany are many well-known scholars. Wilhelm Schott (1802–59), the famous Altaist of the Friedrich-Wilhelm University in Berlin, is one of them, together with A. von LeCoq and A. Grünwedel, who brought back fourteenth-century Mongolian texts from their expeditions to the Turfan oasis in Turkestan. Wilhelm Grube, the Berlin sinologist, added to these collections, as did, later, Professors F. D. Lessing and Erich Haenisch and his former students, until over 671 manuscripts had been collected. Now that the manuscripts are no longer kept in cold storage but are used, one realizes that books and manuscripts not only have destinies, as the centuries-old proverb says, but they also record the destinies of others. Almost every manuscript helps in one way or another to illuminate some dark corner in our knowledge of the remote world of Central Asia.

Until recently, magic and the magical have always bulked large in reports on Mongolia and Tibet and have been presented as a special feature of these countries. When Marco Polo, the Venetian merchant's son who travelled in China and the Mongol Empire seven hundred years ago, writes of lamaist monks and magicians who could make weather and caused a full goblet of wine to fly through the banqueting hall to Kublai Khan's table, then we dismiss the story with an indulgent smile. This sort of thing was to be expected in medieval travellers' reports on distant countries. But then we find on page 68 of the *Peking Gazetteer* of 1876, which was printed in Shanghai, an announcement by the Military Governor of Ili, Yung Tsuan, that a Torgut nobleman, a Djazak taidji, had committed a criminal offence by summoning certain Tanghut lamas to hold a divine service or a ceremony of exorcism for the purpose of curing a disease, and that the said nobleman had opposed an investigation and had resisted all attempts to arrest the guilty persons. The report of the local Torgut prince, which had been submitted to the Governor, ran as follows:

'It had been brought to his notice that the Djazak taidji named Tubchin Keshig received in his house two unshorn Tanghut lama monks with a novice, who performed exorcisms, allowing no one to be present at the ceremonies. They had made the figure of a devil out of green dough. Then they had made an evil-smelling mixture of blood and thrown all this on to the fire. Thereupon the prince sent a group of thirty people from his Banner on 27th February of last year (1875), in order to apprehend these persons. The Djazak, however, concealed the culprits and not only refused to produce them but also summoned a number of people from his Banner, who attacked the prince's men with sticks, swords and spears and wounded some of them. The prince's envoys nevertheless succeeded in carrying off the Tanghut novice and two of the Djazak's servants together with some of the objects employed for the exorcism . . .'

This strange announcement from the *Peking Gazetteer of* 1876 becomes more comprehensible and more intriguing when one reads the hand-written exorcisms and instructions for the casting out of devils and evil spirits.

'This is the ritual for the suppression of demons,' we are told at the end of one manuscript: '(take) two black stones, two pieces of pig-iron and two pieces of iron and make a human figure.

Draw a human form with a dog's head and near the heart a small glass full of grain, on the one side black grain, on the other side wheat, with two tufts of hair in it. Wrap all this in a black cloak and tie it with two golden and black threads. After this ritual has been observed, throw it on the excrement of a red-snouted white dog. Bury it at the crossing of three roads. If such a place is not to be found, bury it under the door of your own house. In this way the casting-out of devils is assured!'

There are exorcisms against dirt-demons and the black demon, which rides on a yellow goat and holds a green crow in his hands. Another manuscript contains sixty instructions for the making of amulets, which guarantee the wearer protection against all threats by natural and supernatural forces. In a mode of living like that of the nomadic Mongols, which was so exposed to the forces of nature, it is understandable that the Mongols should seek every possible means of prevention and protection. The effectiveness of the amulet depended upon precise observance of the instructions for making it. Blood, sweat, semen, urine, plant-juices, Indian ink, medicaments, indigo, red and yellow dyes are the ingredients prescribed. The blood of someone who had died of a particular disease gives protection against that disease. The blood of someone who died young is a preventive against premature death. There is yet another formula which gives protection against unrequited love, a formula which must be 'written with mouse's blood on a piece of ginger-wood, thick as a thumb, which is smeared with the semen of a young man and which is carried on one's person'.

In many Mongolian as well as certain European travel-books a magical long-distance weapon called Zor is mentioned, which the lamaist monks were able to conjure up. The great Russian traveller, A. Pozdneev, has given a detailed description of such a ceremony and of how the magic weapon Zor is thrown. The officiating lama invokes all the forces of destruction into a small pyramid of paste then throws it away, causing misfortune to enemies and adversaries. The biography of the second lamaist High Priest of Peking,

Chang chia Hutuktu Rolpaidordje, which is written in Mongolian, contains a lively account of how in 1767, at the behest of the Manchu Emperor, Chien Lung, he intervened with the help of a Zor weapon in the campaign against the rebellious inhabitants of Yunan. The lamaist priest conducted the ceremony in Peking, assembled all the magical forces into the small paste-pyramid and threw it in the direction of the remote province of Yunan in Southwest China. Some 1,500 miles away as the crow flies a gigantic ball of fire is said to have appeared at that same moment in the midst of the rebels, killing many of them. So, at least, the credulous biographer of Chang chia Hutuktu would have us believe.

In one of the manuscripts in the German collections a prayer called the 'Zor Ritual' was also found:

> 'I, the magic lama, throw away this Zor bread figure,
> throw it at the hated enemies,
> throw it at the evil-scheming devils,
> throw it at the confusion-creating goblins!'

HUMAN SACRIFICES TO THE BANNERS

The manuscripts collected by Hans Leder, the explorer from Troppau, who travelled through the Tibetan-Mongolian border country and Mongolia in 1903, are now in the Linden Museum, an ethnological collection in Stuttgart. There are also other Mongolian manuscripts, which were brought back by those well-known travellers in Central Asia, Sven Hedin, Albert Tafel and Wilhelm Filchner. To judge by the routes the three explorers followed, these manuscripts must have come from the western part of Inner Mongolia and from the Tibetan-Mongolian border area. Long before it had been suggested that an inventory should be made of all the Mongolian manuscripts in Germany and the suggestion was actually carried out, the Linden Museum had asked me to examine and describe its manuscripts. Most of them were copies of Buddhist prayers and teaching manuals. But one of them, which consisted of several incomplete, yellowed sheets, gave me a glimpse of almost unbelievable practices. Perhaps, after all, there was something in the charge made several times in chronicles and historical works, that the Mongols had sacrificed prisoners to their banners and battle-standards. The assertion had been made again in 1620, when Nurhachi, the founder of the Manchu dynasty which ruled China from 1644 onwards, replied to an arrogant letter from the last of the Mongolian Great Khans, Ligdan, and sent it by means of a Buddhist monk, Shiose Ubashi. The Emperor's hope, that Ligdan Khan would respect the messenger's cloth, proved to be false. Ligdan Khan had the bearer of this not very friendly message seized, put in irons and thrown into prison. For a long time the Manchus had no news of their envoy. Then they learned through messengers from more friendly tribes that 'Ligdan Khan, the Chahar, has killed the envoy of the Illustrious Emperor and sacrificed him to his flag'.

At first the Manchus found this hard to believe. But when the same report came in from other quarters, they began to attach credence to it. At least they believed that Ligdan Khan was capable of it. So finally Nurhachi gave orders: 'It is certain that our envoy has been killed. A month has passed since he was seized. Now kill the messenger of the Chahar . . .!' Unhappily one of Ligdan's messengers, named Khanchalbaichu, was present and had to sacrifice his life.

The situation took an extremely embarrassing turn for the Manchu, however, when their envoy, Shiose Ubashi, allegedly offered as a sacrifice to Ligdan's banner, reappeared hale and hearty. He had succeeded in escaping from the Chahar. But the fact that the Manchus had believed the reports of human sacrifice to the flag show that such reports were not regarded as outlandish.

I was reminded of this when I read that time-withered manuscript from Stuttgart. For it contained a sacrificial prayer to Jenghiz Khan's black battle standard, the Chara sülde. The prayer must have been very old. The standard, in which the guardian spirit of the great Mongol ruler was thought to reside, was invoked as protection against enemies, robbers and law-breakers.

Together with a prayer to the Protector of Buddhism, there was the following:

> 'Let the enemy's camp be overrun,
> Take captive in thy hands the enemy's men,
> Goods and possessions.
> Cut off the enemy's warm life at the roots!
> Stir the enemy's white brain
> like sour milk!
> Quaff the enemy's red blood!
> Utterly destroy the evil-doers . . .'

But what was really of interest was the instruction that followed: the sacrifice was to be made 'each month at the first and third of the new moon, on the 15th and 21st, on the 3rd and 9th days' on the top of a high mountain.

'To deal with war and enemies,' the instruction continued, 'as also with hated robbers and brigands, mix the following in brandy in equal parts: the blood of a man who has been killed, swarf from an iron bar with which a man has been killed, and offer this with flour, butter, milk and black tea. . . . When this kind of sacrifice is offered, without any omissions, then one will certainly be able to master anything, be it acts of war, enemies, robbers, brigands, the curses of hated opponents or any adversity . . .'

The blood of a killed man is not always readily available! Did the instruction mean that someone had to be killed for each sacrifice? Or had the words of this old prayer long since lost their meaning and become a mere harmless mumbo-jumbo? Evidence has come to light during the present century to suggest that this was not so. Hermann Consten, the German traveller, who was in Western Mongolia shortly after the siege and fall of the town of Kobdo in 1912, was told by eye-witnesses that Dsha Lama Dambid-shantsan had given orders to cut open the breast of the ringleader of the conquered Kazakhs from the Altai and tear out his heart for religious sacrifice. A Russian observer, Ivan Maisky, who later served as Russian Ambassador in London, confirmed Consten's report. The Dsha Lama Dambidshantsan was a Kalmuck adventurer from the Volga, who had been active in Western Mongolia since 1890 and whose ambition was to make the area independent of China. He claimed to be the grandson of Amursana, the last rebel leader in Western Mongolia, who had died in 1757, a claim which gained him considerable support. In 1926 he was shot by Outer Mongolian troops.

The custom of removing the heart as a Shamanist sacrificial offering was also practised by other Mongolian leaders during the Mongolian wars of independence in 1911 and 1912. This was reported by Maksurchab, one of the most famous of Mongolian freedom-fighters, whose death in 1920 was deeply mourned and who became known as Arad-un chatan batur, 'The mighty hero of the people'. This historically substantiated practice of the ancient and cruel ritual of sacrificing to the banner has even found its place in modern Mongolian literature. The contemporary Mongolian writer, B. Rintschen, introduces this barbaric custom into his three-volume historical novel *Üürün tuya*, 'Rays of the Rising Sun', a magnificent and absorbing account of the fate of a Mongolian family during the years before the Mongolian declaration of independence in 1911, which is based upon actual documents, contemporary reminiscences and eye-witness reports. He describes how Maksurchab sacrificed Manchu prisoners to his banner and how a sung ritual was performed which is very similar to our manuscript:

> 'Holy Sülde (banner), to thee I make offering
> and bow in prayer!
> Graciously grant that the pride of the hated ones
> may be humbled with the black heart,
> Grant ample booty and the good things we desire,
> Remove from our path all obstacles,
> Evils and devils,
> Let the wicked enemy's heart be faint and subdued!'

'And while he chanted this dreadful hymn, Damdinsürüng gave a sign with the arrow in his hand; the executioner's sword was raised and the head of the captive soldier was removed. Then the executioner rolled up his sleeves and drew his knife. He opened the breast of the headless corpse, blood pouring out on all sides, and with one swift movement of the hand tore out the heart, which he handed to Maksurchab. The Mongol leader then reached out for the silken banner, leaving traces of blood on it.

'Maksurchab then handed the heart to Damdinsürüng, letting him taste the blood, after which he himself lifted it to his mouth, drinking the blood, and passed it to his soldiers, who also tasted the blood of the conquered enemy.

'In twos, in fours and in tens they now beheaded the four remaining prisoners, as they had done with the first. The leader anointed the banner as well as the unit flags with the still-pulsating, bleeding hearts. After he had completed this ancient, barbaric ritual and sacrificed a human life to the banner or sülde, the leader Maksurchab spoke . . .'

Each manuscript, each small scrap of hand-written paper contains its own secrets, reveals yet another dark corner of the human soul and uncovers mysteries which have remained hidden for centuries.

AUGUST STRINDBERG'S DISCOVERY

After the Battle of Poltava in 1709, when the army of the Swedish king, Charles XII, following a succession of brilliant victories, suffered a crushing defeat by the Russians, many of the Swedish prisoners of war spent long years in captivity in the eastern provinces of the far-flung Russian Empire. The defeated Swedish king made no attempt to have them freed. But Czar Peter the Great made good use of the skill of these prisoners in the backward areas of Siberia on the borders of China.

Many never returned, many others only saw Sweden again years later. Those who did return brought back astonishing reports from that remote part of the East. One of them, Philipp Johann von Strahlenberg, committed his impressions to paper. His book on the Northern and Eastern part of Europe and Asia, which appeared in Stockholm in 1730, made him famous; quite a number of his theories are still valid today.

A sergeant in the Swedish artillery, Johann Gustav Renat, had suffered particular hardship. Together with his fellow-prisoners he had been transported to Siberia, but only to be captured by the Zungarians on one of their periodic raids across the Russian border.

For seventeen long years, from 1716 to 1733, Renat remained a prisoner of the West Mongolian Zungars. Tsewangrabdan (1665–1727), nephew of the famous Galdan, who had fought against the Manchus right to the bitter end in 1697, had succeeded his uncle. Although he had been at one time allied with the Manchus against his uncle, once he himself became the Zungarian ruler he too acquired the ambition to set up a Western Mongolian Empire between China and Russia. An experienced artilleryman like Gustav Renat, who also knew something of the construction of cannons, was therefore more than welcome. The two men, the Zungars Khan and the Swede, got on well together. When Renat was allowed to return to Sweden in 1734, he brought back two maps which the Khan of the Zungars had presented to him. One of them had been drawn by Tsewangrabdan himself. Both maps, which are in the Kalmuck script, show Zungaria, the Ili region and the border area between Russia and Western Mongolia. They are more detailed than anything on these areas previously available in Europe. The maps, which are on coarse paper, show a colourful landscape with green or reddish mountains and blue lakes.

Renat's maps disappeared into the Linköping Library in Sweden, where they lay forgotten for 140 years, before being rediscovered by August Strindberg (1849–1912), the famous writer, in the days before he had made his name. Strindberg was only twenty-five years old when he took up a post in the winter of 1874, as 'amanuensis', as assistant in the Royal Library in Stockholm. He was given the task of cataloguing a collection of Chinese books, though he was no sinologist. He knew no Chinese. With all the enthusiasm and energy of youth he acquired text-books and dictionaries and set about learning the Chinese script. This involved him in a study of China and Sweden's relations with China. During the four years that Strindberg spent at the Royal Library in Stockholm, he produced several scientific works, which won him recognition from various societies and academies. During this same period Strindberg also became interested in 'the fate of the Swedish prisoners after the Battle of Poltava'. He came upon Strahlenberg's name and then in 1878, after further research, upon the name of Johann Gustav Renat, and his two Kalmuck maps. It was at this time that Strindberg began to acquire a rooted distaste for Charles XII of Sweden, which was to become more and more pronounced over the next thirty years. He regarded Charles XII's war against the Czar Peter I, his attempt to mobilize the Asiatic Turks against Christian Russia as a betrayal of Europe. Shortly after discovering Renat's maps, Strindberg left the library and abandoned his oriental studies.

But the Kalmuck maps, which his quick eye had discovered, had by this time captured the attention of the scientific world. They provided a new picture of the geographical abilities and knowledge of the Mongols, for no one had realized that the Mongols had actually produced maps. For some time, however, efforts to find other examples were unavailing. In 1911 Boris Vladimircov, a Russian Mongolist, who made many interesting discoveries, published a hand-painted Mongolian map of Western Mongolia; but then no more was heard of Mongolian maps and cartographers.

THE GENERAL'S ESTATE

Quite near my house in Peking was a large, palatial residence surrounded by a high wall. Every time I drove to the Catholic University, I passed the narrow alley, one side of which was bounded by this high wall.

I was told that an old Mongolian general from the Manchu period lived there. No one ever saw him or heard anything of him.

Attempts to call on him, in order to ask him about Mongolian manuscripts, were all in vain. Then, one day in 1944, the great gate of the palace stood open. Servants in white mourning-dress were running to and fro. A platform covered with straw mats for the funeral music was erected, and for several days and nights the air was filled with the shrill sound of trumpets and flutes, with the rhythmic beat of gongs and drums. The old man had died and the mourning was long and loud. Then one day there was silence again. The corpse had left the house. The red-enamelled oak coffin on the high, swaying bier had been carried out beyond the city walls and buried.

Now was the time to act, before the general's effects were squandered or even destroyed by ignorant hands. It did not seem to me correct that I should myself make an approach, so I commissioned one of the Chinese booksellers, who had regular access to the house to offer books, to make inquiries on my behalf in the late general's house.

A few days later he came back, smiling proudly at the success of his mission. The dead man, he told me, had held a senior post under the Manchus in the Ministry which, until 1911, administered the Mongolian territories, and he opened the package he was carrying and produced manuscript after manuscript. Material for archives? I did not waste much time bargaining, but bought. When I came to examine my purchase, I discovered more than twenty-six hand-painted Mongolian maps.

These maps later found their way to the Marburg Library in West Germany. Then in 1958, when the German traveller Hermann Consten died, more than 150 hand-painted Mongolian maps were found among his effects. After returning from his memorable jonrney, on which he witnessed the bitter fighting round Kobdo in 1911, he had lived for many years in Peking until after the Second World War, during which he made a special study of the Mongols. He could be seen almost every day, a wiry, compact figure of a man with around, friendly face, exercising his Mongolian ponies on the 'Glacis'. His collection of maps was also acquired for the Marburg Library.

As a result Germany today has one of the largest collections – 180 – of hand-painted Mongolian maps. Even the great State Library of the Mongolian People's Republic only has 360 such maps listed in its 1937 catalogue.

13,000 NAMES

These maps are, in fact, colourful pictures which served a practical purpose. In the bird's-eye view there is always a glimpse of Mongolian landscape. Each of the Mongolian princes had to submit a pictorial map of his principality every ten years to the Ministry for the Outer Marches (Li-fan-yuan) in Peking. Such maps go back to the reign of the Emperor Kang Hsi, who gave orders that the Mongolian princes must notify Peking of any change of residence.

'The mountains, rocks and ruins, temples and monasteries, bridges and gorges and mountain-passes' were all to be clearly indicated, according to an imperial edict of 1690. And so, until 1911, the Mongolian chanceries in all the small principalities copied the old maps, made the necessary alterations, gave a name to every pictorial insert on the map and sent the finished product to Peking.

Tiny villages clinging to wooded mountain-sides can be seen, steep towering cliffs, and figures to show how many days' ride it is to the next habitation. A blue river runs under a vermilion suspension-bridge. Stupas, gravestones and small temples are in white chalk. The snow-white tents of the princes, whose names are given, have gay green and red doors. On the flat roofs of the Tibetan-style monasteries are tall, iron tridents to keep away the evil spirits, while the palaces which the princes built in the Mongolian steppes on the Chinese model have bright crimson pillars and lattice-work.

Many of these monasteries and small palaces have disappeared; much has been destroyed and razed to the ground. But the names on the maps remain. Their historical value is clear.

When my colleagues and I began to study these maps and their place-names some years ago, we had no idea of the amount of work that lay before us. Today we have extracted more than 13,000 place-names from the 180 maps. Any place that was mentioned in a historical work in connection with this or that event can now be located.

IV DANISH EXPEDITIONS IN MONGOLIA

The desk at which I sat from 1953 onwards in the Oriental Department of the Royal Library in Copenhagen, when I was preparing a comprehensive survey of the Mongolian books, is a large, white-enamelled Empire desk with a broad writing-surface covered with green baize. The edges and the embossed feet are picked out in gold. It was the desk of the Danish king Frederick V, a very enlightened monarch, who, true to the inquiring spirit of his age, presented his country with the Royal Library. I still sit at this desk when I am in Copenhagen, working at one or other of the many Mongolian manuscripts. But I am not the only one who has worked so often at this desk; many other scholars have used it – Danes, Englishmen, Americans, a famous man from Ceylon, Dutchmen, Swedes and Finns. The reason why King Frederick V's desk is in such international demand today is the large number of Mongolian manuscripts, which are stacked round it on high tiers of shelves. The room still has a slight odour of joss-sticks, of the incense used in the lamaist monasteries of Mongolia, of mutton fat and arghal, the dried cow and camel dung, which, for want of any other fuel, is burnt in the Mongol yurts. The dung gives off an acrid smoke, which no one who has once smelt it can ever forget.

THE SECOND-LARGEST COLLECTION IN EUROPE

Both in range and in quantity, this is the second-largest, and in terms of content the most important collection of Mongolian manuscripts in Europe; 568 manuscripts and prints, yellow with age, which stem for the most part from the south of Inner Mongolia. How they were acquired and assembled by Kaare Grønbech on the Second Central Asia Expedition of the Danish Royal Geographical Society led by the Dane Henning Haslund-Christensen constitutes an adventure in itself. That they were collected is a tribute to the vision of a scholar and to his determination to preserve and protect them through the sort of crises which can threaten whole cultures and peoples.

THE UNHAPPY 'THIRTIES

During the 1930s Inner Mongolia and its southern tribes were in very real danger. Not only their basic economy, but their very existence as a nation, was threatened. The political situation in Inner Mongolia in 1937 was characterized by the vanished hopes of achieving a united Mongolia and the new hope and trust that Japan would lend support against China. Pro-Japanese but anti-princely nationalists lived side by side with anti-Russian and anti-Japanese and pro-princely Mongols. One thing they all had in common was their opposition to China, which took various forms, ranging from a moderate claim to cultural autonomy for the Mongols within National China to the radical demand for independence from China and the creation of an autonomous Inner Mongolia. The Communist Party was active underground among the Inner Mongolians; the first partisan groups were already being formed to fight against Prince Teh and his pro-Japanese group, either out of anti-Japanese feeling or on instructions from the Chinese Communists.

DISILLUSIONED NATIONALISTS

Even more serious than this political instability, the hope of foreign intervention to help them regain their independence – a dream the Mongols had never given up – was the dreadful economic situation, the appalling poverty among the Mongols, the complete lack of any popular education, hygiene or health service, which was grotesquely out of line with Chinese promises. As the ploughed fields of the Chinese settlers expanded, more and more Mongols in Inner Mongolia gave up their nomadic life. Modern consumer goods, usually of the cheapest Japanese manufacture, began to squeeze out the old hand-made commodities in daily use. In their poverty the Mongols could no longer devote so much care to embellishing saddles and bridles. The artistic silver-work which had once adorned them and the costly silver and coral jewellery for the women's hair became increasingly rare. Here too, under the growing pressure of modern civilization, the old Mongolian customs were slowly dying out. And the broad mass of the Mongol people in Inner Mongolia, at that time a bare million, were accepting this new development with resignation. None of the new political ideas had as yet struck a spark in them, and only a few of the younger generation realized that, if the Mongols were to survive the twentieth century, they themselves must play a part in this development, that they must take a hand in shaping their own destiny. This was the situation in Inner Mongolia between 1937 and 1939. A former member of the great Central Asia Expedition of Sven Hedin, wrote: 'Within a generation of Mongols, Mongolia will have become a pampa, in which herds graze and factory chimneys smoke, in which "corned beef" is manufactured in bulk. Only in the barren country of Western Mongolia will a few yurts survive. There they will create a nature-reserve and reservations.'

The situation of the inhabitants of Inner Mongolia was similar to that of the last Indians, before the United States protected them against decimation by placing them in special reservations.

A LITERARY RESCUE EXPEDITION

It was with this situation in mind that the Danish Central Asia Expedition set out in 1938 with the deliberate intention of preserving as much as possible of the culture and literature of the Mongols, both present and past, before it disappeared – which was bound to happen, unless the situation in Mongolia underwent a major change. This was an expedition whose specific aim was to preserve, to collect. Of course, there had been previous expeditions to Mongolia which had acquired objects in daily use, national costumes and religious pictures for enthnographical collections. The great Sino-Swedish Expedition which had travelled through Mongolia and East Turkestan in 1927–35 (Scientific Expedition to the North-western Provinces of China under the leadership of Dr Sven Hedin), had also collected Mongolian scripts; other and earlier travellers had done the same. But that had been a haphazard process of simply picking up books *en route*, whenever they became available. The Danish expedition was the first to be organized for the specific purpose of collecting as much as could be found of Mongolian culture, language and literature and preserving it from destruction through negligence, ignorance or political unrest. Up till then the work of collecting and exploring in Mongolia had been done largely by the Russians, whose interest had naturally been primarily in those parts of Mongolia in which Russia and later the Soviet Union had a political interest. Namely, Outer Mongolia, the Buryat area and the Kalmuck steppes between the Volga and the Black Sea. No one, apart from the Danish traveller Henning Haslund-Christensen, had so far travelled in Inner Mongolia for the purpose of preserving the old literary monuments, specimens of oral traditions and local customs. Haslund-Christensen, veteran of many expeditions with experience of both travelling and living in Central Asia, had taken part in this expedition under Sven Hedin. He had lived for a long time with the western Mongols of Tien Shan and was loved and respected by the Mongols like so many other Scandinavians who lived among them as traders or missionaries. An avalanche had crushed his leg and for a long time he was lame. But the spell of the great open steppes had proved irresistible. In 1936–37 he travelled alone through the eastern Mongolian provinces of the new Japanese puppet-state Manchukuo, where he recorded on phonograph-cylinders songs and exorcism ceremonies of the old Mongolian folk religion, Shamanism, which was gradually dying out. This rare scientific material survived the war and is still in the National Museum in Copenhagen, although unfortunately no one has as yet gone through it and evaluated it. Haslund-Christensen, by virtue of his unique experience, qualified as leader of the new Danish expedition. W. Jakobsen was responsible for collecting ethnographical material, and the Danish scholar Kaare Grønbech for collecting books.

FIRST CONTACTS

The great adventure began in Kweihwa or Köke Khota, 'The Blue City', as the Mongols called it, which Altan Khan (1507–82) had built at the end of the sixteenth century. At the height of his power the Tumat prince, who until then had lived, like his contemporaries and noble relations from the tribe of Jenghiz Khan, in round Mongol tents, devised a plan to build a permanent city. To be precise, the idea that a real prince must have a permanent residence was put into his mind by Chinese refugees from the China of the Ming emperors, members of the Buddhist 'White Lotus Sect', which was outlawed in China in the late sixteenth century and banned as a subversive organization. The idea came to Altan Khan at a time when he regarded himself as an influential prince; and this, strictly speaking, he was, at least as a source of unrest, which the Mongols of his tribe, the Tumat, and his allies were able to stir up on the long north-west frontier of the internally weak empire of the Ming dynasty. He had also led campaigns against Tibet's eastern borders and the territory of the yellow Uigurs. From there he had brought back Tibetan Buddhist priests, who had preached to him the salvation that lay in the Buddhist doctrine and had so convinced him that he had decided to build a permanent temple for Buddha's religion and his monks. From a temple to a town to a princely palace was a simple progression; moreover, to put such a plan into operation was also easy, for Altan Khan had cheap, willing and skilled labour to hand in the form of the Chinese refugees. The Chinese master-builders drew and measured, the Chinese carpenters worked on tree-trunks which had been transported from remote forests, Chinese masons, tilers and stone-masons did the rest, until, before the wondering eyes of the Mongols, a temple and a prince's palace took shape in the flat Tumat country surrounded by a ring of mountains. Some walls and pillars collapsed and it was only with great difficulty that Altan Khan was persuaded that this was not the revenge of the earth-spirits, who had been offended and enraged by all the digging and building, but merely the result of false reckoning and somewhat amateurish work by men who, before they had fled from the persecution of the Ming emperors, had been engaged in quite different pursuits from building houses and measuring and trimming wooden beams for vaulted roofs. But eventually they succeeded and Altan Khan's palace and temple stood there complete with vaulted roofs and soaring pillars in the Chinese style. It is thus that we see it in a contemporary picture, which has been preserved in an open letter sent by Altan Khan to the Chinese Emperor. The foundation-stone of Köke Khota had been laid. Other temples and buildings were added. Some of them were still standing when Grønbech and the other Danish members of the expedition took up their quarters there and prepared their journey into Inner Mongolia. Some of the oldest buildings are standing today, although Köke Khota, as it is officially called, has become a city with more Chinese inhabitants than Mongols, the seat of many administrative offices and a large University library, which contains thousands of Mongolian manuscripts still untouched.

In October 1938, when the Danish expedition arrived in Köke Khota, there were more Chinese than Tumat-Mongols. Moreover most of the Mongols looked Chinese – an added reason for preserving what could still be preserved and for collecting books in Mongolian script, before someone used them to light the stove.

EXPERIENCES WITH OPIUM-SMOKERS

Grønbech lost no time in trying to make contact with Mongolian book-owners. A lama with a nose for business proved very helpful.

'I have put out numerous feelers,' wrote Grønbech in his diary on 14th October. 'My lama has mysterious plans, which, he has promised, will soon produce results.' Grønbech had been told of one man, who was said to possess an outstanding collection of Mongolian manuscripts, a Mongol named Pao-yueh-ching who had been made director of a bank set up by the Japanese for their occupied territory in Inner Mongolia, Meng-chiang. Grønbech tried to contact him. 'The bank director Pao-yueh-ching is in Kalgan. The family of the Mongol Öldshei has about twenty books. Then there is Söderbom's Mongol friend, who, we have been told by Öldshei, also owns books. But they are in Chahar, where his family lives. Söderbom knows of yet another place, of a chauffeur who buys oil from Söderbom, and this chauffeur drives for a Mongol who is living at present in the house of a Chinese refugee. This Chinese, who was born a Mongol, owns books.'

These were the first titbits of information that Grønbech received. But very soon things began to warm up. After only three days he managed to track down an old manuscript of the Subhasitarat-nanidhi, translated from the Tibetan; this was a list of rules of moral conduct, which had been drawn up in the twelfth century by the Saskya Pandita but had remained popular with the Mongols.

'The book-hunt has now begun in earnest,' wrote Grønbech in his diary. 'We have been in the temple of Shiretu dshun and later visited people. With me were Söderbom, Haslund and Öldshei. The "victims" were the lama who traded with us yesterday, a lama born in Tibet who speaks Mongolian, a lama named Gombodchab who owned books, a very knowledgeable lama who is also a heavy opium-smoker, and finally the widow of a Mongolian prince.

'I finally obtained the spoil from the opium-smoker Tumen bayar. The first time we called on him we had to leave empty-handed, because he was busy smoking and not of this world. But when we came back half an hour later we were offered seats on and near the Kang, and we cautiously came to the point.

'He asked me if I knew Subhasidhi! "No? Ah, but that is really a good book."

'He then took it out of his cupboard. I was able to glance through it. Later he allowed me to take the first volume home with me. In any case, I could not read more than one volume a day and I forbore to mention that I could easily photograph all (eight) volumes in a few hours.'

THE SPELL IS BROKEN

The spell was broken. Grønbech was able, in the cause of knowledge, to photograph with his Leica quite a few valuable works, which their owners were reluctant to part with. In the meantime the Japanese authorities had also relaxed their ban on the departure of the Danish expedition. It had taken them three months to change their minds, during which time the members of the expedition were forced to cool their heels in Kalgan, the gateway to Mongolia, and in Köke Khota. But fortunately these same towns yielded many interesting manuscripts.

The attitude of the Japanese army of occupation and of the civil administration it controlled was the same towards all foreigners regardless of their nationality. The Japanese, who had only marched into Meng-chiang in 1937, were extremely suspicious and were plagued by a fear of spies. The slightest pretext was seized upon to prevent any visitor from continuing his travels and to treat him as a spy. After three months of patient waiting and not a few incidents, their suspicions had at least been allayed and the Danes received permission to travel into the Chahar territory, the heart of Inner Mongolia. The warm summer weather was now definitely over, autumn had begun, and at the end of October the cold can be quite severe in Mongolia. This handicapped them in their work.

BOOK-BUYING AT HEADQUARTERS

They had decided to set up their headquarters in Hadain Sume, an old temple in Chahar, which had been abandoned by the lamaist monks and which had been inhabited for many years by the Swedish merchant and missionary Larson. This was, so to speak, soil in which the seeds of confidence in the Scandinavians and their goodwill had already been sown among the Mongols.

The expedition was to derive great benefit from this. F. A. Larson had been sent to Mongolia from Sweden in 1893 by the Christian Missionary Alliance. He had survived all the dangers and disturbances of the Boxer Rebellion, which had cost so many other Protestant and Catholic missionaries their lives; he had won the confidence of the Mongols and particularly of Jebtsundampa the Eighth, Hutuktu of Urga, the first Head of State of an autonomous Northern Mongolia, which is today the Mongolian People's Republic. He had even been made a 'Duke' and in the early years of the autonomous Mongolian state after 1911 had represented the Hutuktu in Peking. Other Scandinavian missionaries and welfare workers had lived in Hadain Sume after him. The Swedish doctor Erikson spent several years there, helping sick Mongols as best he could. Princes in their palaces and humble folk in their yurts availed themselves of his skill. The Prince of Dörbet appointed him his personal physician. Another Swedish doctor, Dr Ollen, had settled in Gultsagan, also situated in Chahar.

The confidence which had been built up over more than thirty years by Scandinavian friends of the Mongols proved a valuable asset to the Danish expedition. Barely had the news got round that strangers had arrived in Hadain Sume than Mongols came pouring in, filled with curiosity. An entry in a diary for 28th October 1938 gives a vivid impression of the way Mongolian manuscripts were traced and acquired.

'It had always been Larson's custom to invite the many Mongols, who came out of curiosity or to do business, to drink tea in the kitchen and then to receive them in audience. We continued this practice. The population of Chahar and Sunit are, for the most part, very poor and anxious to sell. The first move came with the arrival of Harchin-Hu, a cattleman from Hadain Sume.

'We followed him to his home, which was two yurts a few miles from our headquarters. The dogs were held down by some children and we entered the yurt. It was my first visit to a real Mongol. In the middle of the round yurt a dung fire was burning (this is the only fuel available in Mongolia) and the man's wife was busy cooking. We sat down on the felt matting and were served with Mongolian tea, a kind of corn soup with tea. We were also given ürüm, flat cakes made of dried milk. Then the books were brought out and among them I found a collection of fairy-tales.

'I took the books with me and spent the afternoon reading through them. This was by no means easy. Mongolian books are usually in a shocking state. They are stitched but never bound. In consequence pages are frequently missing at the beginning and at the end, and the bottom of the page is usually so tattered that several words are missing.

'Buddhist books are usually in better condition. But here the pages are loose, so that there is always a danger that something is missing in the middle.'

Meanwhile the news had spread among the Mongols, with the speed of a steppe-fire, that the expedition was collecting Mongolian books and manuscripts and was paying well.

'This afternoon I rode out with Tamirin Suren,' Grønbech recorded in his diary on 14th November 1938, only a few weeks after they had set up their headquarters in Hadain Sume. 'He knew that there were books in a yurt camp thirty li (Chinese miles) away. After a ride through magnificent country we reached the yurts.

'As usual the place was swarming with Mongols and among the many books which they had brought was one of real interest, a ritual book for fire-worship. It contains quite a smattering of Buddhist folk-religion and the Buddhist gloss on it is very thin and transparent.'

From then on the discoveries came to the discoverer. In addition to the rare folk-religious texts, even rarer chronicles appeared. On 17th December Grønbech recorded one of these rare discoveries.

'The weather was marvellous, but I was so engrossed in the books that I hardly noticed it. Around midday the great prize arrived. A man named Bimba came into the kitchen with a book. I took him to my room, where he settled down on the floor, which the Mongols consider to be not only spacious but also comfortable. Then we talked about Haslund, how he was getting on, and about Hedin and how he was getting on, and about Bergmann and how he was getting on, and whether Haslund was now married and how his leg was getting on, and how this leg had been broken not, as they thought in Mongolia, on a heap of stones but in a heap of snow. Then he asked me if I knew various other people. But I did not know them.

'Would Bimba not like a cigarette? This he would like very much.

'Finally we came to the point. He unwound his scarf and produced a crumpled book entitled *The String of Pearls or the Genealogy of the Mongol Ruler Jenghiz Khan*. I immediately paid the fifteen dollars of which Bimba had been dreaming for so long.'

More and more books arrived. On one occasion it was a book of fortunes, on another two Mongolian chronicles, huge books, each of them between a hundred and two hundred pages. Bundles of yellowing, tattered paper and oil- and water-stained volumes and books were piling up. But quite a few Mongols had now been fired not only with enthusiasm for a worthy cause but also with the knowledge that, with a bit of swindling, there was good money to be earned.

'Today the man, who brought chronicles ten days ago, returned with a large pile of books,' the diary reports. 'He was at great pains to show me how splendid they were, picking out passages where the name Jenghiz Khan was mentioned. The whole thing was slightly mysterious. I selected the best of the books and took them off to my room. Before long the man was there again, pointing with his finger. I gave him a few of my own books to look at and was able to continue undisturbed.

'I very soon realized that in one fine book, a history of the Kalka

Mongols, only the first page was chronicle. The remainder was ordinary Buddhist text. The other Jenghiz Khan book, which was bound together with the same suspiciously new, red thread, contained eight pages of chronicle. The remainder was a Manchurian translation from the Chinese.

'But the entire middle portion of another book which had been sewn together contained chapters from the Geser Khan epic, and the remaining books also had something interesting to offer. After prolonged and dramatic bargaining, during which I disclaimed all interest in the books, particularly the two valuable ones, I finally succeeded in acquiring the whole pile.'

In the meantime the other members of the expedition were collecting ethnological specimens, household utensils and articles of clothing from the Chahar, which can be seen today in the Ethnographical Department of the National Museum in Copenhagen and which give a unique picture of the culture of Inner Mongolia in the early part of the present century. In addition to searching for manuscripts, Kaare Grønbech also devoted much of his time to studying dialects and engaged a Mongolian boy to recite folk-tales, which he wrote down.

'Lhisurun, the boy who tells me Mongolian stories, came and started. He is excellent. He has the rare gift of being able to repeat, loud and clear, what he has just said, and my language studies are getting along famously.

'Naturally the yurt, as usual, was swarming with Mongols. Every now and then it would spill over and a handful of Mongols would interpose themselves between an accusative and a gerund. One man brought me a superb manuscript of the Ardji-Bordji stories. But the price was too high: seventy dollars!

'He came back later. Would I be prepared to give ten dollars? Gladly. So now I possess the finest Ardji-Bordji manuscript I have seen here.'

This beautiful manuscript which Grønbech had acquired contains a collection of stories, which are current in various forms in

Mongolia, of King Ardji-Bordji and the thirty-two wooden figures on the thirty-two steps to his throne, which prevent him from ascending the throne by telling him more stories. Mongolian chronicles report that these stories were told to the first Buddhist Grand Lama of Northern Mongolia, Jebtsundampa Hutuktu (1634–1723), by two Indian Buddhist monks, who were on a pilgrimage to Mongolia. The stories are undoubtedly Indian in origin. They caught the imagination of the Mongols, who told and retold them in many variations. Grønbech had succeeded in acquiring one of them. But not all the works which were brought to his notice were for sale. In such cases he would try to persuade someone to copy the book, thus at least preserving the precious contents for purposes of research.

'Other good things also come to light,' he wrote on 30th January 1939 in the diary. 'Today a lama came with a historical work, which he was prepared to copy against suitable payment, the copy to be handed to me. He receives five dollars, if he delivers the book here at headquarters in a week.'

George Söderbom, who had made a name for himself as caravan-leader on Sven Hedin's expedition and had since settled in Mongolia, also acquired several Mongolian works for the Danes. Where he could not buy the books, he asked permission to have a blue-print made of them. This he continued to do while Grønbech was ill following a fall from his horse and had to return to Peking in February 1939.

'Söderbom has acquired several manuscripts for me and has discovered a very simple method of copying books which cannot be purchased. Most Mongolian books consist, on the Chinese pattern, of double pages of quite thin paper.

'When Söderbom wants to copy such a book, he undoes the stitching, so that he can fold the single pages, which are loose, and can take an impression of them on his impregnated paper. This copy then remains for quarter of an hour in a closed tub with ammonia fumes. Later the book is sewn together again and returned to the owner, who not infrequently prefers the new book with its reddish letters to his old familiar book!'

DANGEROUS RETURN JOURNEY

But the moment finally came when the Danes had to say farewell to Hadain Sume, to their friendly and helpful Mongolian neighbours in the nearby yurt settlements and to all the other Mongols whom they had met on their journey. A venture that had seemed to hold out so much promise at the beginning, namely to get the Mongols interested in preserving their old written documents, if only because they could earn money by it, would now gradually be forgotten. The Japanese occupation authorities had given the Danes permission for only a limited stay. Furthermore the political sky in Europe had perceptibly darkened. The storm-clouds were already gathering. It was early summer 1939 when the Danish expedition arrived back in Peking with all their collections intact. Grønbech was still suffering from the after-effects of his riding accident, which continued to give him trouble until his premature and unexpected death in 1956, but otherwise everything was in order and the collections of books and ethnological material had all arrived in Peking. It soon became clear, however, that certain Japanese were after the books. There were frequent visits from people who had all the appearance of being secret agents and who feigned an interest in the expedition's discoveries. There was a very real danger that, on some pretext or other, they would remove at least all the written material from the expedition's luggage, if it was subjected to customs examination. Grønbech decided to forestall any such move. He filled the large chests with all the equipment and mementoes which he regarded as dispensable and which consisted, for the most part, of Chinese *objets d'art* acquired in Peking. These he packed in his dirty linen and the chests, properly nailed down, were sent to the customs.

Grønbech and his wife, who had waited for him in Peking, rolled the rare Mongolian manuscripts up tightly and stowed them away among their personal effects in the hand-luggage. Wrapped up in stockings and covered with articles of clothing, which even the most suspicious of customs officials is usually reluctant to examine in detail, lay the most superb specimens of Mongolian poetry and historical writing which the world of scholarship had ever known. There was no law forbidding their export, they had been collected with the knowledge and consent of the Japanese and many of them had been bought at a high price. But who could know what a spy-conscious customs-official or frontier-guard with a bias against white people would do if confronted with so many hand-written documents? It seemed better to take no risks.

In fact, the precautions taken proved to be fully justified. The heavy baggage was confiscated at the port of Dairen and was only released after long and difficult negotiations. Those who planned to deprive the Danish expedition at the last moment of the treasures it had so laboriously acquired were disappointed. The personal baggage passed through customs smoothly and without incident. When the Danish East Asia Company's boat left Dairen for Europe, it carried the entire collection of manuscripts tucked away among the Grønbechs' shirts and dresses. There were more than five hundred manuscripts and prints, which Kaare Grønbech had collected in Tumat and Chahar in the winter of 1938–39. A splendid fulfilment to a scholar's personal ambition.

But the manuscripts were still not out of danger. During the voyage came the news that Hitler had invaded Poland and that England and France were at war with Germany. True, Denmark was neutral, but this did not make the high seas any more secure. Everyone on board was seized by the U-boat fear. For most of the voyage the ship was blacked out. The Danes' homeward journey was not made any easier by the fact that the ship first called at an English port, before they finally set foot on Danish soil again at Esbjerg. But special security precautions still had to be taken. For the duration of the war the manuscripts were stored in a safe place and they survived the war undamaged. In 1949 they were placed in the Royal Library, where they have remained to this day.

There they now lie on their shelves, neatly arranged according to size. They represent a unique cross-section of ancient Mongolian literature. In terms of volume the Copenhagen collection is undoubtedly inferior to other collections but certainly not in terms of quality. Most important are the manuscripts of Mongolian chronicles. They contain historical works which were previously unknown. I had seen a reference in another historical work to one of these chronicles, the *Book of the Golden Wheel with the Thousand Spokes*, which the learned monk Siregetü Guosi Dharma had written in 1739 and which was based on many older works, but no one had ever seen this chronicle before. Grønbech was the first to have the privilege of photographing it in the library of the Horchin Mongol and bibliophile, Pao-yueh-ching. Until the Mongolian historical works were displayed in the Copenhagen Royal Library, only two or three Mongolian chronicles had been known and made accessible to western scholars. The Russian libraries were known to contain more Mongolian historical works but this did not mean that they were easy of access to the outside world. Now the Danish expedition's collection had made it possible for the first time, in Grønbech's own estimation, to have a coherent picture in western Europe of Mongolian works of history and to gauge their importance to historical research.

DID THE CHINESE HISTORIANS MISREPRESENT THE FACTS?

It is the detailed description that is particularly significant in the Mongolian chronicles. For example, where the official Chinese historians merely make a passing reference to something or, as is often the case, give a distorted account, the chronicles are much more precise or, in some cases, put things in what seems to them the right perspective. This is particularly true of the period of Manchu rule (1644–1911). The Chinese and Manchurian reports, the official announcements and the documents which have survived record only those events which appear to justify the actions of the Manchu emperors on the Chinese throne and which present the deeds of rebels such as Ligdan Khan (1604–34), his contemporary Tsoktu Taidzi, Galdan boshugtu (d.1697) and Amursana, who fought for an independent Mongolian state, as the criminal machinations of bandits against a kind and gracious emperor. This distorted picture is corrected by the Mongolian historians. In fact, one often has a suspicion that the official historians have deliberately lied. Not infrequently they are mere local rumours which have been passed from one anti-Manchurian cabal to another, but if one adds such a rumour to a not unlikely story told by another chronicle, the one supplements the other and, on the principle that 'where there is smoke, there is fire', these hints are worth pursuing.

When Ligdan Khan, the last of Jenghiz Khan's descendants to lay claim to the title and rank of Great Khan, suddenly died on the way to Tibet, his tribe did not hold out very long against the Manchu. His wives and his two sons Edshei Khonghur and Abunai surrendered to Manchu troops in June 1635. The Manchu Emperor married one of his daughters named Makata to Edshei, who died shortly afterwards in 1641, and then to the younger son Abunai. The conquered Chahar princes had also been forced by the Manchu soldiers to surrender the ancient seal of the Mongol emperors, which the Manchu Emperor adopted as his own. This, together with the marriage of one of his daughters with the off-spring of the last Mongol Great Khan, seemed to the Manchu Emperor enough to make him the legitimate successor to Jenghiz Khan. But the Mongols, and particularly those who belonged to the late Great Khan Ligdan's tribe, thought otherwise. Their loyalty to the Manchus was a highly delicate plant, which did not really flourish in spite of Manchu gifts of rank and title to Mongol princes. The Manchu were particularly mistrustful of the Chahar Mongols, although their prince, Abunai, Ligdan Khan's younger son, was the Emperor's son-in-law and a prince by the grace of the Manchu. In 1669 someone – the Mongolian chronicles blamed a prince of the Harachin tribe, which was not very well-disposed towards the Chahar – accused Abunai of nursing rebellious feelings against the Manchu Emperor; the fact that Abunai's Manchurian

wife had died in 1663 lent added weight to this slanderous accusation. So the family bonds, which were no longer so essential
to the Manchu now that they had established themselves, were not
so close as they had been. The Emperor acted immediately, had
Prince Abunai arrested and thrown into prison in Mukden. In
Abunai's place he appointed his son Burni prince of the Chahar.
But, as one Mongolian chronicle puts it, he 'did not see the growth
of others or the light of the imperial sun . . . he was unable to
adapt himself to peace and happiness'. Burni, in fact, sought ways
and means of freeing his father from prison in Mukden. In 1675
he saw an opportunity. Since December 1673 General Wu San-
Kuei, one of the oldest of the Manchu supporters, had been in
rebellion against their rule. The throne which they had worked so
hard to acquire became somewhat insecure and Emperor Sheng Tsu
had his hands full trying to suppress the rebellion of the successful
old war-hero, who in the meantime had proclaimed an empire of
his own in the Chinese province of Hunan.

Burni saw his opportunity to exploit the almost complete absence
of troops from Mukden, in order to free his father from prison.
He called his Chahar to arms and marched on the town.

Emperor Sheng Tsu mustered every man he could find in
Peking – camp-followers, cooks, service-units and untrained
Manchu – and sent them off under Generals Tuhai and Oja to meet
the Chahar Mongols advancing on Mukden. The latter do not
appear to have been strong either in numbers or in fighting-spirit.
But Tuhai had convinced his rough-and-ready army that the
Chahar were immensely rich: if they were victorious, the entire
booty would be theirs. This promise was enough to turn cooks
and raw recruits into supermen. The Chahar were defeated, the
attempt to free Abunai, who was strangled, misfired, and Burni fled.

Shortly after, according to Manchurian and Chinese historians,
Burni fell into a trap and was killed by a Horchin prince. Other
members of his family were executed by the Manchu. Burni's mortal
remains, according to one Chinese source, were allowed to be
graciously buried near his mother's grave.

A Mongolian family chronicle, which was written in 1732 by a certain General Lomi in Manchu service for his grandchildren and descendants and which I found in Eastern Mongolia in 1942, refers to a personal message he received from the second Chang chia Hutuktu Rolpaidordje, the lamaist Archbishop of Peking, who had told him that at that time, around 1732, Burni was still alive.

One's first thought is that the chronicler must have been mistaken. But another Mongolian chronicle, which Grønbech photographed and brought back to Copenhagen and which was written in 1739, also contains a report on Burni's rebellion, how it failed and how his warriors fled. But then it goes on to report that his younger brother was killed by his brother-in-law, Tusiyetu cin wang Shashin of the Horchin. Not a word of Burni's death. Another Mongolian historical work in the Copenhagen collection, which originated among the Chahar themselves and consists chiefly of local legends and traditions, denies that Burni had any intention of revolting against Emperor Sheng Tsu and then reports that Burni was able to flee 'secretly' with three companions and to reach Northern Mongolia, where he settled, unrecognized, in the Khanghai mountains.

Who is right, the Chinese historians or Mongolian tradition? Was this the beginning of a legend, which was still current in the eighteenth century among the Chahar, who were dissatisfied with the Manchu and their rule: 'Our rightful prince is not dead, he lives in a strange land'? The common people love such legends about rulers and princes' sons who fell into disfavour. There were similar legends about the Habsburg Archduke Johann, who, as Johannes Orth, went down with his ship on the way to America with the commoner he had married. But the historian cannot afford to ignore such legends, for they often contain the key to a mystery and reveal things that past generations tried to suppress.

THE FATE OF JENGHIZ KHAN

The real cause of Jenghiz Khan's death is another subject on which the Mongolian chronicles themselves are at variance and also disagree with official Chinese histories. The official version merely records that in 1226 the Emperor was thrown from his horse while out hunting, that a fever set in, of which he died in 1227. But in the Mongolian chronicles of the seventeenth century, which are based on much older historical works and traditions, the view is constantly expressed that Körbelchin, his beautiful 'lizard-like' wife, had done him an injury of which the great warrior had died. Jenghiz Khan, after his victory over the Tanghuts – a Buddhist people with a culture of their own derived from Tibet, who lived in the country stretching from the bend of the Hwang Ho west-wards and south-westwards to the Himalayas – is said to have coveted the wife of the Tanghut king. He had the king executed and took the woman into his harem. One can well imagine that Körbelchin was not greatly impressed by this novel form of court-ing. In any case a whole series of Mongolian chronicles report that, after they had slept together, some 'injury was done' to Jenghiz Khan's imperial body. Körbelchin, so the story goes, fled, pur-sued by the Mongolian guards and flung herself into the Yellow River, which flowed near the camp. Jenghiz Khan died. The injury that he suffered is usually hinted at very cautiously. An early seventeenth-century chronicle, however, is quite specific and records with complete clarity: 'The prince's wife Körbelchin pressed a small piece of metal into her sexual organ and, after she had injured the ruler's sexual organ, she fled, threw herself into the Hwang Ho and died.' The Mongolian historians of the next two hundred years very soon abandoned this naturalistic account of the great ruler's death, particularly as their approach to history became more nationalist. A man who is presented to a growing country as a model and symbol of unity cannot possibly be allowed to die in such circumstances. Marat's death in the bath-tub by the dagger of the beautiful Charlotte is almost heroic by comparison. Thus one Mongolian historian around 1775 condemns this Judith and Holofernes legend as a malicious invention by the Western Mongolians, who had always been ill-disposed towards the Mongols. And Inchanashi, the author of the *Blue Chronicle*, comes to a similar conclusion. One is inclined to bracket the legend of the suicide of Körbelchin with stories of maidens being sacrificed to the Hwang Ho, which are told of the third century B.C. Perhaps it really was a slander perpetrated by the Chinese against their Mongol oppressors, the posthumous murder of a man's good name, which became a Mongolian legend. Many such questions have been thrown up by these hitherto unknown Mongolian chronicles.

SUPERSTITION AND COMMONSENSE

Even more interesting perhaps are certain other manuscripts which Grønbech and his companions collected in Inner Mongolia. They include small scraps of paper, stained with oil and fat and covered with hand-written notes, which do not contain any precise historical data but which do throw some light on what the Mongols were thinking up till a few decades ago, what was passing through their minds – in short, what made them tick. There are traditional prayers and sayings which are still very much in use. One learns considerably more about the character of a people from the anonymous testimony of folk-lore and folk-songs than from works of literature. The manuscripts of the popular Mongol prayers are a veritable gold-mine for any scholar who is interested in the character and culture of these cattle-breeders and nomads. Quite a few of these prayers are addressed to the mother of fire. The Mongol prays to his fire-god in winter in particular, for it is to the warm glow of the fire that he owes his survival. Other prayers are addressed to Tsaghan Ebügen, the 'White Old Man', who gives the herds his blessing, makes them produce and multiply, and protects them against robbers, cattle-pests, sudden snowstorms and lethal drought.

The Mongols believe that Geser Khan, the hero of the great popular epic, lives in the cloud-mountains of the sky and they also pray to him for protection and blessing, especially for their herds. In one of their prayers there is a reference to periods in their history, when, as the spirit or economic necessity moved them, they attacked the Chinese on the other side of the Great Wall:

> 'Son of heaven,
> whose princely body is clad in golden armour,
> . . . deign to be present on this raid
> as leader of the raiders!'

Other manuscripts are collections of songs and sayings which were customary at marriage-ceremonies. The masters of ceremonies on such occasions, the so-called Hondshin, perpetuated these customs unchanged for many centuries and wrote them down in 'Hondshin Tüke', or marriage prayer-books. Other manuscripts give instructions for soothsaying and specify favourable and unfavourable days. My English friend and colleague, Dr Bawden, who has made a special study of these fortune-telling books and the practices described in them, says it is doubtful whether all the various prescriptions, which lay down on which days specific sections of the yurt should be erected, wells sunk and journeys undertaken, could possibly be carried out. But the prescriptions were there and there were plenty of Mongols who tried to observe them and whose lives were governed by them. The Buryat writer Namsaraiev has described this spiritual life of the Mongols, which continued into the early part of the present century: 'Visible and invisible devils and spirits of the dead, Buddhas and gods, the lords of the mountains and the cliffs, the water-spirits, ill omens, good omens and all such stupid superstition oppressed them. In addition there was an appalling number of seers, wise men and quacks, lamaist monks and shamans, who terrorized them and took gold and silver from them in return.'

Other manuscripts, however, reveal the practical commonsense of the Mongols in the form of wise adages and rules, which reflect the qualities to be expected of a good man, a good prince, a son or a daughter. By contrast there are those which show how one should not behave. *The story of the clever parrot*, *The clear mirror*, *The drop that feeds the common man* – manuscripts bearing these titles are to be found in the Copenhagen collection and they contain much homely but also much profound advice.

> 'When you are still young,
> You shall not drink brandy and wine;
> When you drink spirits and are drunk,
> You are laughed at by all!'

And another:

> 'Even if you instruct that stupid animal,
> the cow, it will not follow
> the path of the camel!'

Sometimes the moral precepts are so vividly presented that they are reminiscent of European baroque writing. One of these Mongolian scripts discusses the advantages of a good wife and the disadvantages of a bad one:

> 'Eighth are the women who are uncomely;
> They have hair like a hedgehog's,
> Their bodies smell like an animal's,
> Their speech is like the screech of an owl.
> Ninth are the women no one sleeps with,
> They are averse to washing,
> Spotted like a ram and have drooping lips.
> Tenth are the women, whom no one takes to,
> Their house is like a pigsty,
> They have the nature of a bitch,
> The mouth and lips of a camel.
> Eleventh are the women who are so hard to stomach,
> They are quarrelsome as quails,
> Their behinds are quite enormous and
> Have many nests of felt-lice.'

This might have been written by Abraham à Sancta Clara or by François Villon. But it is the work of an unknown Mongolian poet and it will be worth investigating whether there is evidence here of a Near Eastern influence, of the misogyny of pre-Christian desert ascetics, which might have been transmitted by Syrian travellers.

JOURNEY INTO HELL

Then there are numerous manuscripts of tales, including the Chahar Mongol folk-tales, which Grønbech wrote down with the help of the artful Lhisurun, whose work he described in his diary: five versions of the Ardji-Bordji stories, stories relating 'how the very white lama and the law-king Ardasidi exchanged views', the *Secret Instructions* which show how the Mongols adapted the plots of Persian stories about Prince Ardasin or Artaxerxes. Also their multi-volume Mongolian version of 'Shin Kung-An', a story of the adventures of the judge Si mergen, whose Chinese name was Shih Lüen and who, as one of the Chinese Emperor Kang Hsi's judges, not only passed judgements in court but fought bandits, was captured by them, escaped and eventually received high honours from the Emperor. A Mongolian eighteenth-century thriller!

There is a magnificent, gaily-illustrated manuscript of the story *How the holy, very accomplished Molon toyin repaid his mother for the favours she had done him*, a story of a journey to hell. It is modelled on Buddhist stories going back to the third century and describes how Molon, a rich young Mongol, becomes a monk after the death of his mother, who had led a sinful life, and through prayer is allowed to look for her in the hot and cold hells until her redemption.

Dante was influenced by this story in his description of the infernos in his *Divine Comedy*.

The medieval latin romance *Visiones Georgü*, which was written about 1353, describes a journey into hell by the Hungarian Knight George, whom St Michael leads through purgatory in search of his mother. Coincidence or influence? In any case the descent into hell was a constant source of inspiration to Mongolian story-tellers and artists. There is a whole series of manuscripts of the Mongolian chap-book, well illustrated and embellished with coloured miniatures. The Copenhagen manuscript is one of the finest. With the utmost simplicity the artist portrays the tortures of fire and ice. The flames of hell-fire are red, while the ice-crags of the cold hell are greenish blue, the colours of putrefaction. With artless precision the torments of hell are described, torments to which sinners are subjected by various horned creatures, by devils and fiends with bestial heads. Bodies are sawn in pieces and impaled on pointed blades, bright red blood gushes out, bodies are crushed between cliffs and blocks of ice, liars have their tongues split and those without shame have their genitals removed. But all this is presented in such a way that the motive is not enjoyment of indecency or torment but a simple delight in telling a story.

There are not many illustrated Mongolian manuscripts but those that are known show, like the woodcuts, great artistic skill and a childish transparency and simplicity of presentation. The pornographic element is extremely rare. In all the Mongolian manuscripts which have passed through my hands – and that means several thousand – I have seen only one that portrays a naked couple in the act of coition. And that was not in a pornographic work or love-manual but in a book of fortunes, a handbook in Kalmuck script, which prophesied the most favourable days for married couples to have intercourse.

V THE TRAGEDY OF THE LAST GREAT KHAN

LIGDAN KHAN, THE AUTOCRAT

Even after the Mongol rule in China, the Yüan dynasty, had come to an end and the Mongols had been driven out in 1368, the title and office of Great Khan was retained. The first-born son in the direct line of the last Yüan Emperor, Toghon temür (d.1270) continued to bear the title, but in the two hundred years until Ligdan Khan's succession the office carried in the main little or no power. The Great Khan was *primus inter pares*, more the head of an exclusive family of imperial descent than a mighty ruler such as Jenghiz Khan had been. But the spiritual attributes, the charisma of the Great Khan's office, raised its holder above the other princes. It depended on the individual whether he added power to the title. Most of the Mongol Great Khans in the fifteenth and sixteenth centuries did not do so. Jasaktu Khan delegated his powers to a kinsman, Altan Khan of the Tumat tribe (1507–83), who in a series of brilliant campaigns against the Chinese and Tibetans made the Mongols once again a serious threat to China's northern and north-western borders, brought in Buddhist monks from Tibet and initiated a spiritual revival among the Mongols. His reign brought to its climax a development which had begun under Dayan Khan, the Great Khan of 1480–83. For Dayan had freed the Mongols from the supremacy of the Western Mongol tribes. Under Altan, the Mongols experienced a renaissance of political power. But Altan Khan had no ambition to be Great Khan. The title remained with the Chahar princes. When Jasaktu Khan died in 1604, he was succeeded by Ligdan, the first-born of his late son Manghus taidzi.

There is a gap in the life of Ligdan, this tragic figure of Mongol history, which has remained mysterious and unexplained.

Ligdan was seventeen years old when he became Great Khan in 1604. Lamaism, which had been flourishing again among the Mongols since 1578, seems to have had a marked appeal for the young ruler. He went through various consecration ceremonies at the hands of leading priests, built a number of monasteries in the short space of a year and gave generously to the priesthood. As his spiritual adviser and resident chaplain he appointed Sharba Hutuktu, the reincarnation of Saskya pa-Hierarchen, the former Regent of Tibet under the Yüan dynasty. Very soon, as Great Khan, he received the honorary title of 'Hutuktu Khan', the 'blessed Khan', and was widely believed to be a reincarnation of the greatest of the Mongol emperors of China, Kublai Khan (1260–92), who had been the first to receive the title 'blessed Khan' from the lamaist priests. Ligdan was regarded as one of the great patrons of Buddhism and his outstanding act of devotion was the order he gave that the lamaist holy book, the Ganjur, should be translated from Tibetan into Mongolian.

The Sharba Hutuktu, appointed Court chaplain, brought with him from Tibet the golden statue of a Buddhist divinity named Mahakala, which the Emperor Kublai had once presented to Saskya pa-Hierarchen in the thirteenth century. The Hutuktu's object, of course, was to demonstrate that the lamaist Church regarded Ligdan Khan as the physical and spiritual reincarnation of Kublai. What for the lamaist Church in its newly restored missionary-field, Mongolia, was a shrewd gesture, an almost too naïve form of flattery of a prince's vanity, meant for Ligdan, the holder of the office of Great Khan, a great deal more, namely, the responsibility of power. Before long he was calling himself Jenghiz Khan after his great-grandfather.

There is no doubt that Ligdan Khan possessed a greater measure of political vision than any other Mongol prince of his time. At a very early stage he realized that the growing power of the Manchus, the Tungusian tribe which, from small beginnings in Eastern Manchuria, had embarked upon the conquest of the Chinese Empire, represented a serious threat to his plans and to the cause of Mongolian independence. He began, therefore, to place more emphasis than any Great Khan before him on the central authority of the Great Khanate. The Horchin, the tribe which lived nearest to the Manchus and which had intermarried with them since the early sixteenth century, were given a forceful reminder by Ligdan that they were Mongols and as such were his, the Great Khan's, subjects. The more he tried to tighten his hold on the reins of power from his permanent headquarters – the town near the old Liao pagoda on the crest of the Hsingan mountains – the more restive the other Mongol princes became. What to him seemed a revival of former Mongolian unity, of the old power of his ancestors, seemed to the other princes merely overweening ambition and a violation of the *primus inter pares* position. So one Mongol tribe after another defected. The first to turn their backs on him were those living nearest to the Manchus; then those who lived farthest away followed suit. All gave as their reason Ligdan Khan's lust for power and his violation of law and custom. In an exchange of notes with the Manchus Ligdan referred to himself as master over four hundred thousand Mongols. He ignored the Manchu replies which credited him with the allegiance of only a small section of the Mongols outside his own kinsmen, the Chahar. Reports of his high-handed violations of law and custom, transmitted to the Manchus by the defectors, complete the picture of a headstrong, egoistical prince. Of the war-booty from battles against the Manchus or from raids across the Great Wall into the thickly-populated Amein area of China he always took first choice. And, if he felt like it, he even seized booty which legitimately belonged to other princes. His daughters, whom he had married to various Mongol princes of other tribes, were so arrogant that they used their higher rank as a pretext for hounding their husbands. The Manchus spread a rumour that he sacrificed prisoners of war to the gods of his battle-standards. The enemy who portrayed him thus was later to defeat him.

ONLY A MARBLE MILLSTONE REMAINED

Very little has survived in the way of evidence that might produce a more favourable picture of Ligdan. The inscribed stone which he had put up in Cagan Suburga, the White Pagoda in what is today the Bagharin region, this one-time headquarters, when this old eleventh-century marble monument was restored, has disappeared. In 1895 it was still standing. In 1920 a Belgian priest called Father Mullie found a millstone, which had been hewn out of the white marble stone. In 1941, when I camped for some time at Cagan Suburga, I made a careful search of the great walled quadrangle and ramparts of the almost totally-ruined monastery for any traces of the inscription. But I could find none. A rubbing of this unique document, which was made by the Russian Mongolist Pozdneev and which is said to be in Leningrad, is almost certainly the only one that remains of Ligdan Khan's inscription. It shows him as the great champion of Buddhism, who brought the Sharba Hutuktu in ceremonial procession to the place where the Ganjur was to be translated.

Otherwise there is no original memorial left to Ligdan Khan. The Buryat traveller Žamcarano claims to have seen a portrait of Ligdan Khan and his battle-standard in a temple at Sarachi, a small settlement at Kweihwa near the Yellow River, in 1910. But no more has been heard of them. In the first years of the Sino-Japanese war Red Chinese Mongolian partisans tried to remove the sülde, the Khan's battle-standard, from the temple at Sarachi, but pro-Japanese Mongols and Japanese troops prevented it. What became of the standard and whether in fact it was Ligdan Khan's standard that was the cause of the fighting around Sarachi in 1939–41 is not known.

In any case it is clear that soon after 1626, after Ligdan Khan had given orders for the great inscription to be carved on the white pagoda, the first tribes went over to the Manchus. In 1628–29, when the Ganjur was translated, the Bagharin and Harachin, within whose territory the editorial commission at Cagansuburga was working, also deserted him. Whether this internal collapse was

due to his failure to realize his ambitious plans for a Mongolian
Empire we do not know. Or perhaps I should say: We do not yet
know. Perhaps there are manuscripts in existence which also hold
the key to this mystery. But one thing must have happened at that
time which even Mongolian historical and traditional sources
that are well-disposed towards him all record. They all say that his
mind suddenly became confused, that he caused his wives much
distress and that he turned away from his old religious adviser and
chaplain, the Sharba Hutuktu. And then, it is said, he moved westward, in an attempt to conquer Tibet and put an end to its religion.
He had had good reasons for the western campaign. Abandoned
by his supporters in Eastern Mongolia, who had gone over to the
Manchus, Ligdan had to fall back on the Mongol tribes in the
west around the bend of the Yellow River, on the Tumats of Kweihwa and the Ordos in the Ordos desert, who had not yet fallen
under the Manchurian influence. He took his own Chahar tribe
with him. Thus he hoped to arrest the flanking movement by the
Manchurian forces across Inner Mongolia, which was directed against
the still unchallenged rule of the Ming dynasty in Central China.

But here too the eastern princes opposed the Great Khan's effort
to consolidate his central authority. Once again Ligdan challenged
the other regents. Following the arrival of his troops in Kweihwa,
conditions became so bad that the monks in the Buddhist monasteries had to cook the leather of their boots. Many fled eastward
to seek refuge with the pursuing Manchu army. Ligdan took the wife
of the ruling prince of the Ordos because she pleased him. This
was certainly not the way to win allies or to keep them. In accordance with tradition, the Ordos Mongols preserved the relics of
Jenghiz Khan and his wife in a special place called 'The Eight
White Tents'. Every Great Khan, if time or circumstances allowed,
had taken 'confirmation' before these ancestral relics. Ligdan Khan
followed this custom. But he then took the relics, the white tents
and the sacrificial vessels away from the Ordos.

Ligdan Khan retired westward before the advancing Manchu
army towards Koko Nor on the Tibetan border. On the way he

was afflicted by illness and pangs of conscience and sent the relics of his great ancestor back to the Ordos Mongols. The rest of the story is soon told. In 1634, while he was camping at Koko Nor and trying to form an alliance with Tibetan supporters of the old, non-reformed Buddhist sects, he died. The remainder of his tribe, his wives and his sons surrendered to the Manchu troops.

THE GREAT TRANSLATION PROJECT

The picture which history has so far painted is of a man ambitious, hard, arrogant, filled with his sense of mission to build a Mongol Empire, possessed by the desire to be the greatest patron of the church, greater than his predecessors, greater than Altan Khan, who had actively promoted the conversion of the Mongols to Buddhism. Behind the project to translate the Ganjur, political rather than religious motives must have been uppermost. The aim was to convince the Mongols of Ligdan Khan's great achievements. This was an end that justified any means.

The religious writings of Buddhism had already been sifted at a very early stage, in the first century, and the wheat separated from the chaff. Everything that was considered important was collected in one great encyclopaedia, which was translated into Tibetan and enlarged and rearranged several times in Tibet. This collection of prayers, tracts, didactic writings, rules of obedience and monastic precepts, all approved by the lamaist Church, was called the Ganjur. After the Mongol emperors of China were converted to lamaism in the thirteenth century, they are said to have ordered that this massive collection of more than 1,100 works should be translated into Mongolian. Whether this great undertaking was ever carried out is open to question; at all events none of this collection is available in Mongolian. There is, however, a Mongolian translation of the Buddhist canon. The epilogues to almost all these translations pay tribute to Ligdan Khan the Chahar, last incumbent of the office of Great Khan, 'Ruler of all rulers of men, incarnation of Jenghiz Khan, incarnation of Kublai Khan, incarnation of the ruler of the worlds, who keeps the wheel of religion turning,' the Mongol prince under whose guidance and on whose initiative the great translation project was launched. One Mongolian historical source gives the years 1628–29 as the period in which the work was accomplished. Thirty-five Mongolian and Tibetan scholars and monks under the leadership of Kunga Odser are reported to have translated the 1,100-odd works from Tibetan into Mongolian in that short time. The dates occasionally quoted in the epilogues praising Ligdan Khan corroborate this.

500 MEXICAN SILVER DOLLARS

The translation was distributed in transcript form. Ligdan Khan's copy was written in gold letters on a blue ground. Tradition has it that it was still in existence around 1817, in the possession of one of the princes of the Keshigten tribe in Eastern Mongolia, but since then nothing more has been heard of this show-piece. From a reference made in a Ganjur manuscript, which is now in Leningrad, we know that, when the translation was completed and the special copy was made in golden script, five ordinary copies were also made. But not one of them has been found. In 1910, when Cyben Žamcarano, the Buryat scholar, was travelling in Mongolia, he found in a monastery a manuscript copy of the translation of the Ligdan Khan Ganjur, which had apparently served the editorial commission as a rough copy; for beside words that had been crossed out, corrections had been made with a red brush and whole passages had been erased. The sum of 500 Mexican silver dollars, at that time the normal currency in China, which was the sum demanded for the whole Ganjur manuscript of more than 108 volumes by the Abbot of the monastery, who was as corrupt as he was shrewd, proved far beyond the slender means of the Buryat scholar. As a result, the manuscript remained in Inner Mongolia and nothing has been heard of it since.

In 1923, after the Kalka Mongols of Outer Mongolia had gained their political independence from China, they set up a special committee to organize research into their native territory. In 1961 this committee became the 'Academy of Sciences of the Mongolian People's Republic'. When Jamyang Gung, the first President and founder of this scientific committee, was travelling in his official capacity in the border area between Inner and Outer Mongolia in 1923, he found in a local monastery not only an old manuscript of the *Yellow History*, a historical work from the middle of the seventeenth century, but also parts of a Ganjur manuscript, which was believed to date back to the time of Ligdan Khan. Though he took the historical manuscript with him, he unfortunately left the other manuscripts behind. Nothing more has been heard of them. So when one volume of a Ganjur manuscript was found in Copenhagen it aroused considerable interest.

A hundred years after this version of the Mongolian Ganjur translation had ostensibly been completed in 1628–29, the Manchu Emperor Kang Hsi gave instructions that the Ligdan Khan translation should be revised by a group of lamaist scholars selected from monasteries throughout Mongolia, who were not merely to improve the language but also to cut and print on wooden plates the entire work of 1,055 individual titles in 108 volumes. The whole printing process involved 40,008 pages, printed on both sides and measuring about fourteen inches by twenty-eight. These figures give one some idea how many pages each of Ligdan Khan's thirty-five translators must have translated within the two years 1628–29. It works out at 2,287 single pages per man. And the corresponding number of manuscript pages was even higher. Could each of these men have got through such a monumental amount of work in so short a time? These figures give one good reason to doubt it.

A DELIBERATE SWINDLE

The manuscript in the Copenhagen Library turned doubt into suspicion. Out of twenty-three Tantra translations twelve, according to the epilogues, were the work of a certain Mati bhadra siri badra toyin chorchi, who frequently called himself just Toyin chorgi. He, together with the head of the editorial committee, Kundga-odzer, had translated the last three works. So far so good. Toyin chorgi had also been identified as one of the translators, from other parts of the Ganjur translation.

But a comparison with the printed Ganjur, which is an exact reproduction of the Ligdan Khan Ganjur, gave quite a different picture. One volume of the printed edition contained nine of the same Tantra translations by Toyin chorchi. But the three translations which, according to the old manuscript, he had carried out jointly with the head of the editorial committee were in quite a different volume of the printed Ganjur and the name of the translator was given as Samdan sengge, another member of the 1628–29 committee. The same name was also attached to four other Tantra translations in the printed Ganjur, whereas these same translations in the manuscript were unnamed. Something was clearly wrong.

It could only mean one thing, namely that Toyin chorchi, as the title Toyin indicated, was a lamaist monk from a noble Mongol family who had translated the sixth volume before Ligdan Khan formed his editorial committee. This committee had then retained part of his translation and for other sections of this tantra had rejected his translation in favour of Samdan sengge's. Or could it be perhaps that part of Toyin chorchi's translation had simply been attributed to Samdan sengge? At all events the discovery of this manuscript provided strong evidence that parts of the Ganjur had already been translated some time before 1628–29 and that the group of thirty-five translators had been more an editorial committee and had not translated by any means all the work. And Samdan sengge? His name was mentioned in almost all the epilogues and footnotes in which special tribute was paid to Ligdan Khan and to his achievement in spreading and consolidating Buddhism among the Mongols in the early seventeenth century.

I then recalled that in 1926 B. Vladimircov, a Russian scholar, had compared the epilogue to the Mongolian translation of the biography of Tibet's great wandering mystic and saint, Milaraspa,

as it appears in the printed Ganjur, with the identical translation in
an old Ganjur manuscript, which is in Leningrad. The epilogue to
the Leningrad manuscript, which is in all other respects identical,
named Namudai secen Khan, the Great Khan of the Mongols,
who had lived from 1565 to 1624, as the Maecenas in whose honour,
at whose request and with whose money the translation had been
been made. The same epilogue to the same work in the printed
Ganjur had left out the name of this patron and put Ligdan Khan's
name in its place. Was this a deliberate forgery? Was it in keeping
with the character of this Mongol prince?

TWO MANUSCRIPTS FROM BREMEN

A chance discovery soon strengthened the suspicion that Ligdan
Khan had, for propaganda reasons, taken more credit for the
Ganjur translation than he deserved. The best discoveries are
always accidental! In all the years that I have been searching for
Mongolian manuscripts, I have always assumed that one of the
most likely places to find them, outside Mongolia, must be Europe.
Most travellers in some official capacity, merchants, diplomats,
engineers and globe-trotters, who have landed somewhere in
Northern China since the Boxer Rebellion of 1900 and the increased
flow of travellers and tourists to China that followed it, brought
back mementoes of their stay, whether short or long.

Why should this or that traveller, attracted by the strange
beauty of the script or the splendid brocade or silk binding, not have
brought a Mongolian manuscript with him? I remembered an old
fellow-student who, before completing his studies a few years
before the outbreak of the Second World War, had been in China
and Japan. When he came back, he had proudly shown me his
books, which included a number of Mongolian manuscripts. Then
the war came and we lost touch with one another. After the war I
heard that he had settled in Bremen and one day he came to my
university town on business, and called on me. It turned out that
his library, including his East Asian books and antiquities, had sur-

vived the war, and he suggested that I might like to visit him and examine them.

During my first evening at Bremen I was shown his books, which included several Mongolian manuscripts. I was interested in two in particular; they looked old, and had been found one in Kalgan, the other in an antique shop in Peking.

One of the manuscripts was a thick volume with double pages in the Chinese style; the paper was strong and was ruled with rough, blue lines; the whole thing was bound in coarse, grey-brown linen, on which Tibetan characters had been imprinted. But the linen was so worn from handling and so faded that the characters were almost illegible. It seemed as if, about two hundred years ago, in one of the border markets, some Mongol had picked up a book which Chinese traders had used as a cash-book, had taken it home and bound it with the remains of an inscribed prayer-flag. Such flags with prayers, blessings and magic formulae inscribed on them used to fly until quite recently on long poles outside Mongol tents as a form of protection for the inhabitants. In this case the inscription, as far as I could gather at a first glance, was a moral philosophical text of some kind. I looked for the sort of epilogue that would give details of the work, its author and its translator. There was none. Only the name of the translator was given: Daigüng sikü guosi. It was a name I had already encountered among the thirty-five translators of the Ligdan Khan Ganjur.

The second manuscript was one of those large, unwieldy works in broadside such as were found in the libraries of lamaist monasteries. The stiff outer covers were clothed in tattered, faded, greenish-blue brocade, the script was very old. What was it? Another collection of prayers? On the first page appeared the title: Sanskrit and Tibetan in Mongolian script with a Mongolian translation: *Description of the world we know*. Was it one of the lamaist descriptions of the world, which give a picture of the world as seen by that religion, or perhaps even a geographical work? With the greatest care I turned over the pages of this voluminous manuscript, looking for a chapter-ending or an epilogue. In the middle of the work I came upon the name of a translator: Mayidari dayigung dayun günding guosi. This was another name I remembered from the list of translators of the Ligdan Khan Ganjur. My interest was now fully aroused. On the next page a new work began. Its title was: *How the world we know is arranged.* At the end another translator's name was given: Daigüng sikü guosi. Was this not also the name of the man who had translated the philosophical script? A quick check confirmed that it was. So this much was now clear: I had come upon three translations of works by scholars of the Ligdan Khan period and by collaborators in the Ganjur translation, which were not contained in the Ganjur.

The following day I took the manuscripts away with me to read at leisure and to try to identify with the help of the necessary reference-books. I soon discovered that the thick volume was the translation of a commentary on the Subhasitaratnanidhi, a twelfth-century collection of didactic Sanskrit writings, including parables and animal stories which had been converted into Mongol fables.

When I came to compare the two works on the world, they proved to be two different translations of the same work, the Lokaprajñapti, which presents the Buddhist picture of the world. This was contained in the comprehensive collection of Tibetan commentaries on the Ganjur, known as the Tanjur. It had always been assumed that the Ganjur had not been translated into Mongolian until 1742–49. But I now had before me in one volume two translations of the same work by different translators, who, I knew for certain, had lived in the early part of the seventeenth century. This could only mean that at that early stage preparations were already under way in Mongolia for a translation of the commentaries on the Ganjur. The names of both translators were also to be found in the Ligdan Khan translation of the Ganjur. But whereas in the latter case tribute was paid to the Great Khan in the epilogues, his name was not even mentioned in the other translations. Again there was only one possible interpretation, namely, that these works had been translated at another place and time, that the translators had not worked in the proximity of Ligdan Khan and that he had not yet enlisted their services. Then I discovered that Daigüng sikü guosi had been a contemporary of Siregetü guosi chorgi, the famous translator of Buddhist scripts into Mongolian, who had come to Kweihwa in the Tumat area with the third Dalai Lama, the Supreme Head of the reformed lamaist Church, when he paid his first visit to Mongolia in 1578, and had founded a translation school there. After 1620 there is no further mention of Siregetü guosi. So Daigüng sikü guosi's spiritual home had been in Kweihwa, the ancient seat of Altan Khan, while his successors were on the throne of the Tumat Mongols, whose fame as the first patrons of a Buddhist renaissance among the Mongols Ligdan Khan had tried to eclipse. And it was during that period that preparations had been made to produce a Mongolian translation of the commentaries on the Ganjur. How had these learned monks and translators come to work for Ligdan Khan in Eastern Mongolia twenty or thirty years later? Or had he simply taken the credit for their work?

A CHANCE DISCOVERY

Only a few days after I had looked through the two manuscripts a friend asked me to look at the Mongolian and Tibetan manuscripts which he had brought back from the Mongolian People's Republic in 1956. Some were beautifully written old manuscripts, but they did not contain any new works. My host then remarked that he had another bundle of manuscripts but this had come not from Mongolia but from Tokyo, where he had picked them up quite by chance in an antique-shop. Or perhaps, he corrected himself, he should have said an old clothes shop, for the proprietor dealt in any old goods without really knowing what most of them were. And with that he laid on the table in front of me a bundle wrapped in red cloth.

I unwrapped the red cloth and found manuscripts of varying sizes between two pieces of leather, which took the place of the more usual hard covers. They were all written in the ancient script which was in current use at the beginning of the seventeenth century. I soon found the names of translators. They included names which were also among the thirty-five learned monks who had translated the Ganjur for Ligdan Khan: Toyin guosi, Garma dubsang, Toyin samrub and again Daigüng sikü guosi, who had been responsible for translating the commentary on the Sub-hasitaratnanidhi, which I had found in Bremen. But in this case the names were linked with Tumat princes, who had commissioned these translations. They had lived twenty or thirty years before Ligdan at courts in Southern Mongolia, whereas Ligdan had held court in the eastern part of Mongolia at the white pagoda and waged war against the Manchu. All these translations had been made in the area round Kweihwa, the Blue Town of Altan Khan of the Tumats.

This had been a great spiritual centre of Mongol life around the turn of the sixteenth century. Had Ligdan Khan succeeded in luring all these important translators to Eastern Mongolia? It looks very much as if many of the works, which were allegedly dedicated to him and commissioned by him, had already been translated some time before in the Tumat area by resident trans-lators commissioned by their princes. All Ligdan Khan's editorial committee had to do in 1628–29, if that were so, was to erase the names of those who had commissioned the work and substitute that of Ligdan Khan. The names of the translators and monks of the same faith, even if they lived in remote Kweihwa, were retained by the members of the editorial committee, which in fact consisted only of a few monks who were loyal to Ligdan. So the names of these translators were included by subsequent Mongolian historio-graphers among the thirty-five scholars, who were believed to have translated the Ganjur in the short period from 1628 to 1629. But during these two years Ligdan was already at war with the Tumats. This tends to confirm the suspicion that Ligdan took the credit for the Ganjur translation, in order to win over the broad masses of the Mongols by means of religious propaganda, when he realized that he could not hold them by force. Perhaps the manuscript which will provide final confirmation is still lying in some unknown collection.

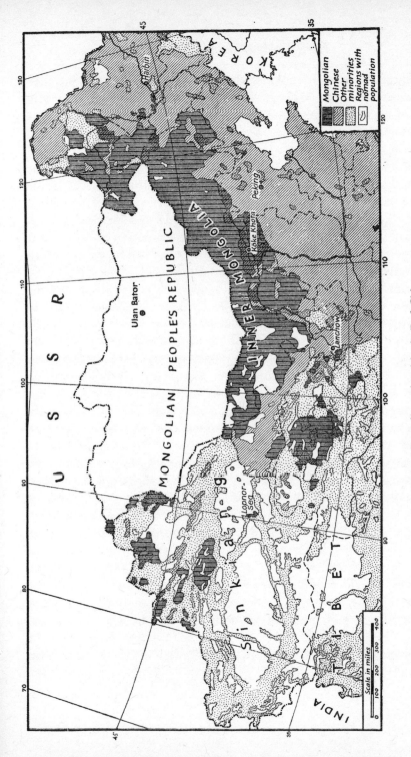

The Mongolian minorities in Red China

VI THE EPIC OF GESER KHAN

THE MANUSCRIPTS OF THE WAX FIGURE

In the early part of the nineteenth century French Lazarist fathers in Eastern Mongolia built their first mission station in the hunting-park of the Manchu emperors in Jehol. Évariste Régis Huc and Father Gabet, whose controversial journey to Tibet during the last century was discussed throughout the civilized world and who wrote an account of their journey which is still one of the most interesting books on Central Asia, were among the missionaries in this area. Later the Mongolian mission was taken over by the Belgian monks of the Scheut Order. They had stations in Eastern Mongolia, in Tumat and among the Ordos Mongols. For more than a hundred years they alone were working in the Ordos area, where, in addition to their religious activities, they did research work and published valuable scientific monographs on the habits and customs of this region. One of them, Father Mostaert, was largely instrumental in developing Mongolian studies into a modern science. Without his great dictionary of the Ordos dialect quite a few works would have remained untranslated. His collection of specimens of the folk-literature which has been handed down by word of mouth in the Ordos area represents a broad cross-section of Mongolia's copious literature. The manuscripts of rare Mongolian works of history, of epics, prayers, the Jenghiz Khan cult, marriage rituals and other semi-religious folklore, which he had collected in the Ordos area during his long stay there, were already known to me. I had even been privileged to make use of some of them for my own work. But was he the only missionary of his Order who had collected Mongolian manuscripts and books?

I wrote to Father Mostaert and asked for his advice. But he had been too long away from the mother-house of the Order in Belgium to be able to give me a definite answer to my question. He did, however, send me a letter of recommendation to his superiors. Shortly afterwards I set off for Belgium by car.

When I arrived at the seminary of the Scheut Order in Louvain, the Father, who looked after the archives, assured me there were no Mongolian manuscripts among the books in the library, but I should see for myself. The archivist was unfortunately right. There was no Mongolian manuscript, although there was an old print in the Mongolian language, the translation of an apologia by Father Aleni, written in 1625. Aleni had lived and taught from 1609 onwards at the imperial court in Peking. But this was all that the archives had to offer. The archivist must have sensed my disappointment. By way of consolation he suggested I visit Father Mullie, who had lived for a long time in Eastern Mongolia in the Bogharin area, and who might be able to give me news of Mongolian texts. It was Father Mullie who, in 1920, had found the remains of the Ligdan Khan inscription on a millstone at the White Pagoda. He knew nothing of any old Mongolian manuscripts in Louvain. All he could show me was a few copies of Peking prints of Buddhist texts, which I already knew. I even had copies of some of them myself. But the old scholar then remembered that he had presented the Sinological Seminary of Louvain University with a few manuscripts.

At the University he laid a thick bundle of dirty reddish-brown linen on the table. It was just as he had bought it from the effects of an itinerant lama who had died. No one had so far shown the slightest interest.

THE LIBRARY OF THE ITINERANT LAMA

The itinerant lamas were one of the strangest phenomena of lamaism. They began as part of the institution of Buddhist mendicant monks, who travelled from believer to believer with begging cup and stick and lived on the alms. But in Mongolia they were very soon performing the function of ministering to what one might call the unofficial religious needs of the population. Their domain was the non-canonized borderland of superstition, the world of popular custom, in which the old folk-religion of the Mongols lived on, despite all attempts by the lamaist Church to suppress it. Astrology, the designation of propitious and unpropitious days for bethrothals, marriages, starting journeys, burials, soothsaying and interpreting dreams were all part of their domain. They prayed for the sick, called upon the wild, occult gods of lamaism for help and protection, where formerly the shaman had been summoned to the house to invoke gods and ancestral spirits. They said purification prayers and made incense-offerings, called upon the 'White Old Man' to protect the flocks and herds, blessed the hunting-weapons and traps, and, when rain was needed, they conjured up rain-clouds. This daily intercourse with the sinister side of life made them feared by the population, while they themselves grew arrogant. Popular Mongolian tales frequently describe how a prince gives a present to a badarchi, or wandering lama, lest curses should rain down on his head. Most of the itinerant lamas did not take the oath of chastity too seriously. They appear to have frequently exploited the fear they inspired by trading a blessing for a willingness to oblige, and holding out the implicit threat of execration and sorcery. They made a substantial contribution to the spread of venereal disease throughout Mongolia during the last century, and one of the first steps taken to reduce venereal disease in the Mongolian People's Republic and Inner Mongolia – successfully, as it turns out – was to eliminate the itinerant monks. But it was their relations with women that made them vulnerable and laid them open to ridicule. 'When in our country', ran one of the many jokes told about the mendicant monks, 'a lama monk did not like work, prayed to Ariyabalu and at the same time deceived everyone with great cunning and guile, imposed upon the credulous and claimed that he would get them anything they wanted, while at the same time he crept around with pious mouth and drooping head and, if he met someone, stretched out his black hand and was importunate, then he was referred to as a badarchi-lama.'

The reference works of such an itinerant lama must clearly be of particular interest, for they will indicate what scripts these monks actually carried with them for the purposes of sorcery and invocation. I was already familiar with two such reference libraries in the Copenhagen collection and I was curious to see how these would compare with them. In fact the contents of the reddish-brown bundle, although in disorder and frequently damaged, proved to be the same mixture of manuscripts on astrology, soothsaying, the designation of propitious and unpropitious dates, and rituals for the summoning of wild deities. The most interesting item was a manuscript of a fire-prayer, evidence of the fire-worship the Mongols had practised for centuries and which may be connected with the ancient Persian cult of Zoroaster that dates back to the seventh century B.C.

I lost all sense of time as I went through the papers, arranging, measuring and comparing them, making notes and selecting certain manuscripts to be photographed for further study. Altogether there were forty-two manuscripts. I was naturally very pleased. But was this really all that had found its way to Belgium after a hundred years and more of missionary work? In Louvain, as I had seen, there was nothing more. Father Mullie then suggested I inquire at the mother-house of the Order, at Scheut near Brussels.

AGITATORS AND SECRET SOCIETIES

While I drove along the broad motorway towards Brussels, I found myself wondering why these missionaries had brought back so little of the literature of the country in which they had worked for so long. It must be connected in some way with the frequent political unrest, to which the Christian mission in Mongolia and the Ordos area had been exposed, particularly in the 1930s.

At the beginning of the 1930s the Chinese National Government could not fail to notice the signs of impending revolution in Inner and Eastern Mongolia, but Chiang Kai-shek's whole interest and energies were directed to the suppression of the Chinese Communists. Mongolia and the Mongols were of no importance to him. In the Ordos area, however, where Chinese penetration had given rise to widespread discontent, the Communists had an excellent opportunity to set up Communist subversive groups under cover of the nationalist movements. In the Otogh Banner of the Ordos League there were two east Mongolian Communist agitators, the Harachin Mongols Öldshei Dalai and Amur. They formed various smaller Mongolian groups into a people's army for the Otogh Banner, which was to oppose not merely the princes of the Otogh Banner but also the European Christian missionaries in the Boro Balghasun area, who had succeeded in bringing the Mongols together and forming a viable agricultural community. In the Uchin Banner in 1929 the old revolutionary and secret-society member Öldshei Jirghal became active again. Since his early youth he had been one of the organizers of the secret societies formed to resist Chinese penetration and tax-privileges. Condemned to death for his underground activities, he had succeeded in escaping to the Mongolian People's Republic.

There he had made contact with the Mongolian Communists, who had trained him and shown a lively interest in his plans to oppose the princes and Chinese domination. They appointed him Commander of the Red Army in the Ushin Banner and sent him back home with a number of armed Mongols and Chinese to form the nucleus of the new army.

Partly by virtue of his old secret connections with the revolutionary Dughuilang Club, which he had once helped to organize, and partly by sheer force, he managed within a short time to get a large section of the Mongolian population in the Ushin Banner to declare their support for Communism and their opposition to the Chinese settlers and to the Prince of Ushin who was protecting them. His 'Red Army of the Ushin area' was incorporated in the

Red Army of Inner Mongolia, which had already been set up in secret, and he became Commander of the 12th Regiment. There was some quite heavy fighting between the Communist Mongols and other Mongol groups in the two Banners of Ushin and Otogh, after the territorial Communist armies in these areas had joined forces. Öldshei Jirghal, whom the Mongolians now called the Shine Lama or New Lama, because of his new doctrine, was killed shortly after in one of these clashes with non-Communist Ushin Mongols. The two bolshevist agitators from the Harachin area, Öldshei Dalai and Amur, were captured by non-Communist Otogh soldiers and shot by their leader Gendun.

But the population of the Ushin area sang this song about Öldshei Jirghal, the 'new lama':

'After the gentlemen, the cunning Wangjugrabdan and
  Bujanchuchak,
The seventy swindlers, had plotted and conspired,
Then they suppressed you.
And even if they suppress you again and yet again,
We have sworn to resist!
The new lama's friends and companions
Are scattered, but they will come together again
And set up an excellent revolutionary government.
Let us follow the path of the New Age . . .!'

These pro-Communist risings in the Ordos area in 1929 proved invaluable as training for the subsequent formation of anti-Japanese Mongolian partisan-groups, the leadership of which fell increasingly into Communist hands and after the Second World War formed the cadres for the Communist Mongolian troops in Inner Mongolia. With the Communist victory in Red China the missionaries were driven out.

A WAX LAMA

On the outskirts of Brussels, in the village of Scheut on the road to Ninove, stands the mother-house of the Catholic Order of

Scheut Fathers, a red-brick building. I was given a friendly but apologetic reception. My long journey had been in vain, I was assured, because there were unfortunately no Mongolian manuscripts in Scheut. I was taken, however, to see the mission museum, which, even if it did not hold any Mongolian manuscripts, at least contained a number of interesting things from that area. There were costumes, pictures, handiwork, furniture from China, archaeological finds from the Sino-Mongolian border area. Then I came to a room, which had been arranged to look like a chapel in a lamaist temple, so as to give the visitor a fairly realistic picture of the lamaist cult, its ritual and its deities. There was an altar with pictures showing the wild gods of lamaism wreathed in flames, but the mysterious semi-darkness which one finds in Mongolian monasteries was lacking. To the right of the altar there was a lifesize wax figure of a kneeling lama in his yellow costume. It was remarkably realistic. The lama was deeply absorbed in reading his prayers. Beside him lay a pile of prayers, sheet upon sheet of rectangular paper, all neatly stacked. The archivist and I exchanged a disappointed glance: the topmost sheet of the pile was in Tibetan script, the language of the lamaist church.

I touched the pile. It was bound together with wire and wax to form a solid wad of paper. Perhaps only the topmost sheet was in Tibetan print, in order to create an illusion of authenticity. I asked permission to detach a few sheets merely to ascertain whether this was so. The archivist, who had become infected by my curiosity, agreed, and I pushed the blade of my penknife under several sheets, carefully raising one corner. The wax binding parted with a crackle of protest: Tibetan script, a page of manuscript. I tried again lower down and a page in ancient Mongolian script appeared.

A pair of scissors were produced as if by magic and the wires protecting the sheaf of papers against accident or theft were cut. Then the whole bundle was taken into another room, where I could examine my discovery more carefully. Among the sheets in Tibetan language and script at the top of the pile were various

Mongolian manuscripts which were in complete confusion. So I had at last found what I was hoping for. But what exactly had I found?

I began to sort out the individual works according to their different scripts. Not all of them were complete. One was the latter part of the Mongolian translation of a handbook in which the Vadshrabhairava was described. These Sadhanas were read by the lamaist monks, when they wanted to form a mental image of a lamaist deity and bring the god to life in their imagination in accordance with the description given in the handbook. The beginning was missing, but the final page with the epilogue proved it to be a hitherto unknown translation by the famous sixteenth-century translator Siregetü guosi chorgi from Kweihwa, '. . . translated in the middle summer month on the 5th day of the female water-snake, 1587.' So yet another of the rare sixteenth-century works had come to light.

Most of the other sheets were covered with fairly uniform hand-writing. If they were part of the same work it must have been quite large. But frequently the same page numbers were repeated, and when I had sorted them out I was confronted with a fairly long fragment of a mystical story, in which Samantabhadra, one of the wise-men, describes the nature of the world to the mythical Indian king, Mahasammata. The beginning and end of the story were missing. I have never been able to trace any other manuscript of the same work, which would enable me to complete the fragment at Scheut. The title, author and date of origin remain a mystery.

I had the impression that the other pages also formed part of a tale. Or perhaps an epic? On one of them, as I was arranging them by numbers, I read the following:

> 'There came from the army of the Nangdulumu Khan
> the black charger with the elephant's back, ridden by
> Shimur, and it had become a blood-red horse.
> The shining armour which it carried had become
> fiery-red armour.
> Petulantly his charger stamped and pranced once, twice.
> Thus he came and spoke! . . .'

A few pages later it ran:

> 'Have I, thy beloved elder brother Dshasa Shikir,
> Not spared thy life and limb.
> My beloved ruler,
> I have always been without house and hearth,
> Lived without sparing myself,
> Let my black blood dry . . .'

It was alliterative epic poetry. Dshasa Shikir and Shiumar were companions of Geser Khan, the legendary hero around whom the Mongols and Tibetans have woven one of their greatest epics. It looked as if I had stumbled on one of the many songs from this epic. It now remained to be seen whether it was a part of the epic that was already known or whether it was quite unknown. The title, which I soon found on one of the last pages I was arranging, namely *History of Geser Khan, ruler of the ten regions of the world,* did not tell me much. Many of the individual songs bore the same title and so too did the whole epos itself.

The existence of this Mongolian epos about Geser Khan had been known in the West ever since 1839, when Isaak Jakob Schmidt had published in St Petersburg and Leipzig *The deeds of Bogda Geser Khan, destroyer of the roots of the seven evils,* a translation of the seven songs then known. In 1716 these seven songs had even been block-printed for the Mongols by the pro-Mongolian Manchu Emperor Kang Hsi in Peking, because they were so popular in Mongolia. The lamaist Buddhist Church did not look kindly on this epos and would gladly have suppressed it. The highest lamaist priest at the Manchu court, the Chang chia Hutuktu, compared the epos to the hideous croak of the raven, the bird of ill-omen. He would have much preferred the Mongols in the eighteenth century to have read nothing but edifying legends about Buddhist saints and have forgotten their many epics and above all the epic of Geser Khan. But they did precisely the opposite. More and more new songs appeared, all woven around the mythical, heroic king, son of the god-king Hormusta, who sends him down to earth to put an end to injustice and evil. Accompanied by his thirty-three heroes,

Geser Khan undertakes this task. The more the Mongols liked these stories, the more tasks Geser Khan undertook, and the number of enemies he conquered grew, and I would not be surprised if even today yet another new song were to appear.

It was only a few years ago that a singer and rhapsodist, Padshai, who comes from the Horchin Banner of Inner Mongolia, created a new version of the Geser Khan epos. Padshai, who served as a young novice in a lamaist monastery, where he acquired a good knowledge of Tibetan and Mongolian literature, left the monastery when he was fifteen, because the urge to become a poet and arrange old songs and epics was stronger than the call of the priesthood. From then on he lived as a wandering singer and became increasingly popular. He survived the Japanese occupation of Eastern Mongolia, which cost so many strong-minded Mongols their lives, by telling stories and singing old epics to the Mongolian gendarmes in Japanese service. Today he is a middle-aged man. His new version of the Geser Khan epic, in which he has dropped the story elements of the supernatural in the hero's exploits – perhaps at the request of the present Communist rulers of Mongolia – is extremely popular and has even been printed. This shows how deeply the Geser Khan epos is rooted in the people and how much the development of the cycle owes to Mongolian singers and rhapsodists. The Mongols have always produced and still produce these guardians of their ancient folk-literature, who themselves add to the stock of songs and stories which have been handed down.

BIOGRAPHY OF A SINGER

Just how a man became a singer and rhapsodist is described by Prof. Dr Rintschen, a member of the Mongolian Academy of Science, famous for his studies in Mongolian folklore and folk-literature. He writes as follows on the Mongolian rhapsodist, Onoltu, from the Huchirtu province of the Mongolian People's Republic, who died in 1953:

'Onoltu's father, Sanchai – Tibetan Sangs-rgyas – "Buddha" was a
cattle-breeder and hunter. He often took the boy with him when
he made the rounds of his horse and camel herds in the steppes,
instructing him in the use of hunting-weapons, so that by the
eleventh year of his life Onoltu was hunting wolves and foxes,
deer and marmots entirely on his own and was also breaking in
young horses from his father's herds. At the age of thirteen, after
a successful hunt on which he had killed nine large wolves, he
received a splendid present from his father – the musket inlaid
with gold and silver, his grandfather's masterpiece.

'It was in winter, when the wolves are mating, that Onoltu was
hunting deer in the mountains. He caught sight of wolves coming
towards him. He immediately hid himself and his great hunting-ox
in a ravine and awaited the beasts of prey. Eight wolves were
running in single file behind a big she-wolf in heat, the strongest
in the lead, the weakest at the rear.

'Onoltu knew that it is very dangerous for the hunter to shoot
the she-wolf first, because then the furious pack attacks the hunter.
So he spared the she-wolf and shot each successive leading wolf in
the chain of rivals, as they raced along the ravine after the she-
wolf. As soon as one of them fell, the others flung themselves
on it, then chased after the she-wolf again. But the bullets of the
courageous young hunter's old musket were faster. And the she-
wolf fell to the ninth shot.

'With the nine wolf-skins hanging behind his saddle, Onoltu
returned home in high spirits and his father was speechless with
astonishment. "It was the foolhardy boldness of youth, my boy,"
he said at last, "to fight alone at your age against a pack of wolves.
But the blue and eternal heavens protected you. Thanks be to the
gods!" The old man was silent for a few moments, then he sighed:
"One should not encourage timidity in the hearts of the young,
but courage and foolhardiness are two different things, my son!"

'That evening Sanchai, who dearly loved his son, invited a
popular singer, who was a kinsman of Onoltu's, in his honour.
For three nights the singer sang and the young and gifted hunter

and rider Onoltu stored up every word in his memory: the great epics of the mighty King of darkness, of the hero who had no mother and was born beneath the river-bank, of the man who had no father and was born in a leather bottle, of the exalted King Jangrai and the mighty King Dawa, who won great victories against the Tibetans.

'The singer was delighted to find such a gifted pupil among his audience and sang yet another saga, the heroine of which was Tsytsen Tsagan gy – "the fat-bellied mare" (In my view this was the story of a shaman spirit in the shape of a mare).

'Near the nomads' camp of the Sanchai family lived the famous singer Chalsan Delek-Debek, the wide-browed. According to Onoltu's description of him, he was a venerable old man with a long, white beard and the face of a sage. He was a member of the great Charanut tribe. In winter, when the day's work was done, the old man was invited into the nomad's camp. Old and young gathered in a circle in the large tent to hear the poetic and wise sagas and to indulge their senses.

'The sagas which had been sung by old Onoltu and Chalsan-Delek formed the repertoire of my late friend, who retained these epics in his memory till he reached an advanced age and sang them to gatherings of his fellow countrymen.'

There had always been men of this kind in Mongolia and one of them had been responsible for this part of the Geser Khan epos that now lay before me. Princely patronage helped to promote them but princely disapproval could do little or no harm, because no prince would dare lay hands on a famous singer and guardian of the past. They sang and still sing their songs to the accompaniment of the 'horse-headed fiddle', the morin-u tologhaitu chur, a single-stringed fiddle, whose neck was decorated with a horse's head. Anyone who particularly liked a song and who could write would then write down what he had heard of the song. As in Mongolia to this day, so in the early middle ages in Europe the first heroic sagas were written down.

THE COPENHAGEN MANUSCRIPT

Quite recently I had come across a manuscript in the Royal Library in Copenhagen, which described one of Geser Khan's many adventures. The manuscript came originally from the Chahar country. In this song Geser Khan called upon his warriors Shiumar, Buidung batur, Hotong Noyan and the twenty-eight-year-old Chargin to arm themselves and saddle their horses. Thereupon the remainder of the thirty heroes took up their arms. With Dshasa Shikir, Geser's brother, at their head, they set out to track down the wild, dangerous, black-spotted tiger and free the world of this menace. Geser, who had the power of sorcery, changed himself into a tiger. He appeared in this form before his heroes, warned them of the strength of the real tiger and of its gigantic, unnatural size and described the terrible deeds committed by this monster, which had already eaten thousands of creatures. After the heroes had thanked their master, they continued their search for the tiger. When Dshasa Shikir caught sight of the tiger in the distance, he reported this to Geser Khan. The heroes spurred their horses to the attack but the horses refused to advance as much as one step towards the tiger.

Geser now turned himself into a horse and led the horses forward. They galloped towards the tiger, which was emitting ear-splitting roars. It grew dark. Geser could no longer hold the reins in his hand. But his magic powers triumphed over the tiger's and it grew light again. At full gallop Geser rode into the tiger's great maw. After he had delivered a short, fervent prayer to Buddha, the eight dragon-kings appeared, riding on golden rams, to help him against the tiger. Geser killed it. The thirty heroes, frightened by the gigantic tiger, had left Geser in the lurch. Reproaching himself for having left his brother and master in the lurch, Dshasa Shikir followed him, but Geser was not to be found. But finally they met and were overjoyed at the reunion. Geser instructed Dshasa Shikir not to destroy the giant tiger's skin, as it could be used to provide armour and tent-coverings for many thousands of warriors. After the heroes had received their share of the tiger's flesh, they returned with Geser to his wife Rogmo ghoa, who prepared a feast in celebration.

The heroic exploits of Geser Khan and his thirty heroes in their struggle against Natshang Khan, who wanted to ravish all women, were described in another section of the Copenhagen manuscript. One passage, which is reminiscent of the old medieval romances, describes a duel between Buidung, a companion of Geser Khan, and an enemy knight, who possessed magic powers:

'Said he: "I will ride down upon him and bring him from
   his horse."
He and Buidung galloped towards each other with great
   bounds.
Once Buidung fell to the ground.
Once the magic knight fell to the ground.
When all this had happened, the magic knight summoned
   all his strength,
Fell upon him, so that sparks flew.
Now Buidung also summoned all his strength,
Rode, so that the sparks flew,
The magic knight stumbled and fell.
As the knight fell,
Buidung cut off his right arm.
When he had cut this off,
He was far from having conquered the magic knight,
Losing control of their horses, they reeled,
Once Buidung struck,
Once the magic knight,
They rode against each other, and
When, with Bodi and Goti together, the three
Had cut down the enemy with their sabres and thrown him,
He turned, came back,
Flung his horse against him,
Persevered, came at a trot, at walking pace, made him reel,
But however often he struck at the magic knight,
The latter was not in the least affected.
Yet when the magic knight retaliated,
Skin and face, hands and legs were covered in blood.
Buidung did not know that

He was drawing on the strength of the other heroes.
Now he attacked,
Now he was attacked, yet
However much the hero shot and thrust,
He could not conquer the magic knight.
Buidung ceased bringing him down,
Shot arrows, sitting on his horse.
Hit by an arrow, the magic knight said:
"More I cannot bear!" —
Turned his grey horse three times into powder,
Put it in his pocket for the bolt of fire.
Transformed his own body,
Appeared now as a mottled brown snake, and said:
"I will entwine myself round Buidung's neck!" . . .'

There were many other songs in the same style, which described further adventures of Geser Khan. There were separate versions of nine and fifteen songs. The songs themselves were not entirely the same. It is becoming more and more generally accepted that the Geser Khan epos has its origins in the border area between Tibet and Mongolia. The epos in its original Tibetan form appears to be the poetic 'fall-out' from the Turkish tribes of Central Asia in the seventh and ninth centuries. At that time the great Tibetan Empire stretched as far as the oases of Chinese Turkestan. The Tibetan versions of the Geser Khan epos are numerous and of considerable scope. The theory that the Geser saga originated in Tibet has become much more plausible in recent times, since scholars in the Mongolian People's Republic discovered a manuscript of songs from the Geser Khan epos, which had been translated from the Tibetan around 1614 for Nomchi Chatun, one of the princesses of the Ordos tribe. These songs show certain similarities with the first seven songs discovered in 1716. But the many other adventures of Geser Khan, which were so popular with the Mongols, must be regarded simply as products of the fertile and absurd imagination of the Mongols themselves. Themes and stories from the many other heroic sagas of the Mongols, from their rich store of legend, were transferred by the rhapsodists to Geser Khan.

For Geser Khan had become a revered figure among the Mongols. The fact that in the epos he was portrayed as the son of Hormusta, king of the gods, had facilitated his adoption as one of the Mongols' popular deities. Despite heated protests by the lamaist clergy, Geser was revered by the Mongols as the god of riders, warriors and herds. The Manchu emperors carried this a stage further at the end of the eighteenth century, when they identified Geser Khan with the old Chinese war-god, Kuan Ti, thereby trying to make a single deity for protecting officials and loyal servants of the empire. They built small temples right up to the northern borders of the Chinese Empire, in which Geser Khan, alias Kuan Ti, seated on his horse and clad in shining armour, was worshipped. The effect this had on the further spread of the Geser Khan cult is not hard to imagine. In the areas where Chinese settlers were penetrating into Mongolia the Geser-Kuan Ti cult began to die at the beginning of the present century. The temples fell into decay. On the wall of my study hangs the wooden horse's head from one of these ruined Geser Khan temples.

But in those areas in which the Mongols were not affected by Chinese penetration, the Geser Khan cult survived until very recent times. In 1943, when I discovered several volumes of manuscript of Geser Khan songs in the Küriye Banner, a densely settled area in Eastern Mongolia, I asked the owners if I might take the volumes home with me for a few weeks to read through them, compare them with the printed versions of 1716 and photograph them, in case they should contain something new. After I had promised to treat these manuscripts with the utmost respect and never, on my journey, to keep them in an unclean place, I was allowed to take them away. A date was arranged on which a messenger would come from the owners to collect them. I was to pay for his journey. To my astonishment the messenger appeared long before the appointed date and, with profuse apologies on behalf of the owners, asked for the return of the manuscripts. The reason, I must understand, was that the cattle had begun to fall sick. It could be that this was due to the absence of the volumes of the Geser Khan epos, and without these volumes it was impossible to pray for the recovery of the cattle. Scattered over the whole area inhabited by Mongol settlers, living on their farms, were small private chapels dedicated to Geser Khan. Naturally I sent the volumes back with the messenger the same day. I hope the cows in the Küriye Banner have been restored to health. The Küriye Banner, incidentally, is a part of Ligdan Khan's old country of residence, and local tradition has it that the local lamaist monasteries have their origins in the monasteries founded by him at the beginning of the seventeenth century.

GESER KHAN GIVES HIS DEAD HEROES LIFE

The manuscript which I had extracted from under the hands of the wax figure at Scheut contained two songs from the epos which had not yet been published. No one knew precisely where these and the other manuscripts had come from. Some priest, who had since died, must have collected them while he was in Mongolia. But no one knew whether the manuscripts came from Eastern Mongolia or from the Ordos area. The Scheut Father who had built the facsimile of the Buddhist temple in the museum and had set up the wax figure of the lama, had also since died. Certain linguistic peculiarities of the manuscript suggested that it came from the Ordos area. I had to let it go at that. After all, the main thing was that, thanks to the wax figure, I had discovered two songs from the Geser Khan epos.

Each time I read them, I was more impressed by their beauty. The first part describes how Geser Khan found his dead heroes again and brought them back to life. After the victory over the twelve-headed man-eater, Geser had taken his beautiful wife Arulu with him. She mixed in Geser's food and drink the potion 'bag', which brings complete forgetfulness, and the great Geser forgot everything except her. He forgot to ask what had happened to his companions, he forgot his own brothers and sisters. But his elder sisters were able to restore his memory. Geser now mourned his lost companions. Hormusta, father of the gods, out of pity for his beloved son asked the Master, Buddha, for the water of life. When Geser sprinkled the bones of the fallen heroes with it, they covered themselves with flesh and came back to life. Geser and his companions celebrated their reunion with a great feast. The Geser of this song has none of the marble-like coldness of abstract heroism. He knows fear like any ordinary man and weeps bitter tears over his dead friends.

The second song contained in the Scheut manuscript is more warlike and full of the poetic exaggerations and blood-curdling details which characterize this kind of epic. Here Geser Khan overcame the fifteen-headed giant king, Nangdulma, who had invaded Geser's territory. No one had been able to defeat him. But Geser with his courage and magic powers succeeded. And when Geser 'came face to face with Nangdulma Khan, he struck off the fifteen heads of Nangdulma Khan with his nine-ell long sword of magnetic iron. Then proceed to dispose of his body . . .' In the end everything that was Nangdulma is wiped out, even to the fifteen-headed son of the demon in his mother's womb.

This meant that two new songs in the Geser Khan series had now come to light. And a few months later I received a new, modern, printed edition of fifteen songs from the Geser epos, based on a manuscript which had recently been discovered in China. The ninth, tenth and eleventh songs in this new edition are more or less identical with the songs I had discovered at Scheut, which shows once again the completely haphazard way in which this greatest of all Mongolian epics was handed down and how much freedom was enjoyed by the individual rhapsodist or writer.

Before I left Scheut, I obtained the archivist's agreement that the rare manuscripts I had found by the wax figure would be safely preserved in the archives for future reference.

VII LAMAIST MONKS DISPLACE
THE SHAMANS

PURCHASES FOR AMERICA

In 1907, less than seven years after the Boxer Rebellion, the American orientalist, Berthold Laufer, went to China. His *Sketch of Mongolian Literature* was the first attempt by any western scholar to prove the existence of Mongolian literary monuments, and led to the Field Museum and the Newberry Library in Chicago commissioning him to make a 'representative collection' of East Asian manuscripts. Laufer, who knew the Chinese, Japanese and Tibetan languages and also had a wide knowledge of the Mongolians and the Manchus, was better qualified than most to carry out the task entrusted to him. In the three years, up to 1910, he collected 1,216 East Asian works. Most of his collection consisted of Chinese scripts. But he also bought any Mongolian block-prints which came his way. There were only seventy two all told, which he acquired in Peking. 'In Peking,' he wrote in his survey of the Chicago collection, 'I acquired all that were still obtainable of the Tibetan and Mongolian books, which had come from the printing-press near the Sung-chu-szu temple.'

'This printing-press', wrote Laufer, 'is owned by Chinese and the entire production of the books is also done by Chinese workers. The block-cutter does not need to read the manuscript, for he sticks the sheet of manuscript, face down, to the wooden block and, so mechanical is his work, that he could well be illiterate. The owners of these plants are printer, publisher and bookseller all in one. They find their customers among the monks in the lama temples in and around Peking and among the Mongolian traders visiting the capital in winter . . .'

By also joining the clientele of the Peking printer and bringing back to America the Mongolian prints he had bought, and by describing them beforehand in his *Sketch of Mongolian Literature*, Laufer aroused the interest of scholars in the Mongolian literature printed in Peking.

But in 1934 Laufer committed suicide, and for many years these literary finds of his were lost sight of. Eventually, an American friend of mine chanced upon some steel boxes stored in the Oriental Library in Chicago. When they were opened, they were found to contain the Mongolian, Tibetan and Manchu prints which Laufer had bought in Peking more than forty years before.

MORE THAN THREE HUNDRED YEARS OF PRINTING

To the west of the old Pei-ta building, the Northern University in Peking, stands a group of temple buildings. One of these is the Sung-chu-szu temple, the 'Temple for sacrifices to the mountains'. Near the main entrance stood the printing-press and the bookshop of 'heavenly purity'. There Mongolian and Tibetan books were printed from old wooden plates, which were often two hundred and more years old.

This was the place Berthold Laufer visited in 1910. The bookshop with its entire stock of plates had survived all the confusion and dangers of the Boxer Rebellion in 1900. According to the City Chronicle of Peking, which had been written and printed in 1787, based on much older accounts, a stone inscription was still to be seen at that time on the nearby temple of Fa-yuan-szu, which recorded that on this spot in the period of the Ming dynasty, in the fifteenth and sixteenth centuries, Tibetan holy books had been translated and printed.

So for more than three hundred years lamaist religious scripts had been printed here in Mongolian and Tibetan. And when I visited the printing-press and bookshop for the first time in 1942, and again in 1945, they were still exactly as they had been several hundred years before. The owners, as Laufer had said, were Chinese, and I was told that all that time it had been in the hands of the same family. Since 1910, when Laufer had been the first to buy Mongolian books, many scholars and tourists had called to buy the beautiful prints made from the old plates.

In 1944 I bought what was still left of the prints. No one, including myself, has ever succeeded in having all the works printed from the plates. There are thousands of plates from the seventeenth and early eighteenth centuries stacked on high racks. A thick folio volume, a kind of sample-book, contained prints of all the title-pages. It was after consulting this volume that the pious Mongolian pilgrims and merchants had placed their orders.

THE ABSENT CLIENTS

But now, in 1944, few Mongols came to Peking. The situation in Inner Mongolia was unstable. Japanese occupation troops were fighting against partisans, and the population was not allowed to travel freely. It had long since been impossible to travel to Outer Mongolia, the Mongolian People's Republic. And for a long time there had been no travellers from that region to buy pious lamaist books. Ever since 1936, when the country had been given a constitution, which was closely modelled on that of the Soviet Union, the frontier with China and the road to Peking had been more and more closely watched. Outer Mongolia sought protection from Russia against possible Japanese encroachment. In the years 1935–37 a counter-revolutionary organization had been discovered at work in two lamaist monasteries in the Mongolian People's Republic. Everything pointed to Japan and Inner Mongolia as the real culprits. From 1936 to 1939 a vigorous campaign was conducted against the lamaist religion in the Mongolian People's Republic.

Some twenty leading lamaist priests were shot; a further five to six thousand monks were put in camps and prisons and the monasteries were used for more worldly purposes as clubs, storehouses and schools. All this meant a severe reduction in the number of clients for the printing of lamaist scripts in Peking.

Throughout the centuries the printing-press of Sung-chu-szu had also bought up plates of many works which had been cut and used by other printers in Peking. This had been particularly true of the first half of the eighteenth century. Even plates of works which had originally been cut in Mongolia had subsequently found their way to Peking and eventually to Sung-chu-szu. So the sample book of titles was a volume of some considerable size. But there was much that could no longer be purchased. The workers, who with skilled hands and years of experience had touched up the rectangular plates with Chinese ink, one after the other, and had then made the print on thin, absorbent paper, had left to find other means of livelihood. Whilst a certain number of prints were still available, new prints were no longer being made. It was not worth the price of ink and paper, the owner told me. Nevertheless in 1944 I was still able to buy a considerable number of Peking blockprints, which in format resemble the Indian palm-leaf manuscripts. The pages, which usually consisted of several layers of thin paper glued together, are printed on both sides. In most cases the first page bearing the title is yellow in colour. Yellow is the sacred colour of lamaism, the 'yellow doctrine'. Miniatures of gods, high priests and lamaist saints adorn the first two pages. Some of the Mongolian prints produced from blocks at Sung-chu-szu in the seventeenth and eighteenth centuries are, as Berthold Laufer wrote, 'Mongolian typographical masterpieces, which, taken merely as samples of the book-printing art, would do honour to any large library'.

But many of the old plates were already very old and worn and the wood was cracked. Most of them were made of apple-wood. There were rumours in the war-winter of 1944–45 that some of the plates had been used as firewood. It was a cold winter. Fuel was scarce in Peking. But this seemed to have been merely a prelude to something much worse. In 1949–50, when the Chinese Communist army was approaching Peking, fuel was in even shorter supply. At that time, it is said, the plates of the Sung-chu-szu went up in smoke. As eyewitnesses have reported that students fleeing before the Communists from Manchuria did not hesitate to burn the gold brocade covers of old scripts in order to extract the minute amount of gold from the gold threads, the burning of the plates seems quite credible. New prints taken from Sung-chu-szu blocks have certainly not appeared on the book-market. The few old prints still extant fetch high prices today, for their value has increased. The prints which I was able to buy are now in the West German Library in Marburg. In almost every case they are complementary to the Mongolian block-prints which Erich Haenisch bought in Peking in 1936.

It so happened that almost all the block-prints which I was able to buy were those that Haenisch could not obtain in 1936, because they had not yet been made.

CONVERSION TO WILD GODS WITH FLAMING HAIR

Between 1650 and 1911 considerably more than two hundred Mongolian block-prints of this kind were produced in Peking. They include small, thin prints of only a few sheets, prayers consisting of only a few verses. But most of them are works of a hundred and more sheets and many of the great religious scripts run to five hundred or eight hundred pages. This is a great deal when one considers that each page had to be cut on a wooden plate and then coloured by hand and printed. There were no machines for this kind of work nor were there interchangeable types. Printing was done entirely from fixed plates, as the Chinese had been doing since the fourth century.

In the second half of the eighteenth century the Mongols again came in contact with Tibetan Buddhism, which was called lamaism after the lama monks who preached it. The effects of lamaist conversion under Jenghiz Khan's successors had either degenerated into crass superstition or disappeared altogether after the Mongols were driven out of China in 1368. The Mongols for the most part worshipped their ancestral spirits: shamans drove out evil spirits and interpreted omens. About 1557, however, some Tibetan Buddhist missionaries appeared in Mongolia and something quite unexpected happened.

The nomads and warriors, who until then had been interested only in the things of this world, turned to spiritual things – or at least were attracted by the promises of salvation held out by the new religion. The new doctrine spread like a fever through Mongolia. Lamaist missionaries were revered like saints. The old beliefs were abandoned unreservedly. What the Mongols failed to understand – and there was a great deal that was beyond them – in the highly philosophical doctrines of Buddhism, they tried to make up for by sheer enthusiasm.

Until now they had certainly not been spiritually capable of surmounting the constant threat to their daily lives that was so explicit in the shamanist world of spirits and demons. They had not created any doctrine of salvation of their own or any doctrine that held out a promise of paradise. This seems very strange when one thinks of the Arabian nomads, who had created the religion of Islam with all its glowing promises of paradise out of the barrenness of desert life.

It was left to the Buddhist missionaries to come and win over the Mongols. And when they came, around the middle of the sixteenth century, the time and the Mongols were ripe for conversion. Uncertainty and internecine wars, the border fighting against the Chinese and the mutual intrigues appear to have produced in the Mongols, during the two hundred years since their expulsion from the paradise of the Chinese host-culture, an immense lassitude and satiety towards the things of this world. The new doctrine satisfied a long-felt desire among them for change. It portrayed a world of deities, in which kindly, compassionate Buddhas were as much at home as fearful gods with distorted faces, with flaming hair and scalps, who carried thunderbolts, slings and arms and rode on bloody human skins instead of saddles.

For the mass of the Mongols only the element of superstition survived. They incorporated it in their traditional beliefs, which Buddhism was never able to eradicate.

At the same time, however, monasteries appeared and from the new generation of monks emerged a group of men who were devoted to religious education and who themselves began to break new ground. Only a part of this new ground – and some of it was spiritually wide of the mark – was reflected in Mongolian script; by far the greater part found expression in the liturgical language of the lamaist religion, Tibetan. In other words, a dual-track literature.

Lamaism in Mongolia degenerated as quickly as it had prospered. The events of the last fifty years have eliminated the enormous number of corrupt priests and stupid monks. But there is no denying that for nearly 250 years the Buddhist influence on the Mongols was a force both for good and for evil and that the 'sacred water of the Ganges,' as Berthold Laufer put it, 'made the barren steppes fertile'.

POLITICS AND GENUINE PIETY

In 1644, when the Manchus came to power in China and founded their dynasty, lamaism had already gained a hold on large parts of Southern Mongolia, and was a force to be reckoned with. The Manchu emperors were not slow to come to terms with it. The Emperor Kang Hsi, the second Manchu ruler on the throne of China (1661–1722), his successor Yung Cheng (1722–35) and his son Chien Lung (1735–99) encouraged the spread of Buddhism among the Mongols. In particular they are credited with having promoted the printing of lamaist works in the Mongolian language in Peking.

This was later interpreted as an insidious move by the Manchus designed to divert the attention of the warlike Mongols from the affairs of this world and thereby weaken them by arousing their interest in the world beyond. 'The not uncommon theory, that it was Buddhism that turned the Mongols from wild conquerors and world-shakers into tame lambs peacefully grazing on the steppes,' wrote one scholar in 1907, 'is one of those legends, which sometimes grow up among scholars and then continue, as unshakeable as a dogma. But who has ever provided any serious proof? Tibetans and Chinese, whenever political interest demanded it, have always carried on their wars regardless of Buddhism, and the same can surely be said of the Japanese.'

The writer of these lines was Berthold Laufer. Research work in recent decades has proved him right. There is, in fact, no evidence to show that the Manchu emperors were responsible for the printing of Buddhist scripts in Mongolian. It is true that Kang Hsi and his grandson Chien Lung, between 1718 and 1720 and from 1741 to 1749, were instrumental in printing the Buddhist canon, the basic teachings of Buddhism, in 108 and 226 volumes for the Mongols. But the Manchu emperors played little or no part in commissioning the many translations and having them printed in Peking.

But in that case who was the driving force behind these prints? In 1650, when the first of these block-prints appeared in Peking, the Emperor Kang Hsi was not yet born. Around 1665, when the next of these Mongolian Buddhist works were printed in Peking, he was twelve years old. It is idle to suppose that a twelve-year-old child could pursue a carefully-planned religious policy.

But the Emperor Kang Hsi's grandmother, who was mainly responsible for his education from the age of ten and who exercised a great influence over him, was a Mongol. Behind the editions of Mongolian works was the Mongolian aristocracy. In most cases, in fact, it is Mongol princes of the Eastern and Southern Mongolian tribes who are named as patrons of the block-prints and the translations of Buddhist religious works from Tibetan into Mongolian. The reproduction and distribution of religious scripts was regarded as a particularly praiseworthy pursuit.

People believed that the 'Copying of religious scripts and the printing of them' was a certain passport to paradise, which explains why these Mongolian princes and nobles of the seventeenth and eighteenth centuries spent large sums on translating and printing holy scripture.

WHAT IS THE PRICE OF SALVATION?

In 1713 the son of a Kalka Mongol prince gave two thousand ounces of silver to meet the cost of printing a work of 4,701 leaves – 9,402 pages. To cut the plates for the 1,300 leaves – 2,600 pages – of the collected works of the Mergen dijanchi cost 140 ounces of silver in 1780–83. The plate-cutters were paid for a period of three years. In the middle of the eighteenth century the ink and paper for a small work of only thirty pages cost one five hundredth part of an ounce of silver.

What was the purchasing-power of an ounce of silver at that time? There are no precise means of comparison. The Mongolian housewife did not keep any household accounts; at least, if she did, none have survived. But one known fact provides some idea of the value of an ounce of silver. In 1743, when the Emperor Chien Lung consecrated the new lama monastery of Yung Ho-Kung in Peking, he bought provisions for the two to three hundred monks worth 3,000 ounces of silver. This supply was intended to last for several years. But more precise statistics are available from the end of the eighteenth and from the nineteenth centuries: a castrated camel cost between twenty and thirty ounces, a horse eight to twelve ounces, a cow eight to ten ounces, and a sheep would cost as little as one ounce of silver, depending on its condition. So when a Mongolian prince spent several hundred or even 2,000 ounces of silver, then his prospects of being reborn in the lamaist paradise were really bright.

CATALOGUE OF GOOD INTENTIONS

By far the greater part of the Mongolian block-prints has an epilogue or 'colophon' at the end. Students of European literature would be happy if there were always such colophons in the literatures of Europe, for it was here that Mongolian authors and translators gave details of time and motive, named their patrons and praised their good and pious intentions. There was an exact record of the pious patron's generosity and of how much silver he had given for translating and printing. Historical data, not available from any other source, were thrown in here and there and cited as background to the actual appearance of the work. Frequently the details given in the colophon smack a little of 'chronique scandaleuse'. For example, at one point, it is recorded that a nun, who had sinned, had written down the work as a form of penitence, and elsewhere, that a prince had commissioned another work in order to atone for some misdemeanour. From the colophons of various works which name the same patron one can deduce the names of his various wives, something which no other document reveals. Most of these epilogues are in rhyme. The authors were often so anxious to display poetic talent that the sense of what they wanted to say and to preserve for posterity was lost. On the other hand, many of the colophons must rank as very fine examples of seventeenth- and eighteenth-century Mongolian poetry.

The colophon of one old manuscript in the Royal Library at Copenhagen makes it clear that this is a fairly early translation from the period of Altan Khan, who did so much for the spread of lamaism and about whom there is so little historical information.

'The reincarnation of the ruler of the worlds,
who in the 25th generation of the succession to
Jenghiz Khan has
achieved great fame as Altan Khan and
adorned with virtue and wisdom only
thinks of the welfare of the inhabitants of this world
and truly, like Esrua, intent only
upon promoting the rule of the pure Buddhist teaching above
all else,
summoned the Dalai Lama Boddhisattva and
so enabled the teaching of Buddha to gain a foothold and
founded the community of monks among the Mongolian
people,

gave orders, with the welfare of the people in mind:
Write down the golden-lustred Sutra!
On this command, Altan Khan's own grandson,
Ilagugsan buyan-u erke Bayagud-un bagatur,
made a beginning before the whole people
by instructing Achirai guosi, Jivandan sangbu erkelur
and other artistic scribes
to write it down for publication
and to distribute it . . .!'

Even more precise are the details given in most of the Peking Mongolian block-prints. On the origins of a 1714 print there is this:

'As Shunchi had become ruler
 by virtue of earlier prayers, he
 summoned the high and exalted Dalai Lama.
 When he then said "What is the nature of the Indian and
    Tibetan sacred scripts?",
 the holy Lama answered as follows:
 "The words taught by Buddha, the 84,000 verses
 are doors through which the wellbeing of all six kinds of
    living creature
 may constantly be increased!" and so by dint of
 repeatedly writing and reciting the same as taught,
 the five evils and the ten cardinal sins were destroyed,
 in order that one may meet the noble, good master (Buddha)
 at one's purest in all states of birth.
 The writing was begun on a propitious day in the
 Intercalary month of the Year of the Blue Horse, in the
 53rd year of the reign of the Emperor Kang Hsi (1714)
 of the great Ching dynasty and was
 ended on a propitious day of the autumn final
 month in the same year.
 The Fu-Dalai by name, living outside
 the gates of permanent peace
 cut it into blocks and published it (in print).

Clearly these words are of the greatest value for literary and historical research. More than twenty years ago, when I set about investigating and presenting in book-form the origins of the Peking lamaist block-prints and the forces that motivated them, I had to rely primarily on the details given in the colophons of more than 220 Mongolian block-prints. I had assembled them from libraries and collections throughout almost the entire world – three hundred and ninety-nine names of Tibetan and Mongolian lamaist monks, high priests, Mongolian princesses and princes were quoted in them. Their aims and motives formed a kaleidoscopic picture of Mongolia's spiritual history between 1650 and 1911. It became evident that it was particularly the Mongolian princes and especially their wives, who supported and encouraged the pious monks in the printing and production of the holy scriptures.

VIII POLITICS IN NOTEBOOKS

'AESTHETIC DEFINITIONS AND MORAL PRINCIPLES'

The custom of keeping literary notebooks was universal in past centuries. They can still be picked up on second-hand bookstalls in Europe; notebooks in which someone has jotted down the fruits of his reading, poems to 'Marianne', some new information on 'Kotzebue's death', and a 'pledge of love' which seems rather long-winded to us today. These notebooks from a period when a book was still a capital-investment and when editions were very limited did not always have a title. People simply wrote down for their own use what had pleased them in a book. But sometimes a small volume packed with notes from the year 1776 would bear the pompous title 'Encyclopaedia of aesthetic definitions, moral principles and philosophical observations on religion, philosophy, literature and the spirit of the age'. Although in 1450 Johann Gensfleisch, better known as Gutenberg, introduced the art of reproducing written manuscript, these notebooks continued for a long time to be important sources for the art of writing. But they are almost the only sources for the Mongolian writing of the last century and the turn of the century.

A MANUSCRIPT FROM THE HERDSMEN'S BANNER

One day in 1943, when a young Mongol from the Jokchin-Ail of the Küriye Banner brought me a thick manuscript, it was some time before I realized that I had one of these important notebooks in my hand. Written on thick, greyish-brown paper, it bore the title

Book of Puzzles, so that I thought at first that young Manidshab had presented me with a collection of Mongolian puzzles. Not that much was known about them either at that time; I could already see myself translating and publishing them.

The Küriye Banner, from which Manidshab came, is a part of Eastern Mongolia which is rich in historical tradition. Ligdan Khan's grandfather had his official residence there in the sixteenth century; later Ligdan, the last Great Khan of the Mongols, himself built monasteries there. The lay population, whom he supplied to the pious monks as helpers and workers, came from the Chahar and Tumat tribes. From the beginning of the seventeenth century the Küriye Banner formed an independent monastic Banner. But the Jokchinar, the inhabitants of the settlement from which this young Mongol came, whom I had to thank for this fine manuscript, had originally been servants who worked in the monastery kitchen or Dshoha. Together with their families these people, who were unskilled workers, settled around temples and monasteries. Over the years families from other tribes joined them, Chinese traders moved in and eventually a village settlement grew up round the monastery; a typical example of how permanent settlements took shape in nomadic pasture-country.

Manidshab had received the manuscript from his uncle, who had died a long time before. He had come from the Sürüg Banner, one of the breeding-grounds of Mongolian nationalism and anti-Chinese resistance. Sürüg in Mongolian means 'herd'. At one time the Sürüg Mongols had tended the Manchu emperors' horses, which were used for the yearly sacrifices before the imperial graves at Mukden. They acted as herdsmen for over two hundred and fifty years, then in 1902 their lands were overrun by Chinese settlers and the peaceful life of the herdsman came to an end.

DID CONFUCIUS WIN?

Throughout Inner and Eastern Mongolia, where the Chinese settlers infiltrated into the Mongolian pasture-lands, the Mongols were in a bad way. The Chinese settlers cut into the grazing-land with their ploughs. For the Mongolians with their large herds wide grazing-areas were essential. The Chinese settlers cultivated the fertile pastures, thus forcing the Mongolian herds back into the sandy, barren areas in the north and north-west. The result was a steady reduction in the number of livestock. The Mongols, living as they did in close contact with the Chinese and forced out of the richer pastures, had no choice but to imitate the Chinese and try their hand at agriculture. But indiscriminate cultivation of fallow land without fertilization produced only a fraction of what the Chinese peasant could obtain from the same soil. If a piece of ground showed signs of exhaustion, the Mongols cultivated another piece of land, leaving the first plot to the weeds. In agricultural competition with the Chinese the Mongol was definitely inferior. In consequence the Mongolian section of the population grew increasingly poorer. The same circumstances which forced the Mongols to become cultivators, because of the lack of suitable grazing-grounds, also compelled them to abandon the nomadic life they had led between summer and winter grazing and to resign themselves to a sedentary way of life.

But the Mongols who had settled led a miserable existence. The round, transportable nomad tent became a rather more solid hut, the walls of which were covered with a rough coat of clay instead of felt. This was soon followed by a clay hut in the Chinese settlers' style with a barrel-vault roof. These wretched hovels were surrounded by brushwood fences. The horses, of which there had formerly been large herds and in which lay the wealth of the Mongols, quickly disappeared. Herds of horses need space. The Mongol settler was now reduced to a single ox; a few goats, sheep and pigs represented his total livestock. The Chinese, by virtue of their superior methods of cultivation, also acquired a superior social status. The poor Mongols imitated the Chinese and adopted some of their customs. They married Chinese women and the children were bi-lingual. Gradually the Chinese language gained the upper hand. But at the same time Mongolian nationalism and anti-

Chinese feeling also grew in those areas which had been overrun by the Chinese settlers. Some of the Mongols cleared out and became bandits, who moved around in the mountains and steppes, hunted by the Chinese police, but who were free and took their revenge on those who had dispossessed them by raiding the prosperous Chinese agricultural settlements.

This was the situation that soon arose in the Sürüg Banner, where Babodshab, one of the legendary anti-Chinese resistance leaders, succeeded in recruiting his famous 'Thirteen Companies'. These gave the Chinese settlers a great deal of trouble. The Chinese police hunted them down as robbers and bandits. The Mongols, however, looked upon them as patriots, whom they helped by bringing them food at night and providing them with local information. Even today many Mongolian ballads still recount the exploits of Babodshab and his thirteen companies.

Another rebel-leader who came from the Sürüg area was Togtok taidshi, on whom the Dshebtsundampa Hutuktu conferred the title of a Duke of Mongolia in 1911 and whom he appointed chief of his bodyguard. During the troubled period after 1902 and the end of the Russo-Japanese war in 1905, Togtok gathered discontented elements round him and became a bandit-chief, who fought against the Chinese settlers. He was joined by more and more Harachin Mongols, who had been driven out of house and home by the wave of Chinese settlers. For the Eastern Mongols, who were embittered by the invasion of Chinese settlers, Togtok and his warriors were a symbol of anti-Chinese resistance. The robber band had soon grown into an army, which inflicted defeat after defeat on the Chinese troops.

> The copper money was distributed,
> then many deserted.
> The number of deserters was large
> And Togtok taidshi led them in battle!
> When silver money was paid
> many looted,

The number of looters was large,
And Togtok led them in battle!
Repeater rifles were distributed,
Rich and poor,
Rich and poor carried them,
And they took the oxen from the plough . . .'

This is only one of many ballads on Togtok and his struggle against the Chinese, which I myself heard and wrote down in Eastern Mongolia as late as 1943.

THE BOOK THAT BRINGS A SMILE TO THE LIPS

The manuscript from the Sürüg Banner, which Manidshab had brought me, was incomplete. As is so often the case with Mongolian manuscripts, the last pages were missing. Thin, fragile paper was far from suitable for anyone leading the life of a nomadic herdsman. Leather or parchment would have been better.

But the manuscript had a foreword, which expressed the kind of ideas that were characteristic of the Eastern Mongolian around the turn of the last century and during the first years of the present one. At a time when everything that was old was being *forgotten*, the unknown collector had put together in his book 'favourite poems, songs and puzzles of earlier times and of today'. And because they could induce laughter, he called his collection a 'Book which brings a smile to the lips'. But what kind of thing made the Mongols laugh at that time? There is a 'Song on recognizing the prince', which is immediately followed by a 'Song of Warning'. After the 'Little Song which consoles the pauper' comes one that 'warns the world'. One poem in the collection envies the flowers and another complains of the way humanity is used. Brandy is praised in one song, blamed in another. And the only prose story, which the anonymous collector thought worth writing down around 1900, is about a monk watching a pair of magpies. The magpies do not trust the human being but eventually become engaged in conversation with him. When the male magpie wants to worship a holy relic which is in a locket round the monk's neck, the monk kills the male magpie. When he is rebuked for this, he says in his defence that he thought the magpie wanted to steal the relic. But the dying magpie enlightens the birds that have gathered round him on the injustice of life. So we have a pious legend which is also a condemnation of degenerate monasticism. What appealed to the collector and writer of these stories and songs was something that reflected the underlying spiritual discontent of the Mongols around the turn of the century, which found expression in passive and eventually active resistance to Manchu rule and the Chinese.

WERE THE MONGOLS AND CHINESE ALWAYS ENEMIES?

There have always been Chinese in Mongolia, just as, throughout the centuries of Chinese history, China's northern borders were constantly threatened by the 'barbarians' and frequently violated by them. A relationship of this kind is inevitable where two economically disparate peoples are geographically adjacent. The history of the Mongol-Chinese conflict is primarily the history of the struggle of the nomads to acquire the additional agricultural produce and the luxury products of a higher culture, which the nomadic economy itself could not produce. The motive behind the great military campaigns by the Mongols' predecessors and by the Mongols themselves against China, the motive behind the countless small raids and border-incursions by the Mongols was in most cases a desire for the additional foodstuffs, which the Chinese peasant produced, and for the luxury goods, which the Chinese urban population manufactured. Where Chinese settlers established colonies, large or small, in the Mongolian pasture-lands, these were mostly military colonies which served as outposts of the Great Wall. Following the Mongol victory over China in the thirteenth century, Chinese settlers were sent to Mongolia to produce additional food supplies for the Mongols. And there were also colonies of Chinese artisans under the Mongol dynasty both in Karakorum and in other parts of Mongolia. Under the Mongol rule, the Mongols were the masters and the Chinese were treated as the lowest grade of citizen in the Mongol Empire. For many decades after the collapse of the Mongol Empire in 1368, Mongolian dress, Mongolian names and Mongolian customs continued to predominate, even though the Chinese had become the ruling people under the Ming dynasty. It required drastic bans and imperial edicts by the Ming dynasty to break the Chinese population of the habit of imitating the Mongolian way of life.

But thousands of Mongols, who had been living or garrisoned in China when the Mongol Empire collapsed, were retained in the service of the new Ming dynasty and they served it loyally. The first emperor of the Ming dynasty, who had led the successful revolt against the Mongol rulers, issued a decree immediately after the collapse of the Mongols rule, that all Mongols, who were living on Chinese soil and had been influenced by Chinese civilization, were his subjects and must be treated as equals of the Chinese. So in the course of a century tens of thousands of Mongols were assimilated by the Chinese and absorbed into the mass of the Chinese people.

In the sixteenth century, when the Ming dynasty lost its grip and the Mongols in Mongolia under Altan Khan represented a serious threat to China's northern borders, there were fifty thousand Chinese peasants, among them ten thousand members of the religious 'White Lotus' sect who had fled from persecution in China, whose agricultural produce provided Altan Khan with substantial economic resources. In all these cases they were Chinese prisoners, as conscripts to the peasants' defence force or as refugees. There had never been until then a deliberate campaign of Chinese expansion or a voluntary migration northward to colonize the Mongolian pasture-lands. This did not begin until the closing decades of the Manchu rule in China, and with it came hate, a conscious clash between Mongols and Chinese. Despite the absorption of tens of thousands of Chinese into Jenghiz Khan's armies and of tens of thousands more in late centuries as agricultural workers under the Mongol Khans, despite the assimilation of many thousands of Mongols in China during the Ming period, the two peoples had remained culturally and spiritually alien to one another· In the course of the centuries the Mongols had undoubtedly proved receptive to certain ideas from Confucianism, the Chinese State-philosophy, from Taoism and above all from its more mystical and magical cults. The prosperous among them had adopted the more agreeable features of Chinese domestic life, but there still remained a deep spiritual gulf between the nomadic herdsmen and the Chinese rural and urban settlers. The Chinese looked – and still look – down on the uncouth Mongols. The Mongols, for their part, regard the walled settlement, the town, with contempt as a restriction of individual freedom.

Recognition by the Mongols of Manchu supremacy had not been by any means universal in the first half of the seventeenth century. True, Ligdan Khan's excesses had driven the tribes of Eastern Mongolia into the Manchu camp, where some had already established kinship by marriage, but Ligdan Khan's dream of a united Mongol Empire did not die with him in 1634. His grandsons tried to stage a revolt against the Manchus, who were already beginning to adopt the Chinese image. In the second half of the seventeenth century the Ordos princes had to be overcome by force of arms. None of the old princes was recognized by the Manchus; a new generation of pro-Manchu noblemen took over as Ordos princes. Renewed attempts were made by the Oirat prince Galdan and his successors Dawachi and Amursana to establish an autonomous Mongolia and there were constant revolts throughout Mongolia against the Manchus and the Chinese in the eighteenth and early nineteenth centuries. The two peoples were separated by more than a cultural barrier; the Mongols were constantly aware of the need and the justification for a separate Mongolian State.

ANTI-CHINESE CIRCULAR LETTERS IN OSLO

Norwegian evangelical missionaries, who had worked in Mongolia, brought back the two notebooks, which are preserved today in the

University library in Oslo. Each over a hundred pages long, these notebooks contain short stories, moral sayings and teachings and one of them also includes pastoral letters from the highest lamaist dignitary of the Kalka Mongols, the 8th Dshebtsundampa Hutuktu. Pastoral letters from a great lamaist priest are nothing new, and the Dshebtsundampa Hutuktu in particular, who wielded so much influence in Kalka Mongolia, left behind a number of these written exhortations. Usually in rhyme, these messages from the spiritual leaders to their flock exhorted them to follow more regularly and more faithfully the precepts of the Buddhist religion. The 8th Dshebtsundampa Hutuktu also issued these episcopal letters, in which he inveighed against the 'Excesses of the Kalka Mongols in sexual intercourse outside wedlock, the injurious enjoyment of tobacco, and black brandy'.

The pastoral letters of the spiritual head at Urga, however, which are preserved in the Oslo notebooks, are of quite a different kind. They show how the 8th Dshebtsundampa Hutuktu, who in 1911 was to become the first and also the last ruler of an independent Mongolia, influenced the Mongols in one of the decisive phases of their modern history and incited them to revolt against the Chinese.

A MAN OF CHILDISH CAPRICIOUSNESS

The 8th Dshebtsundampa Hutuktu was Tibetan by birth, the son of one of the Dalai Lama's officials in Lhasa. At the age of three he was recognized as a reincarnation of the 7th Dshebtsundampa Hutuktu and was brought from his Tibetan home in 1873 to Urga, seat of the Dshebtsundampa Hutuktu and capital of Northern Mongolia. He grew up among Mongols and soon learned to think and feel like a Mongol noble. From the age of seven he surrounded himself with 'gay' companions and led anything but a saintly life. He drank, smoked and enjoyed women. One of his most striking characteristics was his ability to treat those beneath him with unpredictable cruelty. When he died in 1924 he was riddled with venereal disease, blind, an imbecile and an alcoholic.

For the Kalka Mongols the Dshebtsundampa Hutuktu commanded the utmost respect and adoration, however deplorable his private life might be. Alexej Pozdneev, the famous Russian Mongolist and traveller, who met the 8th Dshebtsundampa Hutuktu in 1892 when he was a young man of twenty-two, described him as follows:

'. . . he is a little below medium height and lean. His face is sallow, without the slightest touch of colour. The impression he creates is made even more unpleasant by his permanent expression of childish capriciousness and moody obstinacy but also by the unusually sensual lips.'

This dubious incumbent of the highest lamaist office in Northern Mongolia was shrewd enough to sense the political unrest in Mongolia and to identify himself with it. A start had already been made in the Ordos area with the formation of secret societies to combat the oppressive tax-system of the Manchus, the Chinese settlers and the corrupt nobility. The first of these societies, called a 'Dughui-lang', was formed in the Ushin Banner of the Ordos, an area which was in a constant state of ferment and where later the 'new Lama', Öldshei Jirgal, was to pursue his adventurous course, till he was shot in 1929. In the neighbouring Otok area the first secret society to combat Chinese infiltration was founded in 1861. The members of these secret societies inscribed their names in the form of a circle, so that, in the event of detection, no one would be able to identify the ringleader. The danger of Chinese infiltration increased in the last third of the nineteenth century:

> In 1860 the Chinese government allowed the Chinese to settle on the eastern border of the Kalka Mongols, in the Harbin area.
> In 1878 this permission was extended to include the territory of the Eastern Mongolian princes.
> In 1880 an official Chinese colonization office for the Mongolian territories was opened.

This also alarmed the Mongols of Northern Mongolia, where there was widespread dissatisfaction with the princes, the monks and the

Chinese. But resentment was particularly bitter against the Manchus, the official overlords of Mongolia. The latent unrest was fanned by news of the uprisings by the anti-Manchurian, sectarian Taiping rebels (1870–71) and later the Boxer Rebellion (1900), which had their repercussions as far away as Northern Mongolia.

The 8th Dshebtsundampa Hutuktu was well aware of this development. Although he was addicted to drinking and womanizing, he nevertheless had a keen political brain. The copies of the pastoral letters from the year 1892, which have been preserved in the notebook in the University library in Oslo, reveal how cunningly and secretly he explored the anti-Manchurian and anti-Chinese feelings.

In another of his circular letters from the year 1889, or 1901, which is in the Royal Library in Copenhagen, he suddenly interrupts his pious, spiritual exhortations to ridicule the Manchus: 'When my 5th sacred reincarnation (the Hutuktu who lived from 1815 to 1841) came with many Manchu officials to Urga and they stumbled around there, people said very rightly that they behaved like strangers! But what would happen now if I suddenly expressed a wish to wear Manchu clothes?'

With the help of religious embellishment and imagery the Dshebtsundampa incited his flock even more openly against the Chinese in 1892. In the notebook which is now in Oslo he recounts a dream he had during the night of the 15th New Year month:

'And suddenly someone appeared sitting on clouds of five colours. He wore the clothes of a person of rank with a hat-button, but the hat was the hat of the priesthood. He bowed politely before me in a kowtow, pressed the palms of his hands together and said: "Khan Hormusta has sent me from heaven and commanded me thus, for he had the sorrows of the Mongols before his eyes . . ."'

The Dshebtsundampa deliberately made use of the Mongols' ancient belief in an old prince of heaven named Hormusta, who is master of heaven and earth. Anything that came from him was a divine commandment! And the words he uttered were taken as a commandment: 'Now it was said that a Mongol must die, if he imitates the Chinese with a white hat and Chinese shoes. When an end has been put to all this, it will never happen again and the good time of the Mongols has begun.' All strange events in the year 1892 are 'signs that a new era is beginning!' But this is followed by the divine commandment 'from the first of the fifth month (1892) to ride south and to destroy the many Chinese, who make the soil yellow and dry by their ploughing!'

No one rode against the Chinese in 1892. But the people knew that their spiritual overlord also hated the Chinese and Manchus. Moreover they were dissatisfied with their princes. In 1891 there were riots against the Tüschijetü Khan of the Kalkas, in 1897 there was trouble with Baiti princes and with monks in Ulankom. Then in 1900 the garrison of Kiachta revolted against the Manchus. Although the revolt was suppressed, a beacon had been lit. The Chinese Resident Sangdowa, the political representative of the Manchu Emperor in Urga, began to give the Mongols an ugly demonstration of the power of the Manchus. In 1910 he gave orders for barracks to be built in Urga for the Manchurian troops. The Mongolian nationalists decided at a secret meeting to break with China. In June 1911 representatives of the Kalkas and of Inner Mongolia went to St Petersburg to enlist Russian support. When the revolution broke out in China, the Mongolian nationalists also struck. The Chinese Resident was driven out and Outer Mongolia, with Czarist Russian support, was declared independent. On 9th October 1911 the 8th Dshebtsundampa Hutuktu was proclaimed the first Head of State of an independent Mongolia. He may have been a drunkard who was quickly going blind, but for the mass of the Mongols he was also a symbol of their fight for independence. In his pastoral letters he had even called upon the people to fight against the Chinese. The proof of this is now in the library of Oslo University.

CHINA'S PERVERSITY

Despite the announcement of an autonomous Northern Mongolia, the Chinese Republic continued even after 1911, after the overthrow of the last Chinese Emperor, to cling to the view that the whole of Mongolia was an integral part of China and was subject to Chinese sovereignty. This claim was even upheld in 1924, when the Mongolian People's Republic emerged with strong support from the Red Army, and when the last Chinese soldier had left Northern Mongolian soil. Up till 1945 Chinese maps continued to show the Mongolian People's Republic as a part of China and on 5th May 1936 the revised constitution of the Republic of China still referred to Mongolia unreservedly as belonging to China.

China's claims were based on the Tripartite Convention of 7th June 1915, which she had concluded with Outer Mongolia and Czarist Russia and in which China and Czarist Russia agreed that Outer Mongolia, that is the territory of the present Mongolian People's Republic, should remain part of China but should have complete autonomy in the administration of its internal affairs. China deliberately closed her eyes to the fact that this had made Mongolia a semi-independent State under Russian protection and that after 1924 she had been unable to exercise any influence on this Russian protectorate. The unofficial view of officials and leading circles of the Chinese Republic was that Russia had cheated China of her rights in northern Outer Mongolia.

The Chinese Republic was left with the Inner Mongolian territories inhabited by the tribes of the Yeke Dshu confederation in the Ordos bend of the Hwang Ho, then, to the east, the Ulanchab confederation and the Tumats of Kweihwa, the Shilingol tribes in Chahar and the Mongols in the western part of Manchuria, who lived mostly on pasture-lands along the watershed of the Hsingan mountains, as far as the Bargha country in the north. Altogether there were about 2,000,000 Mongols, twice as many as in Outer Mongolia. One might have thought this would have induced the Chinese Republic to adopt a conciliatory policy towards the Mongol minority, for it was in precisely these areas, Inner and Outer Mongolia, that the Mongols had bitterly resisted the infiltration of Chinese settlers. In the Ordos area the first secret societies or Dughuilang had been founded to combat the Chinese infiltration and in 1912 an attempt had been made to join up with Outer Mongolia, an attempt which had only been foiled by Chinese 'pacification campaigns'. The whole Bargha country and the Horchin Banner in Eastern Mongolia tried to link up with Outer Mongolia and thereby share in its independence. These attempts, in which Prince Utai and the living Buddha of the Gegensüme played a leading part, had to be crushed by Chinese troops. In the Bargha area, which was Outer Mongolia's nearest neighbour to the northeast, the situation never returned to normal. In 1915 China was forced to grant the area autonomy, although in 1928 she tried to abolish it by a decree of the President of the Republic. The flames of revolt flared up again. Soviet troops marched into Bargha, where they remained until 1930.

CHINESE EXPANSIONISM

With the opening of the East Chinese railway and of the line from Peking to Suiyüan, thousands of humble Chinese settlers poured into the pasture-lands of Inner Mongolia. From 1926 there were around a million of these Chinese immigrants a year. In the years 1928–29, after the railway from Taonan to Solunshan in Western Manchuria had been completed, 40,000 Chinese arrived in the Taonan area alone. By 1930 two-thirds of the territory inhabited by the Mongol tribes in the eastern part of Inner Mongolia were already colonized by Chinese, and the Mongols, who were greatly outnumbered, had been forced back from the fertile grazing-grounds to the more barren partly steppe areas near the Outer Mongolian frontier. There was a similar situation in the south of Inner Mongolia. The proportion of Chinese in the population of the Ordos area rose to seventy per cent. The number of Chinese in south-eastern Chahar showed a similar increase, the Tumats in Suiyüan gradually lost their national characteristics and became sinicized. With the exception of the Shilingol tribes in northern Chahar all the tribal territories of Inner Mongolia were overrun by Chinese settlers in the 1930s. Small wonder that discontent increased among the Mongols of Inner Mongolia. Various political groups emerged, which, though opposed to one another, were all products of the same deep-rooted discontent with the Chinese administration and the lack of autonomy. The 'Young Mongols' under Mersai, young men who had been educated at Soviet or Japanese schools and universities, stood for a large measure of autonomy which would lead eventually to a fusion with the Mongolian People's Republic. Other more nationalist-minded groups formed under the leadership of princes in Eastern and Inner Mongolia. Their demands ranged from complete political independence from China to a compromise solution in the form of cultural autonomy. Contacts were made with Japan, who was formulating her own plans for expanding into the mainland of Asia. Contacts were also made with the Soviet Union, with the Mongolian People's Republic and with Nanking, the capital of the Chinese Republic since 1927. But the Mongols of Inner and Eastern Mongolia never succeeded in sinking their political differences and achieving unity of purpose.

MINORITY POLICY À LA CHINOISE

Sun Yat-sen, the spiritual father of the Chinese Republic, in his fundamental 'Principles of the People', had always referred to the 'unity and equality of rights' of the five nations of China, one of which was the Mongols. This conception had been embodied in the constitution of the Chinese Republic. Yet very little was in fact done to treat the Mongols as equal partners in the Chinese State. The Chinese National Government of Chiang Kai-shek set up a special government office in Nanking to deal with 'Tibetan and Mongolian Affairs' and even appointed Mongols as President and Vice-President, but neither this office nor any other body took up the just demands of the Mongols for a halt to be called to the Chinese immigration and for cultural autonomy. On the contrary, it was believed that the problem of the territories beyond the Great Wall could best be solved by inducing the Mongols to abandon their nomadic way of life, by subjecting them to the Chinese influence and by opening up additional living-space for China's surplus population.

All that was offered to the Mongols in the form of education was on the Chinese pattern and was designed to impress upon the Mongols, and convert them to, a Chinese culture which was greatly superior to their own and which certainly regarded itself as such. The Chinese National Government, which was imbued with the ideas of the Kuomintang, remained convinced of the superiority of Confucianism over the primitive barbarians of the north. At conferences which were held at various times between representatives of the Mongols and the National Government, the Mongols were promised all that they asked for, namely, Mongol unity and the economic and cultural development of the backward areas of Mongolia. Detailed development programmes were worked out but nothing practical ever came of them. Nanking, National China's capital, was very far away from Mongolia.

WORDS AS A SAFETY-VALVE

Several notebooks with literary entries have been found in Mongolia. They were nearly all compiled around the turn of the last century. It almost looks as if during those years the Mongols had sought refuge in the written word and in their rather homely philosophy. The Royal Library in Copenhagen possesses two thick books of this kind, which were acquired in Chahar by the Danish expedition under Kaare Grønbech. The anonymous writers were primarily interested in moral maxims, didactic sayings and poems. Most of these were compiled by a lamaist monk and must be classified as religious tracts. A historical work was interpolated. As it had previously been unknown, this was an important discovery. Similar entries are also in another notebook from Kalka Mongolia, at the State Library of the Mongolian People's Republic at Ulan Bator (formerly Urga). But scattered throughout one of the notebooks at Oslo in a variety of separate entries and collected together in a notebook at Ulan Bator are short rhyming stories which bear the strange title: 'The Words'. The fact that they recur so frequently shows that in the late nineteenth century and early twentieth they were very widespread and very popular among the Mongols. *The words of the orphaned young antelope, The words of the old cow,* and *The words of the steppe-marmot* are all in one of the notebooks at Ulan Bator. A particularly frequent one is *The words which crows and magpies exchange with one another.* A spidery handwriting in Copenhagen relates *The words which the mouse said for fun.* Here the mouse reminds a greedy monk, from whom she has stolen a few breadcrumbs only to be caught by the angry cleric, that as a member of the priesthood he should not kill but must be charitable. In these 'words' human judgements are put into the mouths of animals. What could not be said openly by the Mongols, so long as they were exposed to extortion by their princes, squeezed out by Chinese settlers and heavily in debt to Chinese traders, was expressed here in literary guise, and satire was clothed in the animal fable, a form which Buddhists had introduced centuries before. It is not known who wrote all the words or who first thought of this poetic safety-valve for the general discontent. Most of the 'Words' are anonymous folk-lore. The authors of some particularly popular 'Words' are, however, known. Among them was the Lama from Urga, Tshisangbuu, who, like Kulichi Sandag in the second half of the nineteenth century, wrote his ironical and melancholy 'Words' in rhyme. His *Words of a wolf, which has been tracked down by the beaters* is also included in the Oslo notebook. They express what the simple Mongol must have felt in the critical years at the close of the last century, when he was defenceless against the despotism of the princes. No prince's spy, no fawning time-server could quote these words against him and no prince could punish him for them.

'In the steppe I was born
I, the blue wolf.
Have robbed and eaten men's cattle,
Went back to my lair and
Thought as I went; I'll have a sleep right here in the steppe!

With the Banner Prince at their head,
Who was followed by many warriors from the whole Banner,
Who rode on their good, fast horses,
They came rushing up like a whirlwind.
For beggars who acquired a paunch,
For robbers who lost courage
Hell is the place to go to! —
But what is to be done here?
There to the north are the distant mountains,
Here is the wide steppe before them.
I say: the tendons of the horses' hindquarters are meeting.
I say: is the dun horse coming nearer?
As I look around
They are already coming to catch me.
As I leap up
They are already coming to seize me.
This morning has no evening.
What I caught and ate
With the eagerness of hunger
I can no longer digest.
This is no matter for mere talk,
This is not chance – only evil fate,
This is no heritage of which one can speak
This is nothing in me – only evil fate!
One of many children later
Skinned, cut and ate
The lizard —
I am as wretched as that animal!
Even if heaven pities me, it is too late.
I ate an animal I had killed,
I swallowed something that tasted good.
Now that I contemplated my future,
I saw only one great sin.
I was born in the plain,
I, a mangy, bad wolf.
Although I thought many thoughts,
I could no longer find the cunning to flee!
Now you must be merciful, my Lord!'

In the 'thirties, when the political situation of the Inner Mongolian
tribes, which had been forced to remain in China, seemed quite

hopeless and the internal friction between Mongols and Chinese had become almost unbearable, the East Mongolian poet Muuökin, who was born in 1906, expressed the feelings of the Mongols in sterner words. In one of his songs he wrote:

> 'The Prince of the Banner is a tiger,
> The evil Regent a wolf . . .
> The sheep is Muuökin, the singer.'

A BURYAT FOUNDATION

That many such works have been preserved in western libraries is due to European travellers, collectors and scholars. But it seems quite natural that the Mongols of the Mongolian People's Republic should today have the largest and most comprehensive collection of Mongolian manuscripts and block-prints. This is due above all to one Buryat scholar, Cyben Žamcaranovií Žamcarano. In 1921 he founded the Mongol Committee of Sciences. The Russians abbreviated the Russian name 'Mongol'skij učenyi komitet' to Utschkom. In 1962, forty years after its foundation, the Committee of Sciences became an Academy of Sciences.

IX THE TWENTIETH CENTURY

THE CULTURAL AVANT-GARDE

About 300,000 Mongols – approximately a tenth of all Mongolian-speaking people – live in Buryat Mongolia, one of the autonomous Soviet republics of the Soviet Union. Its centre is Lake Baikal. Since the Treaty of Nerchinsk between Russia and China in 1689 ceded this area to Russia, its Mongolian inhabitants have been in continuous contact with the Russians. The Mongols there went to school at an earlier stage than anywhere else. As early as 1816 the Russians built the first school for Buryat children, and this Russian initiative bore early fruit. In the first half of the last century Buryat scholars such as Dordshi Banzarov, who died young (1822–55) and the Lama Galsang Gomboev (1822–63) made important contributions to research into Mongolia and her culture. Both were educated in Kazan, which at that time was the training-ground for the spiritual and cultural expansion of Czarist Russia towards the east. It is to them that we owe the translations of various Mongolian poems. Gomboew also translated the historical work *The Golden Button*. From the middle of the last century the number of educated Buryats increased by leaps and bounds. They were influenced by the ideas of European nationalism and independence. A Buryat politician of the 1920s, referring to the part played by the Buryats, said that they 'formed the cultural *avant garde* among the Mongol tribes and introduced and directed the revolutionary ideas of our time'.

The educated Buryats were Mongolian nationalists, who dreamt of a greater Mongolia – while at the same time helping the Russians in their efforts to gain influence both under the Czars and in the first phase of Communist expansion in the Far East. Time and again the Russians referred proudly to the cultural achievements of the Buryats as having been made possible only with Russian help and support.

RED PARTISANS

The severance of Outer or Kalka Mongolia from China in 1911 was an act of dissatisfaction with China. It was the answer to China's attempt to oppress and sinicize the Mongols. The nationalist refugees from the areas of Inner Mongolia which had remained with China exercised a considerable influence. In 1915 the Chinese moved back into 'Independent Mongolia' in the person of General Hsu, who because of his stunted growth was known as 'little Hsu'.

The rule of the Dshebtsundampa Hutuku was becoming more and more of a farce. An increasing number of young Mongols were disappointed both with the renewed Chinese intervention and with the official representative of Mongolian independence, the Dshebtsundampa Hutuktu. Like Choibalsang, who later became Minister President of the Mongolian People's Republic, most of them had come in contact with Russians at an early age, they had visited the Mongolian school, which had been established in the Czarist period in the Russian consulate at Urga, and they had subsequently been influenced by Russian Communists and their ideas at Irkutsk.

In 1919, when it had become abundantly clear that 'little Hsu' intended to restore Independent Mongolia to China, these young Mongols, led by Sükebator, the national hero of the Mongolian People's Republic, and Choibalsang, decided to make an organized resistance.

This cell, which was to grow into the revolutionary Mongolian movement, was strongly influenced by two Russian agitators from Irkutsk, Kucherenko and Gembarshevski.

THE BALTIC BARON UNGERN IS DRIVEN OUT

When 'White Russian' troops led by the Baltic Baron Ungern-Sternberg, a comrade-in-arms of Ataman Semjonov, advanced into Outer Mongolia to outflank the Red Army, which was attacking the Whites in Siberia, Sükebator and Choibalsang formed the first Mongolian Communist partisan units in the present town of Altan bulag and on Lake Khosho gol, near the Russian border. They were later to be expanded into the Mongolian People's Army. On 4th February 1921 Ungern-Sternberg stormed the town of Urga, the seat of the Dshebtsundampa Hutuktu. He drove out General Hsu's troops and set up a government consisting of princes and the priest-king. But the one-eyed Balt was secretly toying with the idea of making himself Emperor of Mongolia. Choibalsang and Sükebator declared unofficial war on this feudal government and Ungern-Sternberg with a steadily growing number of partisans and with the support of the Far East Soviet Republic which had been established in 1920.

On 1st March 1921 they founded the Mongolian Revolutionary People's Party at Kiahta on the Russo-Mongolian border. Žamcarano drew up the party's programme. Despite the Communist jargon, it was fundamentally a Mongolian nationalist document. Clause two stated: 'In view of the fact that the peaceful existence of the Mongolian tribes and their links with the culture and knowledge of the enlightened peoples requires the formation of an independent, self-governing Mongolian national state and not enslavement and oppression by foreign imperialists, our People's Party strives for the ultimate goal of a union of all Mongolian tribes in one single, autonomous state.'

On 13th March 1921, a few days after the party programme was adopted, a provisional government for Outer Mongolia was formed at Kiahta. Its chairman was Chakdurzab. In addition to Choibalsang and Sükebator there were three other ministers.

The provisional government then asked the Soviet Government for help against the 'white' occupation of Mongolia. International law having been involved by the formation of a government at Kiahta, Soviet troops, supported by Mongolian partisans, occupied Urga on 6th July 1921. There a government of the Mongolian People's Republic was set up.

Both in its composition and in its aims the new government was considerably influenced by Buryats. Erdeni Batukhan, the Minister of Education, was a Buryat, as was Dashi Sampilon, the Mongolian Minister of Economy. Rinchino, another Buryat nationalist, was, in effect, Minister President of the Mongolian People's Republic in 1928–29. Their major political aim was the unification of all Mongols. At the Third Party Congress of the Mongolian Revolutionary People's Party Rinchino said: 'We must also bear in mind that millions of our race, the "inner" Mongols, are groaning under Chinese oppression.' In November 1924 he addressed this challenge to the great People's Assembly of the Mongolian People's Republic: 'We must become the cultural centre of our race, we must draw the Inner Mongols, the Bargha Mongols, and others, to us.'

Cyben Žamcarano translated this challenge into action in 1921 when he founded the Committee of Sciences in Ulan Bator, the capital of the new Mongolian State. It began its life in a small building with a staff of only thirteen people. One department was to specialize in the Mongolian language and literature, while another built up a library. In 1924 a museum was added.

Žamcarano, who was born in Buryat Mongolia in 1880, already had a successful scientific career behind him. On various expeditions sponsored by the Russians he had travelled throughout Mongolia as far as the Ordos area and had collected specimens of Mongolian literature. When he founded the Committee of Sciences in Ulan Bator in 1921, he had already collected valuable specimens of folk traditions and folklore which had been passed down by word of mouth not only among the Buryats but also among the Kalka

Mongols and the tribes of Inner Mongolia. How he came to do this, he himself described in 1914:

'From early childhood, I learned to love the whole people, the Buryats, to love fatherland and home, sagas and shamanist hymns, folklore and folk-religion. My eighty-year-old great-grandmother related memories from her childhood of "devils' tricks", of the struggles between the shamans and the lamas, of the great spirit of the Shasan mountains, who was so alive that he spoke to the children. My grandmother described the famous exploits of Geser and his battles with the many-headed monsters (mangus). My grandfather spoke of the ukhar (demons) of our family, which, the nomads believe, only disappeared when they have lured away the member of the family who pleases them most. All this enchanted us as children. It transported our imaginations into a fantastic world of heroes and giants, shamans and werewolves, and such was our faith that there could be no doubt of the reality of that world. Sometimes my father read aloud the trilogy of Geser Khan, Ardji-Bordji Khan and Vikramijid as well as the Indian allegories from the "White Lotus" book. Then there was a poem about Jenghiz Khan's two horses, a delightful affair.

'Later I wrote down the epic songs my father sang. He was a good singer and they are still the best of all those which I later wrote down among the Buryats.

'And my childhood love for this people, for the old epic tunes and the world of shamanism cast a more and more powerful spell over me!'

Within a few years Žamcarano and his colleagues, fired with enthusiasm, had amassed a magnificent collection of Mongolian manuscripts and block-prints. In 1926, when the famous Russian Mongolist, J. B. Vladmircov, visited the Committee of Sciences at Ulan Bator, he remarked admiringly that this 'important collection' of Mongolian manuscripts and xylographs 'is excelled only by the collection in Leningrad. The library of the Mongolian Committee of Sciences contains rare documents which other collections completely lack.'

The Committee of Sciences did not hide its treasures away. It placed them at the disposal not only of Russian scholars, such as N. Poppe who is now teaching in America, and of the Frenchman Paul Pelliot, but also of the German scholar, Erich Haenisch, who discovered the *Secret History of the Mongols* and who studied the manuscripts at Ulan Bator in 1936. A catalogue published in 1937 listed 589 historical works alone together with many other manuscripts and rare books.

FOR AND AGAINST THE SPIRIT OF THE PAST

In the meantime Japan had occupied Manchuria. The Russians established themselves in Mongolia. Choibalsang, the old partisan-leader of the struggle for independence, was appointed Marshal.

In 1935, Gendun, who had been Minister President for many years, expressed the view in public that the Communist economic system was not practicable in Mongolia. Both he and the Defence Minister Demid were suspected of espionage and sabotage in the pay of Japan. The case for the prosecution before the Central Committee of the Mongolian Revolutionary People's Party was preserved by the newly-fledged Marshal Choibalsang, who indicted his old comrades. The insane process of Stalinist purges began in Mongolia. When very conveniently a counter-revolutionary organization was discovered in two lamaist monasteries of the Gobi, there was near-hysteria. Outstanding Mongols, including scholars, were placed under police-supervision or exiled to the Soviet Union. Among them was Žamcarano. He worked for some time undisturbed in Leningrad at the Academy of Sciences but in August 1937 he was arrested and disappeared. By 1940 he was dead. Presumably he died in a concentration-camp on the White Sea.

In April 1936 the Soviet Union had concluded an aid agreement with the Mongolian People's Republic, which was designed to halt Japanese expansion in Manchuria. There were purges throughout the country of 'untrustworthy' elements. Everything Mongolian was regarded as nationalist and was therefore suspect. In the years that followed, up to the end of the Second World War, many of the Mongols' cultural values disappeared as a result of this policy of destruction. The Mongols themselves refer to what was done during that period as 'deeds of Mongol brawn and Russian brain'.

After Stalin's death there was a change in the cultural policy of the Mongolian People's Republic. The State Library is housed today in a modern building and has one of the finest collections of Mongolian literature. Expeditions cover the entire country in search of old manuscripts and old literary works. At the University of Ulan Bator there are several Chairs for Mongolian literary history and language. In 1962, on the fortieth anniversary of the Mongolian People's Republic, the Committee of Sciences was elevated to an Academy of Sciences. There are institutions which publish good editions of Mongolian poetry and literature, which are sent to scholars and institutions throughout the world. A realistic attitude has also been taken towards the past. Even the Chairman of the Central Committee of the Mongolian Revolutionary People's Party acknowledged in May 1963, when the cultural and literary policy was under discussion, that the ancient works also had literary value.

At the same time he stressed the importance of warning the modern reader against the pitfalls of the feudal, bourgeois, reactionary and religious thinking of the past, pitfalls which lay concealed in these recognized works of old Mongolian poetry. Cyben Žamcarano is dead, but he has been rehabilitated as a victim of Stalinism and his memory and achievements are honoured.

In 1952 the State Library at Ulan Bator had 150,000 European books, Mongolian and Tibetan manuscripts and prints.

JAPANESE CULTURAL OFFENSIVE

Ever since 1932 Japan had been pressing forward into the Chinese mainland. To begin with, the greater part of the Mongol population of Inner and Eastern Mongolia was pro-Japanese. The Japanese had promised to put a stop to the invasion of the Mongols' grazing-grounds by large, state-sponsored groups of settlers and they had promised in particular to halt Chinese cultural subversion of the Mongols by meeting the Mongolian demands for education. During those early years, however, Japan's Mongolian policy was dominated by propaganda against the Soviet domination of Outer Mongolia. So, for the time being at least, the Mongols' ambitions and dreams of unifying all Mongolia were kept alive.

But the first blight began to fall on these hopes soon after Japanese troops had occupied Inner Mongolia and the Meng-chiang Federation had been created under the pro-Japanese Prince Teh Wang. The Mongols had expected that at least the Mongols living in the four Hsingan provinces and the new Inner Mongolian Federation would be united in an autonomous Mongolian State under Japanese protection. The Japanese, however, made no move in this direction; they even began to seal off the Mongols in Manchukuo from those in the Inner Mongolian Federation.

Then in the summer of 1939 came the incident at Nomonhan on the border between the northern Hsingan province and the Mongolian People's Republic. What was in reality a trial of strength between the two Great Powers, the Soviet Union and Japan, apppeared to be merely a trial of strength between the Mongols of the eastern tribes and the Kalka Mongols. Mongols were fighting on both sides. Japanese prestige among the eastern Mongols and in Inner Mongolia suffered severely when the Japanese divisions, which were thrown in, were decimated by the Russians. The border incident was soon settled by agreement. But the Japanese loss of face was not so easily forgotten by their Mongol subjects.

The next source of disillusionment for the Mongolian Nationalists of Inner and Eastern Mongolia was Japan's educational and cultural policy. Undoubtedly the Japanese had gone some way at first, and very quickly, towards meeting the Mongols' demand for education. In 1940 there were more than a thousand elementary schools and sixteen high schools in the eastern areas of the Hsingan provinces. The teachers were both Japanese and Mongol, and more than 50,000 boys and girls attended these schools.

The number of schools and scholars there had increased four times in one year, but the Japanese realized that they needed an educated middle-class if they were to keep the Mongols firmly under control. So in Wang-yeh-miao, now called Ulanhoto, they founded an academy with a mixed Japanese-Mongolian staff of teachers, who trained young Mongols, selected from all the Banners of the Hsingan area, to become government officials and officers, very much on the Japanese pattern. There was a similar situation in the Japanese-occupied areas of Inner Mongolia. In addition, Mongols were sent to universities in Japan and to the State University of Manchukuo. To begin with, there was strong support for the tendency among the Mongols to restrict the influence of the Chinese language and culture in favour of the Mongolian language and script. Apart from the schools there were also courses in further education for adults. The small printing-presses belonging to Mongolian Nationalist groups, such as the Bökekeshik Press in Kailu, were turned over to the production of Japanese propaganda. In 1941 a State Translation Office was set up for the Mongols in the capital of Manchukuo, Hsingking, under the direction of a Harachin Mongol, Kcshingga, who had also directed the East Mongolian book-printing press at Mukden. A publishing house and a printing-press for Mongolian works were also set up in Inner Mongolia by Prince Teh Wang, which were run by one of the Prince's secretaries named Chogbadarag and were more independent of the Japanese than any other similar institutions. Chogbadarag, a native Eastern Mongolian, always had strong pan-Mongolian sympathies and is said to have been sent by Prince Teh Wang before 1945 to hold secret talks in the Mongolian People's Republic behind the backs of the Japanese.

All these publishing-houses and printing-presses now began producing books in Mongolian for the increasing number of Mongols who could read, thanks to the improvements in education. In addition to Japanese political propaganda, they published works on the Mongolian Nationalist movement, on administration, language and hygiene.

The main feature of their output, however, was the publication of old Mongolian historical works, and from time to time, after the Japanese Buddhists had persuaded the Japanese occupation authorities that Buddhism was an important weapon against the Communist ideology, a certain number of old lamaist works were also printed. The newspapers which appeared in the Mongolian areas occupied by the Japanese were, for the most part, no more than organs of Japanese propaganda. Whereas in 1939 they had adopted a martial, blustering tone towards the Mongolian People's Republic, from 1941 onwards, the year in which Japan concluded a non-aggression pact with Russia, they quickly transferred their state-controlled interest from Russia and her Mongolian satellite, the Mongolian People's Republic, to the 'ABC Front' as they called the American-British-Chinese front against Japan. This meant that they lost sight more and more of the original function for which they had been created, namely, to produce something that would halt the spread of Chinese literature. In fact, ever since 1938 Japanese culture in Mongolia had been a disappointment to the Mongols, for in that year almost all Japanese organizations began to encourage the adoption of Japanese as second language. In February 1944 in Manchukuo and even earlier – in 1942 – a campaign was launched in the Inner Mongolian Federation to introduce 5,000 Japanese words into the Mongolian language. The specific aim of the campaign was to base all word-formations of a modern and particularly of a technical character on Japanese. However understandable such a scheme may have been from the Japanese viewpoint – they were out to involve occupied Mongolia in their economic planning and this called for a class of Mongols to whom technical work could be entrusted – this use of language by the Japanese as a political weapon found little favour among the Mongols. For nothing contributed more to the deterioration in Japanese-Mongolian relations than the economic exploitation that went on during the Second World War. Originally Japan's economic policy had been to develop Mongolia's natural resources. The original aims of the occupation authorities as well as of many industrial concerns which were mainly financed with Japanese capital had been to exploit and process these natural resources with the help of Mongolian labour and to modernize and improve the country's main source of wealth, cattle-breeding. But the more isolated Japan became on the East Asian continent during the war the less attention was paid to economic development. The existing agricultural stocks and in particular the cattle population were drained off, regardless of the consequences, to feed the Japanese armies in Northern China and Manchukuo. The economic plight of the Mongols grew worse year by year throughout the war. The number of herds steadily decreased. Materials for clothing, leather for the traditional Mongolian boots and even the most elementary consumer goods were unobtainable. So acute were the shortages that millet, a staple diet of the Mongols, was rationed, and it was quite impossible to obtain rice or white flour. So the efficient, smooth-working administrative machine which the Japanese had built up in the occupied territories served little or no purpose. And what had been achieved by creating a stratum of young, well-trained Mongolian officials and intellectuals, who were informed on all questions of modern politics? For this was a development that the intellectuals themselves, whose fathers had demanded cultural autonomy and improved education of China, took for granted. As for the monumental administrative buildings in Hsin-king, Wang-yeh-miao and Kalgan, the capital of the Mengchiang Federation, they made little impression so long as the ordinary people were denied basic food-supplies. For this stratum of young Mongols the Japanese represented their only hope of developing and modernizing the country's agriculture, industry and transport; these young Mongols, most of whom had been educated in Japan, hoped with Japanese help to bring their country into line with the twentieth century. They did not, however, regard Japan as a leading power in Asia and were fairly critical of Japanese propaganda claims of this kind. They were anti-Russian, because they believed that the Soviet presence in the Mongolian People's Republic was an obstacle in the way of the unification of the Mongolian People's Republic with other parts of Mongolia occupied by the Japanese. Their stand against Communism was not, therefore, based on any ideological or philosophical grounds but purely and simply on political and utilitarian considerations. The more Japan's policy on the Chinese mainland seemed doomed to failure, the more inclined young Mongols were to look round for another patron to protect them against renewed Chinese infiltration.

The alternative was the Communists, who had deliberately reverted to the old tradition of the Mongolian secret societies in the late nineteenth and early twentieth centuries, the so-called Dughuilang, which fought against the Manchu rule and Chinese infiltration. There was no pure Communist propaganda. The sole enemy was the Japanese occupation forces. The Chinese National Government was increasingly tolerant towards the Chinese resistance movement, because it had no means of its own of resisting the Japanese in the occupied territories of Mongolia.

The first partisan groups were created in Eastern Mongolia in 1932 and 1933 with the active support of the 8th Chinese Communist army and the moving spirit behind them was a young Tumat Mongol from Kükehot, named Ulanhu, who was subsequently to play a distinguished part in Inner Mongolian politics. Ulanhu's career is typical of the young Mongols who had turned to Communism. For many years he was a member of the Chinese Communist Party. Born in 1905, his parents were simple people, who like most Tumat Mongols in the Chinese province of Suiyüan, had already settled on the land. He went to the local elementary school and was then selected, as one of the more gifted pupils, to attend the Tibetan-Mongolian school at Peking. In February 1924, when the Russians made their first attempt at Communist penetration of China under Borodin, he joined the Communist Youth Union and before long he had become its secretary. While in Peking he played an active part in revolutionary student activities and worked as a Communist agitator. In 1925, at the age of twenty,

Northern China in their dealings with the Mongolian partisans made them national martyrs. Thus Rinchenhorlo, the leader of a Mongolian partisan group in the Muumingan area who fell into Japanese hands in 1942 and died during interrogation, became something of a legendary hero to the Mongols and his death made the anti-Japanese feeling even more intense. The Japanese clamped down on everything that seemed to them resistance to their occupation and policy, and they came more and more to identify Mongolian nationalism with acceptance of the radical, revolutionary ideas of the 8th Chinese Communist army. Finally Japanese mistrust extended not merely to active partisans but also to the Mongolian nationalists, who had originally welcomed Japanese intervention in Mongolia as a means of achieving the national aims.

Amongst those arrested by the Japanese was Bökekeshik, director of the Mongolian book-printing concern in Kailu, Eastern Mongolia and a member of a group of Mongols who had at one time been at the Peking State University as students and teachers. Bökekeschik, with Japanese support, had carried on his printing business for many years 'with the object of preserving Mongolian culture and the Mongolian nation'. But he was accused of having failed to support and even to have sabotaged the efforts of the Japanese from nationalistic motives. In 1943 the Mongolian daily newspapers announced the sudden death of the man who had done so much to promote the cause of Mongolian literature. From information published in America after the war it became clear that the Japanese had, in fact, condemned Bökekeshik to death.

The passive resistance and sabotage, which the Mongols were able to carry out, ranged from a certain obstinate indifference to Japanese propaganda to the failure to carry out Japanese orders, particularly in the field of culture and propaganda. What can only be regarded as an act of great courage was the publication by the Mongolian State Translation Office of the Manchukuo government of the caustic poems of the Chahar monk Ishidangchinwang-chil, which he had written in 1902 in protest against the Chinese infiltration and the oppression by the princes. They seemed topical to the Mongols again, for in them the poet had said many things which the Eastern Mongols found highly relevant to their plight in the years 1942-45. Here is one example:

> 'It is shameful not to be aware of the poor, shivering slave,
> When one is warmly wrapped in fox and lamb (skins);
> It is shameful not to notice the hungry slave's lethargy
> When one sends currants and sugar, meat and butter as presents;
> It is shameful to know nothing of broken bones and flesh,
> When one has the strength and will to punish and flog;
> It is shameful not to recognize the exhaustion of the poor
> servant,
> When one is trotting along quickly on a good horse or carriage;
> It is shameful to have one's subjects as serving-people outside,
> When one is surrounded oneself by clinging wives and
> girls . . .'

Right up to the end of the war the Japanese control authorities never understood why this book was so popular, otherwise they would not have allowed another edition to appear in Inner Mongolia shortly before the end of the war. Membership of the resistance movement and the partisan units had long since ceased to be confined to small revolutionary groups. The nobility and the intelligentsia were represented side by side with herdsmen and peasants, and many of the young Mongols, whom the Japanese had educated, were members of the anti-Japanese resistance, in spite of their official positions in a pro-Japanese administration. Many a peasant or Mongolian herdsman, who worked peacefully during the day, exchanged his agricultural tool or milking-stool at night for a gun with which to fight as a partisan. Mongolian women also took part in this anti-Japanese fighting. The wife of the Prince of western Urat and a woman in the eastern Urat Banner both became well-known leaders of partisan groups operating in the Japanese-occupied area of Inner Mongolia. In 1944 the situation was not unlike that of the Italian partisan groups or the French resistance movement. By organizing the resistance and the partisan groups, the Communists had won the confidence of the discontented population. They came to be regarded more and more as the representatives of the Mongols' national cause and of the demand, which the Japanese had failed to satisfy, for Mongolian independence. The Mongols of Inner and Eastern Mongolia were now hoping to achieve this independence after the war by joining up with the Mongolian People's Republic. Champions of these demands for independence were the partisan groups led and controlled by the Communists. The target which had been set by Russian agitators at the first meeting of the Mongolian People's Revolutionary Party in 1925 for Ulanhu and others to achieve, a link between the Mongolian national liberation movement and the national revolutionary forces in China, had been largely realized. The ground had been prepared for further development.

THE YALTA CONCESSION

In the meantime at the secret conference of the Allied heads of state on the sunny hilltop of Yalta in the Crimea in 1945 a decision had been reached, which was eventually to set the seal on the separation of the various parts of Mongolia. A protocol dated 11th February 1945 and signed by Joseph Stalin, Franklin D. Roosevelt and Winston Churchill ran as follows:

'The leading statesmen of the three Great Powers – the Soviet Union, the United States of America and Great Britain – have agreed that in two to three months after Germany has surrendered and the war in Europe has terminated, the Soviet Union shall enter into the war against Japan on the side of the Allies on condition that:

1. The status quo in Outer Mongolia (Mongolian People's Republic) shall be preserved . . .!'

This was the demand presented to the West and to National China by the Soviet Union to guarantee her sphere of influence in the Mongolian People's Republic, and the demand was accepted. Having achieved this Western commitment, the Soviet Union then demanded that the Mongolian People's Republic should join in the war against Japan on the side of the Soviet Union by invading the Japanese-occupied areas of Inner Mongolia and Manchuria.

The Mongolian People's Republic only joined in the war after an official exchange of notes with the Soviet Foreign Minister. These official preliminaries to Mongolian intervention in the Second World War on the side of the USSR are an interesting reflection of the 'independent' status of the Mongolian People's Republic, which has been repeatedly stressed by the Soviet Union.

On 10th August 1945 the Mongolian People's Republic declared war on Japan, one day after the Soviet Union's declaration. Units of the Mongolian People's Army amounting to 80,000 men, supported by Soviet troops, marched across the Gobi and through the Hsingan mountains to Kalgan, Dolunnor and the province of Jehol. From there the mixed Mongolian-Russian units advanced towards the Bay of Liaotung.

One Mongolian-Russian detachment, on reaching Dolunnor, turned and marched on the railway-junction of Chengteh in Jehol, which was a key communications-point between Dolunnor, Wei-chang and Peking, and the most important strategic point north-east of the Kupeikou Pass. At the same time Soviet infantry and artillery units advancing on the Bay of Liaotung penetrated the great Hsingan mountains and occupied the Manchurian basin. Other units of the Mongolian army, after crossing the Gobi, turned southward and occupied Kalgan, thereby driving a wedge between Manchuria and the Japanese-occupied parts of Northern China, between the Kwantung army and the northern Chinese army.

The Mongolian intervention came as a complete surprise to the Japanese. They had assumed that the Gobi and Hsingan would present insuperable obstacles. Hsingan and the ranges running parallel to it had been fortified by the Japanese, who had taken similar precautions in the mountains round Kalgan. These fortifications were taken by the Russo-Mongolian troops. The Mongolian cavalry and the mechanized units were not held up by the difficult terrain. Problems did arise from the absence of any inhabited settlements and therefore of fodder, water-points and wells. The Mongolian cavalry covered up to thirty miles a day, while the mechanized units covered altogether six hundred miles from their original assembly-points on the border of the Mongolian People's Republic. Large sections of the opposing Mongolian army of Prince Teh Wang and Mongolian units of the Manchukuo army, the Hsingan Cavalry, did not fight and offered no resistance but sent representatives to negotiate terms of surrender. Some of the units went over intact with their commanders without firing a shot. At Wang-yeh-miao, the administrative centre of the four Hsingan provinces of Manchukuo, where the Officers' School of the Hsingan Cavalry was also situated, and at several other places Mongolian officers and soldiers placed their Japanese superiors and instructors under arrest. All arms in the possession of Eastern and Inner Mongolian units were immediately withdrawn. The old order and any buildings associated with it were systematically cleaned out. Officials under the Japanese occupation, big landowners, landed proprietors and high lamaist priests were brought before People's Courts.

The greater part of the East Mongolian population did not receive the army groups of the Mongolian People's Republic as enemies. The Mongols on both sides hoped that the Eastern and Inner Mongolian territories which had been freed from the Japanese would now be incorporated in the Mongolian People's Republic. Any obstructions which might have been expected at one time from the land-owning princely families were now virtually non-existent. The ruinous economic exploitation practised by the Japanese in Mongolia had led to substantial reductions in property. But what the Mongols feared most of all was that the Eastern and Inner Mongolian territories would once again be made subject to the Chinese provincial administration. This would have meant that the Hsingan provinces, Jehol, Chahar and Shilingol, which had enjoyed cultural autonomy, would again have been flooded with Chinese settlers and the Mongols would have been subjected once more to Chinese indoctrination. So the greater part of the population hoped for union with the Mongolian People's Republic. But shortly after the conclusion of the campaign the Mongolian People's

Republic troops and the Russian troops were withdrawn from Inner and East Mongolia to be replaced by Chinese Communist units in the east, while troops of Chiang Kai-shek's National Government moved from Ninghsia and Ordos into Chahar and Shilingol. When the Mongolian and Soviet troops left, they took with them a large part of the cattle stock from East and Inner Mongolia as well as any movable property they could lay their hands on. Subsequent observers spoke of a systematic dismantling such as the Russians had also carried out in another form in the industrial areas of Manchuria.

But the troops of the Mongolian People's Republic also took a number of Mongols from East and Inner Mongolia as hostages or for indoctrination. Among the hostages were the wife and children of Prince Teh Wang, who had managed to save his own skin by going over to the Chinese National Government. Amongst those selected for indoctrination was the former commander of the 9th Mongolian Division, Ölchi Odzer, together with two hundred members of his staff, who reappeared shortly afterwards as one of the key figures in East Mongolia. The fact that the troops of the Mongolian People's Republic took Mongols back to the Republic for indoctrination proved that the idea of incorporating East and Inner Mongolia in the Mongolian People's Republic was still being pursued.

But it was not to be. Following the successful campaign in Inner and East Mongolia the troops of the Mongolian People's Republic were praised for their discipline and courage in both Russian and Mongolian army reports, in speeches by Stalin and the Mongolian Head of State Choibalsang, in newspaper articles and in decrees by the Supreme Soviet. Marshal Choibalsang received the Russian Order of Suvorov First Class, while Mongolian generals and other officers also received Russian decorations.

But not a word was uttered about the fate of the Mongols in East and Inner Mongolia. What had happened? Unhappily, the Yalta Agreement had cut clean across the Mongols' ambitions for unification. On 24th August 1945 Chiang Kai-shek, head of the Chinese National Government, had made a speech at a meeting of the Supreme Council for National Defence and the Central Executive Committee of the Kuomintang, in which he said:

'. . . it is also our endeavour in the interior of the country to give all racial groups of the nation self-administration; this applies particularly to Tumat and Outer Mongolia. In the year 1924 Outer Mongolia sent a message of greeting to the Kuomintang. We have never oppressed the Mongols as the Peking government has done. In the year 1922 Outer Mongolia declared itself independent. At the present stage we have a good opportunity to revive the old friendship. Faithful to the principles of the Kuomintang we recognize the independence of Outer Mongolia . . .!'

Only two days later the National Chinese Foreign Minister Wang Shia Chieh handed a note to Molotov. This threw further light on a step by the Chinese National Government, which seemed, on the face of it, so surprising. Mr Wang informed Molotov that, in view of the demand for independence which the people of Outer Mongolia had repeatedly made, the Chinese Government would recognize the independence of Outer Mongolia within its existing frontiers – after the defeat of Japan and on condition that a plebiscite of the population of Outer Mongolia confirmed this demand. This statement became binding after the Treaty of Friendship and Alliance signed by China and the USSR on 14th August 1945 had been ratified. Following this offer, any further hope on the Mongolian side of influencing China in favour of Mongolian unification had to be abandoned. It is not clear whether Chiang Kai-shek's acceptance of the Yalta decision only fourteen days after the occupation of East and Inner Mongolia by Outer ,Mongolian troops was simply a clever move to prevent their remaining. It is certainly true to say that he thereby barred the door to any plans for Mongolian unification and annexation.

The Chinese would have found it difficult to prevent a union of the Eastern and Inner Mongolian territories with the Mongolian People's Republic, as long as the Mongolian People's Republic was still officially an 'integral' part of the Chinese Republic. Such was the situation now, however, that the Mongols had no option but to withdraw behind their own frontier. Preparations were made as quickly as possible for the plebiscite in the Mongolian People's Republic and it was held on 20th October 1945 in the presence of Chinese observers. There was a hundred per cent vote and 487,409 votes were counted. All were in favour of national independence for the Mongolian People's Republic.

China had, therefore, abandoned a claim – largely nominal, it is true – to the territory of the Mongolian People's Republic, to which she had been clinging since 1911. As regards the Mongols, they, for the time being at least, had to give up all hope of a Greater Mongolia; this was the price they had to pay for the recognition in international law of the Mongolian People's Republic.

THE HEROES RIDE AGAIN

It has been said that the Soviet armoured units, which had conducted the lightning campaign with the Mongolian troops into East and Inner Mongolia, only withdrew to the frontier of the Mongolian People's Republic, where they remained stationed, in order to forestall any annexation plans the Northern Mongols might have. But in the Inner Mongolian territory, which had been 'liberated' from the Japanese, the Chinese Communists or, more precisely, the Mongolian People's Revolutionary Party were operating under the leadership of Ulanhu. By 1951, following the Communist victory in China, the greater part of Inner Mongolia was in Red Chinese hands. The land reform which was carried out in Red China was well received in parts of Inner Mongolia.

But many of the owners of herds were not in sympathy with the land reform. Resistance to the Communist rule in Inner Mongolia was focused on Prince Teh Wang, the former Head of State of the pro-Japanese Inner Mongolian government from 1939 to 1945. When the Chinese National Government collapsed, he had succeeded in making his way through the Communist lines before the fall of Peking and reaching Inner Mongolia. From his retreat at

Tingyuanying in the Ala Shan mountains he tried to form an anti-Communist Mongolian shadow government. Large numbers of former supporters, soldiers and groups of people who were dissatisfied with the Communist rule flocked to join him. Very soon he had mustered a fairly large force, which kept Communist Mongol and Chinese units busy for several years and kept Inner Mongolia in a state of permanent insecurity. In fact, opponents of the Communist régime kept the Mongolian cavalry units and the security forces of Inner Mongolia fully occupied. Political control was extended and tightened. A security officer was stationed in every settlement and a security office was set up in every Banner.

Every Mongol or Chinese received an identity card, which he always had to carry with him. Former members of National Chinese units or of the former National Chinese administration were placed under special supervision. Nevertheless internal security was frequently threatened by acts of sabotage and anti-Communist resistance groups. The Mongolian Communist troops conducted major campaigns against these groups.

This struggle is a special feature of the modern literature of Red Inner Mongolia. Accounts of it were widely distributed for propaganda purposes. In style they differ very little from the old epics. The sabres gleam, the horses trot, heroism and courage triumph. The capture of an anti-Communist 'bandit leader' is described as follows:

'The chase lasted another twenty-five or thirty yards, till the horse with the white fetlocks stumbled and finally fell to the ground. The figure in the black woollen cloak quickly jumped clear and landed firmly on his feet. The veteran bandit calmly set his feet apart, without showing the slightest sign of nervousness when he saw Harko and the boy throwing themselves on him with the fury and speed of a whirlwind. With deadly calm he raised his carbine and aimed it at little Li. But Harko whipped his horse, turned it and had reached the man so quickly that the eye could not follow it. With all the power he possessed he brought the silvery blade down on the black felt hat. The man uttered a wild cry and threw both arms in the air, as the steel of the sabre pierced his left shoulder. Slowly he fell to the ground. But a second later his sound hand was reaching into his coat pocket for a pistol.

'Harko flung himself head-first from the right side of his big, black mare on to his enemy. "Don't move," he roared and placed his nailed boots on the man's breast. Harko and little Li quickly took the bandit's carbine and the American automatic pistol, then kicked him until he stood up. The fellow was bleeding now and his black woollen cloak was smeared with blood. Little Li bandaged the prisoner's wounds and then they led him up the hill to the place where Bator had fallen. "You are one of the bandit's bodyguard, aren't you?" asked Harko, who was very pleased with himself.

'The fellow pulled the rim of his black felt hat down over his nose to hide his dark, fleshy, pimply face. "Oh, no! Not a bodyguard, your obedient servant is just an ordinary soldier."

'"If you are not a bodyguard, you must at least be a staff officer. Judging by your appearance, your horse and your arms you are not an ordinary bandit. No one who is right in the head will ever believe that," said little Li. The fellow suddenly stopped and over his face came a sly grin: "You have sharp eyes, dear brothers, you have not been deceived, I am a bodyguard of Pao, the Senior Commander, and, dear brothers, if you allow me, I would like to say a few words to you, may I?"

'"What sort of damned trick are you up to now?" asked Harko, who was finding it difficult to suppress his mounting fury.

'The fellow fished a gold watch from a pocket of the woollen sweater he was wearing under his cloak. Then he took a step forward: "We are Mongols, all of us! We are all Horchin . . . And if you think nothing of the bonds of blood that unite us, then, brother, at least set me free for the sake of our common birthplace! Let me go free! I will never forget that you were a friend in this moment of misfortune. And the day will surely come when I will be in a position to pay you back your noble generosity in full. There is not a soul here apart from us three, no one in the world will ever know – only this watch – it is a very unworthy and modest gift...!"

'"Who wants your stinking watch?" little Li interrupted.

'"Oh... isn't it enough?" The fellow took another step forward. "You can have two gold rings as well."

'"Give it to me!" Harko tore the watch out of the other man's fingers and threw it furiously in his face. "Here," he shouted, "take it to hell with you!"

'All the units of the company had now assembled on the hillside. Standing on one side, tired and dejected, were the prisoners and the captured horses.

'"Harko and little Li approached on their horses, driving a man before them. Loud cries came from the rows of men as the group approached: "Perhaps that is Pao Tsun-feng? It is Pao Tsun-feng."

'There was no doubt. The prisoners soon confirmed that the man in the black woollen cloak was none other than the Senior Commander Pao.'

Another work of contemporary Inner Mongolian literature which had a wide circulation and was even dramatized, the short story *On the Horchin grasslands* by the Inner Mongolian writer Malchinhu, describes in much the same way how a young Mongol girl called Sarin pursues and captures a counter-revolutionary and saboteur:

'The storm was raging over the plateau, claps of thunder and flashes of lightning gave her the feeling that the end of the world was near. A wild and empty wilderness stretched away before Sarin's eyes. She could only judge her direction and the nature of her surroundings by instinct and was guided solely by her years of experience as a cowherd. But it is difficult to advance even a few inches in meadow-land when it is raining, for there is a great deal of muddy ground. Occasionally the horse slipped and then both rider and horse fell into the muddy water. But Sarin would not give up. After every fall she remounted her horse and continued the chase. Each time her burns came into contact with the water, the pain almost made her faint. "How far shall I have to follow him in this broad plain?" she wondered. At that moment a flash of lightning made it possible for her to see a few footmarks in the mud and this gave her the courage to ride on. She thought: "To the west is the Sharamöringhol. As a result of the heavy rain, it will have overflowed its banks. He won't go there. The only possibility is northward." She could see ahead of her the dim outline of a small hill with some young elms. Often in the past Sarin had brought her cattle there and it was on this same hill that Sambu had first proposed to her. Various kinds of flowers grew on the hill and she remembered how Sambu had placed two blooms in her hair . . . In her mind's eye she saw Sambu's beautiful mouth and his gay smile and for a moment she forgot everything in the recollection of her love.

'Suddenly she heard a short bark from the hill and Sarin's heart stopped beating for a moment. Whether from joy or from fear she herself could not say.

'"Galu must have found the saboteur," she thought. She forced her horse to walk slowly and softly, while she rode up the hill and tried to pierce the darkness with her eyes. She hoped that her Galu would give another signal, but the dog was silent.

'"Ha! Try biting me again, damned mongrel!" A deep, male voice echoed triumphantly from the hillside four or five yards away. Sarin stared ahead anxiously and was just able to distinguish a dark form climbing up the hill. Behind it lay another dark form on the ground.

'"The ruffian must have killed Galu!" she thought and, filled with rage, she gave rein to her horse and fired. The black shadow ran like the wind. "He has no gun!" she thought. "I must not kill him; it is better if I take him alive." She caught up with him and struck him down with the butt of her rifle. He fell to the ground and uttered a cry. Her finger on the trigger, Sarin cried: "Don't move!" She remembered that the soldiers shouted something of the kind. The black form did not speak and did not move.

'"I have probably knocked him senseless," she thought.

'She sprang down from her horse and was about to run over and tie his hands, when she heard the click of a safety-catch behind her and a voice cried: "Stop! Don't move or I'll shoot!"

'A shudder ran through Sarin's body. "Now it's all over. I've run into a trap and they've surrounded me! But I must be a good Mongol and not show any sign of fear!"

'"Who are you? If you come any closer, I will shoot," she cried back as loudly as she could.

'"Eh! Is that Sarin?" It was the voice of the man she knew and loved. Then the light of a torch shone on her mud-smeared figure.

'"It really is you, Sarin, dear child!" cried Amugulang, jumping down from his horse. There were others behind him.

'"Grandfather, Amugulang, Sambu!" Never had their names sounded so wonderful to Sarin. With tears in her eyes she ran up to them and embraced Amugulang tenderly.

'"Good girl! But wait a moment! Tell me, did you just fire a shot?"

'"Yes, I took the saboteur's gun from him and knocked him unconscious."

'Sarin also embraced Sambu, then she took his torch to shine it on the black, lifeless form. By the light of the torch they saw a man with a pock-marked face scrambling to his feet, ready to run away.

'"So you'll run away, will you, you rat? Stop!"

'Amugulang walked across to the terrified ruffian and asked: "Who are you? What are you doing here?"

'"I . . . am an ordinary citizen!" Gold teeth gleamed when he spoke.

'"Oh, I know you. You're the second-in-command Bujan from the Aru-Horchin Banner!"

'"That is not true. I'm from the Horchin Banner."

'"You think you can talk yourself out of this? Then think again!"

'"This is the ruffian who set fire to the northern pasture!" said Sarin indignantly.

'Bujan rolled his eyes and said nothing.

'"No more bandying words with a counter-revolutionary," said Amugulang to the militiaman. "Tie his hands and take him away."

'The sight of the enemy's hands being tied made Sarin inexpressibly happy. Then Sambu came over to her and pressed her hand and said: "Sarin, you have had a hard time!"

'"No, that was my duty." They laughed. "Sarin is right. This is the duty of every Mongol."'

Such is the tone of the official modern literature of Mongols in Red China. What they really think may perhaps be reflected in a few decades from now in notebooks filled with poems, songs and stories.

X THEATRE IN THE YURT

As recently as 1945 in the Sung-chu-szu temple in Peking I was able to see more than eighty Mongolian prints being made from plates which had survived from the Manchu period. Almost all of them were lamaist prayers, hymns and guides to ritual. A very small number were tales, but they, too, showed traces of Buddhist influence and local colour.

The title of one of these works particularly appealed to me. It ran: 'A tale of the moon cuckoo with the blue throat, which was a Bodhisattva, called ear-jewel of those who know that the world is worthless.'

I realized, as I read it, that this was not an original Mongolian work but a translation from the Tibetan. But as such it was a work of art. The epilogue made this clear. It was the work of one of the best-known and most famous translators of the eighteenth century.

Dai guoshi Nawangdambil, a learned monk of the Nordabagha-nar tribe, one of the Inner Mongolian federations, translated this work from Tibetan into Mongolian in 1770. He undertook this laborious task when he was seventy-one years old. None other than the highest lamaist dignitary at the Manchu court, the Chang chia Hutuktu Rolpaidordje, had asked him to translate 'The tale which relates how someone assumed the body of a cuckoo and became a cuckoo'.

Was this just another of those pious, high-minded Buddhist tales, which the lamaist priests in the eighteenth century employed to suppress and supplant the exuberant imagination of the

Mongolian story-tellers and singers? The Chang chia Hutuktu in particular was known for having conducted a forceful campaign against the pagan epic. He had once compared the Geser Khan epic to the 'evil croaking of the ravens'.

So when I started reading the *Moon Cuckoo*, I was to some extent prejudiced against it. Very soon, however, I was captivated. It was not so high-minded as I had feared and even contained some real drama.

It was the story of the strange fate that befell the son of an Indian king. The young prince grew up in the care of a pious mother. By his father's wish, Lagayana, the son of a Minister, was assigned to him as playmate although both son and mother had a vague feeling that they could not trust Lagayana.

So the two boys grew up together. One of their teachers was a Brahman who had magical powers. From him they learned how to animate a corpse with their own souls and inhabit the body of the dead.

This story also has it that the king's son wanted to become a monk and to turn his back on the world. This is a feature of almost every Buddhist tale. But in this case the father, who saw a threat to the succession, forbade his son to enter a monastery. Instead he married the young prince to Altan, the beautiful daughter of the neighbouring king. She was not only beautiful but also clever. With sympathy and understanding she brought out the religious trait in her husband's character. The two found mutual pleasure in studying and practising the Buddhist religion. Altan cast such a spell on the young prince that one of the concubines felt unduly neglected. She was overcome by jealousy to such a point that she persuaded Lagayana, the prince's playmate, to remove him and take his place.

At first Lagayana manfully resisted the insinuations of the beautiful seductress. But finally she succeeded and the prince's playmate agreed to her evil plan.

When the prince and his household were on their way to a beautiful garden near the city gates, they came upon the corpses of two dead cuckoos. The birds showed no sign of violence. At the sight of the birds a plan blossomed in Lagayana's brain, by which he could remove the prince. On the other side of the river lay a beautiful wood, which did not belong to any other prince. Lagayana persuaded the prince to explore this wood with him. But this, he explained in a whisper, could only happen in another form, if they were to avoid a ban by his royal father. What had been the object of learning to assume another form? It was an easy matter for them to make use of the two cuckoo corpses.

As Lagayana had suggested, the two boys animated the cuckoos' bodies. They left their own exanimate bodies behind on the bank of the great river and flew over the river into the great wood. There the prince was lost in amazement at the rare frui' and flowers, at the birdsong and the colours.

In the meantime, however, the deceitful Lagayan v back over the river, left his cuckoo's body and entered the princ dy which had been left on the bank. He threw his own exanimat ody together with the cuckoo's corpse into the river. Then he returned lamenting to the prince's household and said that his beloved playmate Lagayana had fallen into the river and drowned.

The courtiers, who took him for the prince, believed him. Only Altan, the prince's favourite wife, had doubts about the genuineness of the one who had returned. By contrast with the real prince, he showed no interest in Buddhism or in religious practices and prayers. So before long the false prince repulsed her and turned his attention to the concubine who had incited him to betray the true prince.

The prince had remained on the other side of the river in the form of a cuckoo. At first he believed that some mishap must have befallen his friend Lagayana. But then Buddha appeared to him and told him about his friend's treachery. Filled with pity, Buddha also assumed the form of a cuckoo so that he could keep the prince company in the wood. He predicted for the future that the prince would have to live as a blue-throated cuckoo among the birds till a famous lama monk called Tsogtu appeared to instruct him. So the poor prince lived as a cuckoo among the birds and preached Buddhism to them.

The theme of an old Indian legend, that of Buddha preaching to the birds, is cleverly woven into this dramatic story of transformation and intrigue.

With the appearance of the Lama Tsogtu, the didactic character of the work and the element of conversion, which have been cleverly concealed, at last emerge. This gave the author an opportunity to introduce various stories and long-winded moral passages. Everything that happens is interpreted, in accordance with the Buddhist dogma, as the consequence of previous evil or good actions. Lagayana's treacherous behaviour towards his friend, the prince, is also explained by the fact that in a previous existence the two had been neighbouring kings who were hostile to one another.

The prince finally succeeds in bringing home to his parents, his wife and his friends the treachery of which he has been the victim. But, faithful to his destiny, he remains to the end of his existence a cuckoo among the birds and continues to preach the true doctrine to them.

The whole thing was an astonishingly compact and thrilling story, if one overlooks the didactic passages. But after all the *History of Dr Faustus* was originally a didactic play to be performed by students in medieval monastery schools.

In the story of the *Moon Cuckoo* the dialogue was so fluent that I sometimes felt as if I was reading the script of a stage-play.

But was there such a thing as a theatre in Mongolia in the eighteenth century? The possibility could not be ruled out altogether.

SHAMANISM IS DESTROYED

When the lamaist missionaries and devotees again converted the Mongols to Buddhism around the turn of the sixteenth century, they forbade the Mongols to practise their old folk-religion, Shamanism. In this religion everything – every stone and every mountain – was believed to be inhabited by spirits of good or bad ancestors. The industrious lamaist missionaries collected the idols of felt, wood and skin together and burned them.

Around 1650 one such collection alone among the Eastern Mongol tribes, particularly the Horchin, produced a pile of ancestral idols as large as a round Mongolian tent, which was then burnt. This represents a funeral pyre about ten feet high and about twenty feet in diameter.

The Buddhist proselytizers were not content with this. In strict accordance with their belief in the negation of all life, they also condemned all other expressions of the life of the Mongol people, which had been adopted during the turn of the century. All that was not Buddhist must disappear. Songs, marriage-customs, felicitations and blessings were forbidden as being just as heretical as dances and other Mongol traditions. By way of compensation the lama monks devised new prayers. They offered the Mongols the rich and varied treasure of Indo-Tibetan Buddhist tales, rules of life and stories of the descent into hell.

Nevertheless the bans imposed by the lamaist missionaries did not produce any lasting or profound results. The Mongols' folk-religion and old traditions proved too strong. The folk-religion still lives on today, enriched by concepts from lamaist doctrine and cloaked in Buddhist phrases. Yet another influence came with the Tibetan lamaist missionaries of the sixteenth and seventeenth centuries: the pantomime masked dance. At a certain time each year masked dances with strong religious undertones were performed in the best-known monasteries. They were called Cham.

The idea behind these performances and exhibitions, which were designed to have a mass propaganda effect, was to present in mime the dreadful, terrifying tutelary gods of Buddhism and their struggle against the enemies of religion. Dressed in garishly-coloured costumes of unusual design, the personifications of the various gods and demons danced round to the beat of penetrating, rhythmic music. In front of their faces they carried cunningly carved or papier mâché masks, which usually presented wild and horrifying features: death's heads, deformed animals' skulls with snouts, protruding eyes, enormous faces with horns and strange adornments. This was how the Russian Mongolist and Buddhologist, Boris J. Vladimircov, described them in 1925. Numerous specimens of these dance-masks are to be found in European museums. In places such as Nepal, Bhutan and Sikkim on India's northern frontier, where lamaism is still free from government restrictions, the cult of the masked dance is still practised and the lama monks still produce new masks when the old ones have become worn and cracked.

In Tibet in the late seventeenth century the first pantomime-dances were performed in which figures from other than religious ...es were represented. During the reign of the 6th Dalai Lama (1683–1706), a young man who was more interested in earthly things than in the hereafter and who became better known for his Tibetan love-songs than for religious tracts, the secular dance was already established.

Gradually the religious pantomime-dances gave way to a pseudo-religious theatre. The figures began to speak and to answer one another. The original Cham dance became less and less common, until finally a proper stage-play was produced in its place. Scenes based on the life of the famous Tibetan wandering ascetic Milaraspa (1040–1123), who has been referred to as a Tibetan Francis of Assisi, were particularly popular. His songs were among the finest of Asia's literary creations.

SONGS IN THE YURT

It was not long before the new quasi-religious theatre had spread across the broad steppes of Mongolia. The Mongols were particularly receptive to such performances, for at the princes' courts and in the close circles of the yurt families they had passed countless long winter nights with a similar form of entertainment: antiphonal singing by several voices.

These songs were entirely secular in character. For the most part they were dramatic songs in praise of all-conquering love which stopped at nothing and shrank from nothing. The sort of love that featured in these songs was that of a mighty prince for a poor shepherdess. One of the songs was called 'Princely Pleasure', while another, which had spread from the Chahar area of Southern Mongolia to the south-east and to the north, told of the illicit love of the Bedshing Lama, a lama monk from the capital Peking, for the beautiful Mongolian girl Dshiujar and made fun of the love-sick priest. Dshiujar divides her attentions between the lama and the Mongolian prince Samiya. In the end she decides in favour of the prince. The rejected lama is left with nothing but ridicule.

It is hardly surprising that the powerful and influential priesthood of the lamaist monasteries of Mongolia should have forbidden such worldly part-songs. The Mongols were soon compelled to indulge their taste for this sort of Mongolian 'operetta' in secret.

The pseudo-religious theatre, therefore, had an added attraction in that it helped to satisfy something of the urge to act with which everyone is more or less born and which the lamaist church was only prepared to tolerate if its own image was favourably reflected. The interesting point was that the theme of the play was taken from the tales which had come to Mongolia from Tibet and India with the Buddhist mission.

In this way the Mongols turned the Indo-Tibetan fairy-tale of the fairy Manuhari, who was caught by a fisherman on the banks of a lake and later became the wife of Prince Manibadara, into a stage-play.

In 1781 Baron von Asch, the senior surgeon of the Russian army and correspondent of the Göttingen Society, sent a Western Mongolian manuscript of this story back to Göttingen with this comment: 'Is said to be a comedy. About the sorrow of Luin Khan, to wit the king, when he is compelled to hand over Zilma erdeni to the hunter Tusat. He has the power of magnetism, with the help of which he obtains the Khan Ginar's daughter, the beautiful Manicharja.'

This remark by Baron von Asch is simply the translation of the Russian gloss on this manuscript, which the Russian collector had written on the title-page. But nothing is known of how the Mongols in 1781 and probably later presented this central Asia version of the fairy-tale *The Fisherman and his Wife* on the stage. For there was a Mongolian Theatre in the eighteenth and also in the nineteenth centuries. There are frequent references to performances in the monasteries based on episodes from the life of the Tibetan hermit and poet Milaraspa.

THE LADY CHOIDSHID DESCENDS INTO HELL

The *Journey into Hell* of the noble Lady Choidshid was also a particularly popular story. This too derived from a Tibetan religious play. The Mongols embellished the dialogue from other popular stories of descent into hell.

The noble Lady Choidshid, while suffering from a grave illness, dreams of her own death. She experiences her descent into the Kingdom of the Prince of Hell, before whom she appears for judgement. After the Prince of Hell has consulted the archives in which an account is kept of every man and his deeds, the Lady Choidshid is informed that the time has not yet come for her to die and repent her sins. Before she is allowed to return to the kingdom of the living on earth, she witnesses the passing of judgement on the sins and good deeds of the dead from all classes who appear before the Prince's throne. Laymen and monks, rich and poor, men and women pass before the infernal judge as in a medieval dance of death and answer for, defend and explain away the lives they have led.

Having returned to her own people on earth, the Lady Choidshid relates these experiences and exhorts all who hear her story to lead virtuous and meritorious lives.

There are several manuscripts of this particular religious drama in Ulan Bator and Copenhagen. They are all more or less paraphrases of the same original text. One must therefore assume that the various actors presenting it lengthened, shortened or improved upon their parts depending on their ability, their ambition and their memory.

In Urga, as the capital of the Mongolian People's Republic, Ulan Bator, was formerly called, this drama was even produced as a block-print during the last century. It was still popular in the early part of the present century. Almost all young Mongols, who came to Berlin between 1923 and 1928 to study or as members of a special mission from the Mongolian People's Republic, could recite passages from it by heart, just as we today can remember a passage from the 'Threepenny Opera' or 'My Fair Lady' which particularly appealed to us.

In those early years a play was produced about the 'Moon Cuckoo' in various monasteries in Northern Mongolia, the Mongolian People's Republic of today, and especially in the southern Gobi desert and in Inner Mongolia. But the scholars had not heard of it. The Mongol theatre had not yet become a subject for literary research. When it did become one, when it was finally realized that the religious theatre of the nomads was an absorbing subject, it was almost too late for research.

CHANGES IN THE SOCIAL STRUCTURE

The last Dshebtsundampa Hutuktu, who had been made Head of State of Mongolia since it became independent of China in 1911, died in 1924. With him died theocracy, the rule of the clergy in Mongolia.

Its place was taken by the Mongolian Revolutionary People's Party, the Mongolian version of the Communist Party, which, under Russian guidance, assumed power in Mongolia. The Mongolian People's Republic became more and more closely tied to the Soviet Union, and became Russia's first satellite. Its internal development was closely modelled on that of the Soviet Union. The country was more and more isolated from outside contacts.

Between 1929 and 1938 the entire social structure was transformed. The social groups which until then had held the leading positions and owned property were removed or deprived of their former influence. The Communist doctrine, which was now dominant, was irreconcilable with Buddhism or Lamaism, which were regarded as backward. A large part of the national economy was in the hands of the clergy, so war was declared on them.

The monasteries were expropriated, destroyed or closed down; many were converted into museums, clubs or children's homes. The monks were forced to return to private life and the property owned by the monasteries was confiscated.

According to the record of the seventh Great Chural, the People's Assembly of 1935, the property owned by the lamaist monasteries in 1932 was worth two million Tuchrik. The Tuchrik is the Mongolian unit of currency. Within three years the figure had dropped to one million Tuchrik.

Buddhism ceased to be the official State religion, and with the passing of the monasteries, the dance-masks, the religious pantomime, the religious theatre and the text-books of the plays also disappeared. Moreover, in Inner Mongolia the acute economic hardship to which the Mongols were exposed during the Japanese occupation made deep inroads into their cultural life. In the early 'forties when I inquired about religious drama-productions in Eastern Mongolia, people knew nothing of them. Only the more ordinary masked dance with its ritualistic movements was performed around the turn of the century. According to Mongolian sources the situation in the Chahar area of Inner Mongolia about the same period was quite different. But a foreigner travelling through the area learned nothing of this, for the Mongols at that time treated foreigners with suspicion. So the block-print of the *Moon Cuckoo*, which I had found in Peking, was for a time one of the few vague pointers to the fact that, at some stage or other, religious drama had been performed by the Mongols.

AN INCOMPLETE TEXT?

In 1959, Damdinsürüng, the Professor of the History of Mongolian Literature at Ulan Bator University, visited the Gandang monastery, the only lamaist place of worship that has been reopened in the

Mongolian People's Republic for some years. In it a small number of lama monks, most of them elderly men, live and pray. They also draw large congregations. The abbot of the monastery, Gombodo, apart from his normal functions, also plays an active part in the International Peace Movement, which is directed from Moscow.

When Professor Damdinsürüng, who, in addition to being a teacher and research-worker in the field of Mongolian literature, is also one of the leading modern lyrical poets and short-story writers in Mongolia, entered the library of the Gandang monastery on this occasion, his attention was caught by about ten large, thin volumes of manuscript among the collection of manuscripts and prints of religious works.

The title, however, did nothing to raise his hopes further. It was the *Life History of the Moon Cuckoo*; Damdinsürüng assumed that what he was holding in his hand was one of the many copies extant in Mongolia of the block-print from the year 1770, which I also had managed to pick up in Peking.

I can well imagine Professor Damdinsürüng's feelings. While I was investigating collections in Oslo, Copenhagen and the German libraries I frequently came upon similar copies of old block-prints. They have no particular literary or historical value, and are only of interest in rare cases where, so far as is known, no specimen of the original print exists and one can learn from the epilogue of the copy that the work was in circulation a hundred or two hundred years ago in block-print. If one also learns, as I did once from a dirty, tattered manuscript in Copenhagen, that the cost of paper, ink and printing from the blocks in the middle of the eighteenth century was five-hundredths of a silver ounce for about fifteen sheets, then one is especially grateful, for even today very little is known of book-prices in Mongolia in past centuries.

Damdinsürüng glanced through a few pages of this familiar *Life History of the Moon Cuckoo* and found that it was the well-known story – but then again it was not. There was dialogue but no continuous narrative. It finally proved to be the script of a play on the moon cuckoo, which was not the same as the Peking block-print of

1770 or as the story told in it. On reading further, Damdinsürüng came upon the name of the author. It was Rabdshai, the fifth Noyan Hutuktu, one of the high lamaist dignitaries of Northern Mongolia.

A PLAYWRIGHT-MONK

By pure chance a literary discovery of the first order had been made. The fifth Noyan Hutuktu Rabdshai was one of the great Mongolian writers of the last century. There had been persistent rumours that he had written a play, but no evidence had ever been found to substantiate these rumours.

No discovery, however exciting, is ever perfect and in this case only parts of the text were found. There were, in fact, several copies of volumes one, three and five among the ten thin volumes of manuscript, but the remainder of the text was missing.

All the information Damdinsürüng could obtain for the time being was that a man from the Gobi area, a certain Sayabadar, had brought these volumes with the text of the drama to the Abbot of the Gandang monastery.

Rabdshai or, to give him his full name, Dangdshinrabdshai, was a high lamaist priest. In spite of this, his works lack any trace of pious affectation. They are conspicuous rather for their vivacity and deep feeling. Rabdshai's life-story, as it emerges from his biography, the reminiscences of his contemporaries and stories told about him, is characteristic of the development of many important writers and personalities in Mongolia.

MODEL OF A POET'S BIOGRAPHY

Damdinsürüng collected all the information he could about Rabdshai with great diligence and ingenuity.

Rabdshai was born in 1803 in northern Sunit in Inner Mongolia, where his father was a poor herdsman. His mother died while he was still a baby. The father brought him up almost unaided and the relationship between the two must have been very close. In his poems Rabdshai frequently refers to his father, Duluitu, whose sole possessions were a tent and a horse. When Rabdshai was five years old, one of the appalling droughts which sometimes afflict Mongolia forced father and son to leave their home.

The child rode on the horse, which also carried their few belongings. The father led the horse, and they travelled like this through the drought-ridden country looking for water and food.

When they reached the Ongki river, which flows today through the Mongolian People's Republic, a misfortune befell them, which had a decisive influence on both their lives. During the night a wolf ate their horse, their only means of transport. The despairing father could think of no way of continuing with the small boy, now that the horse was gone. To save the child, he gave him to the nearest monastery to be trained as a monk. He hoped that on his own he might survive.

The little novice blossomed forth in the shelter of the monastery. His poetic gifts became apparent very early. At the age of seven Rabdshai began to write the first of the fifty songs and nearly thirty poems which have been ascribed to him and are widely known among the people.

Other Mongolian poets and singers were also destined in their youth to become monks, without being asked and, in most cases, against their will. Ishidangdshinwangdshil (1854–1907), a Chahar Mongol, entered a monastery at the age of seven. He is generally accepted as the author of the poem 'Exhortations of the enlightened one from the Duke's temple', a social satire which reflects the profound internal unrest of the Mongol population around the turn of the century.

Padshai, the Inner Mongolian rhapsodist and singer of epics, who is still alive, was placed in a monastery by the Jarut prince, whose bondsman he was, against the will of his parents, and he soon began writing poetry and singing.

The wandering beggar-monk Shagdar, who later escaped from the monastery and who was known among the common people as 'the madman', had been placed in a monastery in the Bagharin area by his impoverished parents in 1875 at the age of seven. A number of picaresque stories are told in the Mongolian vernacular about this figure, which were not his work. But the majority of the anecdotes told by him, in which he censures the corruption of the princes, the libertinism and intrigues of the lamaist monks, are based on experience, and most of the satirical poems ascribed to him were in fact written by him.

For the sons of poor cattle-breeders, of herdsmen who were the serfs of princes, entry into the community of the lamaist monks opened the door to education and culture, to reading and writing. But above all it meant freedom from taxes and from the oppression of serving the Banner princes. The same development took place in Mongolia at the beginning of the present century which had led to the formation of a literary stratum in European society in the early Middle Ages.

Many of these reluctant monks were destined to rise to high positions and to achieve great freedom within the hierarchy of the lamaist Church.

One of these was Rabdshai.

Whether it was due to his early talent as a poet or to other causes we do not know. In any case Rabdshai, the boy left in a monastery by his father on a desperate journey, was suddenly recognized as the reincarnation of the fourth Noyan Hutuktu.

His predecessor had been stabbed by a drunken monk during a service in Erdeni dshuu, the chief monastery of the Kalkha Mongols. Representatives of the monastery and followers of the murdered Buddhist dignitary travelled round the Kalkha area, seeking a successor. In the small, laughing eight-year-old, who was already composing beautiful songs and writing poems, they recognized the reincarnation of the dead Noyan Hutuktu.

Rabdshai's whole life was transformed. From now on he was one of the privileged few in the lamaist Church of Central Asia. He had become a saint. For in Mongolian Lamaism, as in Tibet, it had been an article of faith since the late sixteenth century, the time of the third Dalai Lama, that important priests in the lamaist Church were incarnations of godheads and were always reborn in a successor.

While this dogma of reincarnation had been confined originally to the highest church dignitaries, the number of holy reincarnations increased with the centuries. Every monastery wanted to have its own living Buddha. Even this pious doctrine was not immune against ambition, the lust for power and the glamour of high office. By the eighteenth century the doctrine of reincarnation had become so debased and the number of reincarnations in Mongolia and Tibet so large that the Manchu Emperor, Chien Lung, had to instruct his Ministry for Border Territories, the Li-Fan-Yuan, to issue certain regulations which governed the recognition of such reincarnations and their acceptance in accordance with these rules. From then on candidates for reincarnation had to be submitted by the monasteries to Peking, where a selection was made by drawing lots.

The date of birth, forty-nine days after the death of the predecessor, certain birthmarks and the laying-of-hands on objects or persons from the dead man's household were regarded as sure signs of reincarnation. Frequently the dying man hinted where his reincarnation was to be found. Ambitious families and pressure-groups sometimes put utterances and prophecies of this kind in the dying man's mouth. In short, there were many ways in which a child might be recognized as a reincarnation. In the case of Rabdshai, who was intelligent, poetically gifted but poor, the monks in his monastery seem to have realized at quite an early stage that the boy's talents presented distinct possibilities. That is doubtless why they recognized in him the reincarnation of the recently murdered fourth Noyan Hutuktu.

HIS HOLINESS FOUNDS THE FIRST THEATRE

His elevation to the reincarnation of a high lamaist priest did not mean that Rabdshai had to abandon all worldly interests. He was fortunate in that his predecessor had belonged to the old red, non-reformed lamaist sect, which does not believe in celibacy or mortification of the flesh. Rabdshai was free to marry, and took two wives.

After he had been consecrated, he founded several monasteries in the northern Gobi. He spent most of his time, however, travelling from monastery to monastery, from one prince's residence to another, accompanied by his wives and his household and indulging not so much in religious abstinence as in contemplation of the present-day world with a mixture of light-heartedness and somewhat melancholy wisdom.

His works appeared in rapid succession and were soon enjoying wide popularity. The people liked his songs. Rabdshai touched a chord which appealed to them. They understood and enjoyed the subdued, almost sceptical wisdom of the *History of the Paper Dragon*, which Rabdshai wrote in 1833.

During his travels in the northern Gobi, the borderland between Northern Kalka Mongolia and the country of the Chahar and Sunit, he had plenty of opportunity to see the splendid Cham dances and performances of semi-religious plays in the monasteries. This inspired him to write the *Moon Cuckoo*, a play based on the theme of the Peking block-print of 1770. The play was written about 1831.

For almost ninety years after it was first performed, with the Noyan Hutuktu himself directing it, the *Moon Cuckoo* was produced in many monasteries in the eastern Gobi and Chahar. The parts were played more and more by the laity, both male and female. It was not until the troubled period when the Mongolian People's Republic was emerging that the play was forgotten and the time came when it was no more than a popular rumour that the Noyan Hutuktu Rabdshai had ever written such a work. But in fact the *Moon Cuckoo* had quite unintentionally prepared the way for a national theatre.

From the turn of the century onwards groups of drama enthusiasts sprang up, of laymen, who produced their own plays and devised a new form of drama from the old traditional part-songs. They borrowed wherever they could, particularly from the Chinese theatre and from the spectacular scenery of the Chinese opera. But before long they had devised a style of their own. Plays such as *The Hero Temüdshin*, a Jenghiz Khan drama, *Maral Shara, the yellow hind* and others were performed.

In 1930 Mongolia's first professional theatre was opened in Ulan Bator, the Mongolian capital. Today the Mongolian State Theatre is a large, imposing building, which presents both drama and opera. Shakespeare's *Othello* in Mongolian is as much a feature of the repertoire as Goldoni's operas.

The accent, however, is on developing plays and operas by Mongolian authors and musicians. The themes are frequently taken from Mongolian history and the poetic style and the melodies are modelled on the old poetic forms and folk-songs. The picaresque tales of Balansengge, which are told in every yurt, were used by the Mongolian writer T. Oyun as the basis for a popular comedy. The libretto of the popular opera, *The three magic hills*, which was written by the late Natsagdordsh, is strongly reminiscent of old Mongolian fairy-tales, particularly of the *Huntsman and his beautiful wife*.

SEARCH OVER FORTY THOUSAND SQUARE MILES

Damdinsürüng was fully aware of the importance of his discovery at the Gandang monastery. But further inquiries in Ulan Bator produced no result. If there was anyone who knew about the play and its performances, then it could only be among the older people in the eastern Gobi. It was just possible that someone there might also have the remains of the manuscript. All that Damdinsürüng was able to obtain from inhabitants of Ulan Bator was a list of ten or twenty names of acquaintances in the southern and eastern Gobi who might perhaps know something.

The eastern Gobi district of the Mongolian People's Republic covers an area of 40,000 square miles and has only 20,000 inhabitants. So Damdinsürüng postponed his search for the remainder of the Rabdshai manuscript until April 1960, when a Russian jeep was placed at his disposal.

Damdinsürüng began his search in the eastern Gobi district, where the Noyan Hutuktu had formerly lived. He looked for old people who could remember productions of the *Moon Cuckoo*. A sixty-seven-year-old monk at the Gandang monastery in Ulan Bator had suggested this line of inquiry, when he told Damdinsürüng how, at the age of eighteen or nineteen, he had twice seen the *Life History of the Moon Cuckoo* at the Rashijant residence of the Mergenwang Noyan.

The Mergenwang area corresponds to the modern eastern Gobi district. It must have been about 1911 that the old Rendshendordsh saw these performances. In the eastern Gobi district Damdinsürüng soon met other seventy-year-olds, who confirmed this. But a former monk, who was well over eighty, remembered seeing a production of the *Moon Cuckoo* at the age of ten. He had particularly enjoyed the jokes which were told between the acts by comedians.

Another remembered a particularly popular actress, who had played the part of Matimahani and who, he believed, was still alive somewhere in Northern Mongolia. A third referred to the stage-like platform in front of the Kökenidün monastery, on which the play had been presented. And one even recollected the clothes which the actors had worn and was able to hum a few bars of a song from the play. But no one had any texts.

Then at last came the day when one of the workers at the oil-well at Dzhunbayan appeared with a book. It was a copy of the third act. Another period of fruitless search and questioning followed before there came another discovery. This time it was an elementary schoolteacher, who handed Damdinsürüng another volume, which contained part of the second chapter with a dialogue between the prince and one of his dignitaries.

SOUNDINGS IN THE SAND-DUNES

One day Damdinsürüng was told that a certain Awangdshundui had another part of the play. All that remained was to find this man, who was said to live in a place called Shara dubu – 'Yellow Hill'. It was soon established beyond doubt, however, that Awangdshun-dui had died some years before.

But what had happened to his books? People in Shara dubu explained that, a year before his death, old Awangdshundui had taken two chests full of books into the desert outside the village and, with the help of a girl named Tsetsek, buried them.

Damdinsürüng then set out to find Tsetsek. When he eventually tracked her down and questioned her, she told him that three years before, when she was thirteen and was watching the cattle, old Awangdshundui came up to her with his two chests and asked her to help him. No one, apart from herself, knew the spot.

Daminsürüng's attempt to find anything failed. A few months later however the village schoolteacher, Dshanabadshar, and a few scholars accompanied by an old man were successful in discovering two chests. These were packed with rare old Mongolian works, which would otherwise have been left to decay in the desert. But unfortunately there was no manuscript of Rabdshai's *Moon Cuckoo* among them.

There were several other disappointments of this kind. Then Damdinsürüng heard that an elderly cattle-breeder, who lived to the west of the oil-well at Dzhunbayan, had a manuscript of the *Moon Cuckoo*. Was this just another false alarm?

Damdinsürüng went to see him and this time the information was correct. Old Darchanbalbar really had found three volumes of the *Moon Cuckoo* play. They were the missing volumes one, three and five. Damdinsürüng now had all nine volumes of the manuscript of the first Mongol secular drama. This made it possible to reproduce the first performance of the Mongolian national theatre almost a hundred years after the death of the author.

Although old Awangdshundui's chests did not contain any of Rabdshai's manuscripts, they did reveal many other old and rare manuscripts, thus confirming yet again that there must still be many other manuscripts hidden away in various parts of Mongolia. Some of them were stored away only a few years ago. Others have lain hidden since 1937 and the period of the Stalinist purges, during which much of Mongolia's old cultural heritage was destroyed. Others again have been lost for centuries, ever since they were put in a safe place to preserve them against some invading enemy.

No effort should be spared to trace them. The example of the *Moon Cuckoo* shows that a determined search can be successful.

XI ARCHAEOLOGICAL DISCOVERIES

The time has come to say something about archaeology and the results of excavations in Mongolia. The question inevitably arises whether archaeological excavations in Mongolia have not unearthed any Mongol literary treasures.

Until a few decades ago, archaeological research in Mongolia was extremely difficult. The superstitious mentality of the population, which the lama monks had fostered, presented an almost insuperable obstacle. The people believed – and to a large extent still believe – that any excavation of the soil disturbed the earth-spirits, the so-called 'Lords of the Earth', the genii loci or local gods. Roused from their contemplations, the angry Lords of the Earth would bring misfortune and disease down upon the inhabitants of the areas affected, punishing them with dead cattle and drought.

When a rich and powerful prince wanted to build himself a permanent residence – and only such a man could venture to do such a thing in earlier days – and the ground had to be excavated in order to lay foundations, the lamaist priests soothed and pacified the restless, angry 'Lords of the Earth' by prayer and sacrifice, banished the evil spirits of the place and made them docile. In such circumstances it is understandable that systematic archaeological excavation in Mongolia ran into considerable difficulties. Any attempt to dig the soil was soon met by protests from the lama priests or from an alarmed population. The German geophysicist, Wilhelm Filchner, reporting on his great geophysical exploration along the Mongol-Tibetan border in 1934–36, describes how he was not even allowed to sink stones in the ground as fixed points for measuring the terrestrial magnetism; they were immediately removed by the superstitious population and carried off.

As a result, any major excavations of burial-grounds in Mongolia had to be deferred until such time as the influence of lamaism as a religion had receded. It is only in the last two decades that Russian and, in increasing numbers, Mongolian scholars have begun to excavate old towns and settlements in Northern Mongolia and particularly in the Mongolian People's Republic.

MASS-DESTRUCTION OF ARCHIVES?

For a long time it was thought that nothing whatsoever remained of the literary works or of the archives from the Mongol period in the thirteenth and fourteenth centuries. A group of scholars took the view that the responsibility for this lay with the Chinese, who, after almost a century and a half of oppression by the Mongols, had given vent to their pent-up hatred. After the Chinese national independence movement had brought about the collapse of Mongol rule in 1363 and the Chinese, led by a former Buddhist monk, had placed a national Chinese dynasty, the Ming dynasty, on the throne of China, such was the thirst for revenge on the part of the Chinese against their former oppressors that they destroyed all the evidence of Mongol rule. According to this school of thought, Mongol writings also disappeared during this outbreak of mass-emotion. But was it really credible that every hand-written document could have been destroyed or could have disappeared, which covered a period of 162 years – if one reckons from 1206, when Jenghiz Khan united the Mongols, until 1368, when the Chinese drove the last Mongol Emperor, Toghon temür, out of Peking? The story of the *Secret History* alone suggests otherwise, as I have shown in Chapter I.

According to another school of thought, the barbaric, half-savage Mongols were so bowled over by the high culture of the Chinese that they quickly, within a few decades, adopted the Chinese script and language. The result was that in those two centuries nothing was written in Mongolian.

As things turned out, neither of these two views was correct. In the first instance, the only discoveries that were made in Mongolian language and script from the period of Jenghiz Khan and his immediate successors were made in the outlying provinces and border areas of the Mongol Empire in the middle ages. They were mainly coins from the Golden Horde in Russia, from Persia, East Turkestan and Siberia. There were also a few documents, which the Mongol rulers of Persia, Argun and Öldsheitü had addressed to the French king, Philip the Fair, in 1289 and 1305. In Russia a number of hand-written decrees from the Mongol rulers of the Golden Horde had also been found in the archives. But all these manuscripts merely threw some light on the administration of parts of the Mongol Empire and on their political relations with the Occident. There was nothing from the Mongols' own country. None of the letters and decrees which have been discovered throws any light on the poetry and literature of the Mongols.

Yet another school of thought sprang up. It argued that few if any documents were likely to be discovered concerning the heart of the Mongol Empire, in other words modern Mongolia and China, since in 1294 the Emperor Kublai, Jenghiz Khan's grandson, had commissioned his adviser in religious and cultural affairs, the Tibetan Buddhist monk Phagspa, to devise a special script, which he then introduced as the imperial script. According to this third group of scholars, this new imperial script of Kublai's replaced the old Uigur-Mongolian script throughout the whole of the central Mongol Empire. Was this perhaps the reason why, right up to the end of the last century, almost no documents in the Uigur-Mongolian script had been found?

DISCOVERIES IN EAST TURKESTAN'S OASES

About 1900, when the British explorer of Hungarian extraction, Sir Aurel Stein, was travelling in the oases of Eastern Turkestan, he came upon a Buddhist cave-temple at Tunhuang, in which he found concealed in a small box-room thousands of scrolls and sheets of manuscript in Chinese, Uigur, Tibetan and Soghdian script from the seventh century A.D.

Such was the reverence felt by the devout Buddhists for anything written that they had not thrown away or burnt manuscripts which were either illegible or incomplete, but had bundled them together with other odd leaves of manuscript and stacked them all in a remote but safe part of the temple, where they were to be left unused for the rest of time. This form of reverent burial of incomplete manuscripts was practised for centuries. Almost every lamaist monastery in Mongolia and in Tibet had a tiny chapel called the Bungchang, in which manuscripts which were no longer needed were stored. For the research-worker these manuscript-cemeteries were veritable treasure-houses.

Sir Aurel Stein's first expedition to Eastern Turkestan and its oases was followed by an invasion of western scholars. Paul Pelliot, the famous French orientalist, brought a rich store of manuscripts back to Paris. From 1902 onwards the first and until 1907 the second and third Prussian Turfan Expeditions worked in the desert oases of northern East Turkestan round the Turfan Depression. Under the leadership of Albert von LeCoq and A. Grünwedel they discovered not only the wonderful wall-paintings in the abandoned cave-temples, which are now exhibited in the Ethnological Museum at Berlin-Dahlem, but also hundreds of fragments of manuscripts in Uigur, Syrian, Tibetan, Chinese and Turkish script with works from the field of Buddhism.

When these were examined in Berlin, it was discovered that in 1904 certain manuscripts in a variation of the Syrian script had been found in the Turfan oases, which F. W. K. Müller, the versatile philologist of the Ethnological Museum, had identified as relics of the lost literature of the Manichees. It was found possible to put other manuscript fragments together and reconstruct Buddhist works in Sanskrit and Chinese, while others gave an insight into the unknown literature of the Uigurs.

Side by side with Buddhist texts in the almost indecipherable Soghdian script there were Nestorian-Christian tracts. The de-

ciphering of these fragments that had one particularly happy out-
come was the rediscovery of an Iranian literary language, which
had once been widely used but had since completely disappeared,
namely Soghdian, the language of the inhabitants of ancient Soghd
or Soghdiana with its twin capitals, Samarkand and the rich and
famous city of Bukhara.

The deciphering of these manuscripts took a great many years.
The preliminary work was done by the two men who had discovered
them, LeCoq and Grünwedel, and F. W. K. Müller.

Work on this rich store of manuscripts, which throw more and
more light on the religions and cultures of Central Asia in the
middle ages, is still continuing and is likely to continue for a long
time to come. It has, however, produced something new for the
student of Mongolia.

Among the many fragments of manuscripts and scraps of printed
paper, which the Prussian Turfan Expeditions recovered from the
sand, there were twenty-five pieces of Mongolian manuscript and
prints from the fourteenth century. This disproved, at least par-
tially, the theory of mass-destruction by the Chinese. The Mongolian manuscript fragments were not identified for some time.
The Uigur script on the many Uigur documents that were found
and the Uigur-Mongolian script of the fragments are remarkably
similar. The credit for distinguishing the Mongolian fragments
from the thousands of Uigur fragments must go to the former
Berlin sinologist, Erich Haenisch.

Among the scraps of manuscript was a letter from Öld-
sheitemür and other local Mongol rulers. Among the fragments of
fourteenth-century prints were Buddhist hymns, prayers and, most
important of all, several pages of a Mongolian translation of a gloss
on a didactic Sanskrit work, the so-called Bodhicaryāvatāra.

This gloss on a book of instruction how to live in such a way as
to bring reincarnation as a Buddha-like Bodhisattva even carried a
date. The work of the famous translator, Chosgi odser, a Tibetan
in the service of the Mongol emperors, it had been cut into plates
and printed in 1312.

There was also a hymn to a tutelary god of lamaism, written by the same Chosgi odser. Only the conclusion of the Bodhicaryāvatāra fragment was there, a few longish pages in large format. But they served to prove something that had only been hinted at in the postscripts to editions of the same work from the early eighteenth century: that there actually were Mongolian printing-works in the fourteenth century. All this information has, of course, only come to light in the last twenty years, for it was only then that scholars began to take an active interest in the twenty-five Mongolian fragments from Idikutshähri near Turfan, which Le Coq had found there in the winter of 1902–03.

THE MONGOLS SANG OF ALEXANDER THE GREAT

Among the fragments of manuscript was a small bundle of papers, some of which were torn, while other pages were missing altogether. The first pages were in Turkish, giving the impression at a first glance that this was another of the many notebooks full of monetary data from the Uigur area in the ninth century. But then Nikolaus Poppe, who has since become Professor in Mongolian studies at the University of Washington in Seattle, discovered that the later pages contained a substantial portion of an epic. The hero of this song was called Sulkharnai. This is the Arabic name for Alexander the Great.

The song began:

> In ancient times there lived in the East
> In the town named Misir
> A man by the name of Sulkharnai.
> Reaching the age of a thousand years . . .

And it ended:

> 'It is over, is ended, ended!' thus spake he.
> 'Old men, be happy, all is vanity when one dies and comes
>   to an end!
> It is ended. Be happy.
> When one dies and comes to an end, all is vanity!

Let us be happy!
Let us be prosperous!'
Thus spake he. 'It is ended,' he said.

The song describes Alexander's adventures. He wants to live to the age of three thousand, crosses a long bridge of life, climbs up a high mountain, descends to the bottom of the sea, constantly searching for adventure and longevity. After he has crossed the land of darkness, he waters a tree with the water of life, and thereafter the tree remains for ever green. At the end of all his adventures he gathers his companions round him and tells them that he is the only king of the earth, who is destined to live for three thousand years. Then he gives instructions for his burial when the time comes for him to die.

A Mongol, who knew how to write, had heard this song of the adventures of the great Greek king, an excerpt from the Persian-Alexandrine romance, by some fireside in a caravanserai and had written it down in Mongolian.

Six hundred years later this relic of a native Mongolian literature in the thirteenth century was unearthed from the desert sand, which had preserved it for so long. The remainder of the volume contained a didactic Buddhist poem. But it too proved to be an original Mongolian work and not a translation. The manuscripts had to be stored away during the Second World War, so that half a century had passed since their discovery before the Mongolists Haenisch, Poppe and Cleaves identified and translated them.

IN THE RUINS OF KARAKOTO

In the first decade of the present century it seemed as if the golden age of research and discovery had begun in Central Asia. One major expedition followed another.

From 1907 to 1909 the Russian explorer P. Kozlov travelled through Mongolia and the Tibetan-Mongolian border area of Amdo to the ruins of the ancient capital of the Tangut kingdom, which Jenghiz Khan had conquered in 1226–27. It was a Russian Geographical Society expedition, which set out to reach Karakoto, the 'Black City', as the ruins were called. The massive square walls surrounding the ruins, each side of which is about 500 yards long, stand in the middle of the Gobi desert near Edsin Gol (41° 45' 4" latitude; 101° 5' 15" longitude).

'When we were no more than half-way we could detect traces of a former culture which were reminiscent of Karakoto,' Kozlov wrote in his diary. 'We found millstones, remains of irrigation-canals, pieces of clay and china dishes, etc. But by far the most amazing sight was the ruins of the gateways and the funeral pago-das, which stood singly, in pairs or in rows of five along both sides of the road leading to the ruined city.'

The expedition continued on its way to the ruined city over sand-dunes and dry river-beds. On a low terrace of coarse sandstone lay the ruins of the ancient walled city of the Tanghuts with its pattern of rectangular streets. Temples and many other buildings had been razed to the ground and were mere mounds of rubble, which con-sisted of sand, stones, potsherds, broken vessels and, here and there, a few metal objects usually of cast iron but occasionally of copper and very occasionally of silver. It was here that one of the most important discoveries of fourteenth-century Mongolian documents and prints was to be made.

Karakoto was the capital of the prosperous kingdom of Tanghut, which lay between China and Tibet proper. When Jenghiz Khan grew more and more powerful and became the real ruler of Inner Asia, the Tanghut king gave nominal recognition to the Mongol ruler's supremacy. But at that time the Mongols were busily engaged in campaigns against the wealthy city-states of Central Asia, so nominal recognition and the tributary payments it involved did not seriously affect the Tanghut state.

The Tanghuts were a sedentary and highly cultured people. Devout Buddhists, merchants and traders, they had a rich literature of their own in a script which has not yet been fully deciphered. Only where glossaries and texts in two languages are provided, in which the Tanghut characters are accompanied by their Chinese equivalent, do we know what the Tanghut characters of the Hsihsia

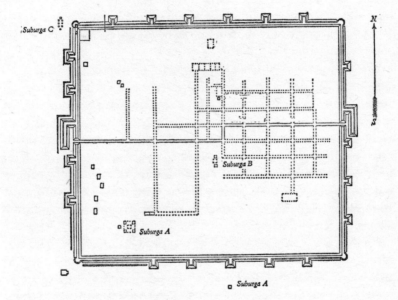

Ground plan of Karakoto

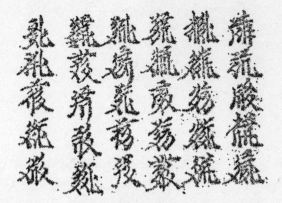

Tanghut characters

script mean. Otherwise the Tanghut manuscripts are still an unsolved riddle.

When Jenghiz Khan had returned from his conquest of Central Asia and was preparing to launch a major attack on China, he demanded troops from the Tanghuts amongst others. This was a binding obligation on a people which had submitted to Mongol domination. When the Mongols began their invasion of Northern China, there were, however, no Tanghut troops. Jenghiz Khan took his revenge for this breach of loyalty by his Tanghut allies in a ferocious punitive expedition on which the king of the Tanghuts was killed. According to Mongol legend he was slain by Jenghiz Khan in single combat, although he tried all the arts of sorcery.

The *Secret History of the Mongols* reports laconically: 'After he had turned the Tanghut people into slaves, the Ilukhu Burkhan into Shidurgu and then slain him, he gave orders for the Tanghut people, mothers and fathers and the whole community, to be exterminated to the last man.'

Among the Tanghut towns and settlements destroyed was Karakoto with its temples and fine buildings, its trading houses and caravanserais. The land of the Tanghuts, having been subdued, was incorporated in the administrative system of the great Mongol Empire.

By the time Jenghiz Khan's grandson Kublai had ascended the throne, normal life had been resumed in the Tanghut kingdom. The old script had been revived. In the many temples thousands of Tanghut monks prayed to Buddha. The Venetian traveller Marco Polo, who spent seventeen years in the service of the Mongol Emperor Kublai, reported in detail on life in the land of the Tanghuts.

Karakoto also took on a new lease of life. From 1286 it was a Mongol garrison town, until some time after the end of Mongol rule in China, after 1368, the garrisons were withdrawn and the city gradually fell into decay. When exactly this happened is not known. Shortage of water, due to the drying up of the Gobi basin, must have been a decisive factor in its decline.

The Torguts of Western Mongolia, kinsmen of the Volga Kalmuks who live with their herds on the Edsin Gol, had known Karakoto as an abandoned ruin for many generations and kept anxious watch over it, lest the repose of the dead city and its spirits should be disturbed. Now and then a particularly courageous Torgut had entered the empty city to look for hidden treasure which, according to local hearsay, lay buried under the ruins.

In March 1907, after Kozlov had spent several days digging in Karakoto, he had to pay a visit to the prince of the Torguts. He was given a very friendly reception. At the end of the audience the prince offered to take a charred sheep's shoulder-bone from the fire and read the future in it, as the Mongols had done for hundreds of years. This kind of fortune-telling was a highly-respected art. In Western libraries today there are manuscripts containing the rules for this form of prophecy.

When my English friend and colleague, Dr Charles Bawden, examined these manuscripts some years ago, he followed the rules laid down in them and burned many sheep's shoulders in the open fire of his house in England but his family finally persuaded him to stop. In the first place, they were tired of eating mutton week after week, and secondly the smell of the smouldering bones was too much even for the patience of a scholar's family.

In 1907 the Torgut prince made the following prophecy from

the charred sheep's bone: 'Tomorrow the leader of the expedition may expect two joyful events. The first will bring him very great joy. The other will bring him less joy but will nevertheless be very welcome. And the great joy will come from a very rich and very important discovery from the excavations . . .'

The following day in the ruins of Karakoto Kozlov actually found a large number of manuscripts in all kinds of Inner Asian languages.

Kozlov's greatest discovery at Karakoto, however, was not made until April 1909, when he was on his way back from Amdo and, on behalf of the Russian Academy of Sciences, carried out further excavations in the ruined city. This time conditions were much less favourable. Summer was approaching and it was already hot. The enormous clouds of dust imposed a heavy strain on the excavators. To make matters worse, the initial discoveries they made were negligible. Kozlov therefore decided to dig in a pagoda outside the walls.

The change of site was more than justified. 'Here,' reported Kozlov, 'we found an entire store of antiquities which had remained untouched since time immemorial. A whole library came to light, countless scrolls and manuscripts, together with some three hundred Buddhist graven images, a number of statues, wooden busts, models of Suburghans and much else besides. All these objects were intact, due to the continuous aridity. Most of the discoveries, although they had lain under the earth for centuries, gave an impression of complete freshness.'

When the Kozlov expedition had returned to Russia and examined its discoveries more closely, it found that they included seventeen Mongolian documents. Most of them were fragments of letters, which give an insight into the daily life of a Mongolian garrison town. One letter had been written to announce a gift. In another letter the writer complained of the theft of a horse. Many of the fragments were of loan-contracts and loan-repayments. Debtors, guarantors and witnesses had given their names and affixed their sign and seal. One manuscript consisted of thirty-four folios, giving rules for determining auspicious as well as unlucky days.

Finally there was one sheet of paper with only fourteen lines of the old Mongolian script. It gave the name of one of Jenghiz Khan's most faithful companions, the Bugurchi noyan. It also contained one of Jenghiz Khan's rules of life, which have been preserved in various earlier manuscripts and in Mongolian works of history, after having been passed down by word of mouth among many Mongol tribes. But none of these utterances of the first Mongol ruler could compare with the old fragment from Karakoto.

Among the relics found were the remains of block-prints in Mongolian language. 'Up to the present,' wrote Professor Kotwicz in 1923, until then the only one who had studied the Mongolian texts from Karakoto, 'we have never found a Mongolian print which goes back farther than the middle of the seventeenth century.' Kotwicz clearly had not yet heard of the large print-fragment of 1312, which the first Prussian Turfan Expedition had discovered in 1902–03.

The fourteenth-century Mongolian scripts and prints found at Karakoto were removed from their dry, protective coffin of desert sand in 1909, but ever since then they have been lying in the archives of the Soviet Academy of Sciences in Leningrad. Apart from the first general description by Kotwicz and the photographic reproduction of one of the promissory notes, nothing has been seen or heard of them since. The spirits of the dead Mongol soldiers from Karakoto still keep their secrets.

A SOLDIER'S GRAVE ON THE VOLGA

The next discovery of a classic of old Mongolian literature was made quite by chance.

In 1930 an agricultural worker on a Kolkhoz on the Volga came upon a grave. When he looked more closely at the bones, he noticed a bundle of birch-bark, which the dead man had been holding when he was laid to rest. The birch-bark was covered with strange characters which the worker had never seen before. Fortunately he did not throw it away, although the sheets of bark had been saturated by moisture from the corpse and was heavily discoloured.

He took the bundle of bark to someone who was interested in the antiquities of the Volga area.

Archaeologists examined what remained of the burial garments. They came to the conclusion that it was the grave of a simple Mongol soldier not of a nobleman of the 'Golden Horde'.

It is here in Southern Russia on the Volga that the descendants of Jenghiz Khan's eldest son Jochi, who had been allotted the western part of the Empire, had their seat. Under Batu Khan (1237–56) this branch of the Mongols strengthened their hold on Russia. On one arm of the Volga not far from the modern Stalingrad, now known as Volgograd, Batu Khan built his capital Oldsarai, to which the Mongol armies came surging back after they had beaten the German-Polish knights at Liegnitz in 1241 and had wiped out the Hungarian knights at Mohacz. It was here on 8th August 1253 that the Flemish Franciscan monk Wilhelm von Rubruck, whom King Louis IX of France had sent as an emissary, met Batu Khan. The Mongol camp was so vast that Rubruck, who was after all not unfamiliar with large encampments, was struck dumb with amazement: 'For the tents belonging to him alone,' he reported, 'gave the impression of a great, elongated town and they were surrounded by settlements to a depth of three or four miles.'

The simple Mongol warrior, in whose grave the written sheets of birch-bark had been found, must have been a descendant of the Mongols who took part in the great Western campaign. For on the reverse side of these bark-sheets are words in the square script which the Emperor Kublai introduced after 1294. So the dead soldier can only have been laid in the grave *after* that year and with him the birch manuscript.

In Central Asia people frequently wrote on birch-bark. If there was no other suitable material for writing ready to hand, the thin, white bark was stripped from the birch-tree and was then used for paper.

A few texts on birch-bark had been found in Turfan. More than a hundred years ago a Mongolian-Buddhist text from the early seventeenth century, which is written on birch-bark, was regarded as one of the curiosities of the Royal Library in Copenhagen.

But the birch-trunks only provided relatively small pieces of bark that were suitable for writing. So even a short message had to be written on many sheets of bark. Only a few sheets have survived.

The manuscript found on the dead soldier on the Volga consisted of some twenty-five sheets, nineteen of which had writing on both sides. Age, water and decay combined had made long passages illegible. Only seven of the nineteen sheets were written in old Mongolian script. The remainder were in Uigur but completely illegible. Only isolated names could be deciphered.

The sheets covered with Mongolian script contained a poem in alliterative rhyme. Here and there parts of the rhyme were missing but there was no doubt that it was a poem.

It was the song addressed by a son to his mother, sung during the campaign out of longing for her and for his home. There is no trace of excitement over the campaign, no word of praise for the ruler. Simple longing for his mother, brothers and companions is reflected in these lines.

> ' . . . there will I go,
> O mother mine, heart's dearest!
> In the grass on the meadows the sap is rising,
> Dear friends begin to come,
> So I too am making for my dear home!'

And the song ends:

> 'And at this moment, as I fly up,
> I call to
> My mother, my heart's dearest:
> The mountains are full of meadow-grass,
> The dear brothers are preparing to come,
> Now I am returning home, to be there always!'

This was as much as could be reconstructed of this song, one of the earliest specimens of thirteenth-century Mongolian folk-poetry. The former owner of the text, an unknown Mongolian warrior, was not granted his wish to return home. Today his song is preserved for science in the great collections of the Hermitage in Leningrad.

Archaeological Discoveries

Mongolia, both Inner Mongolia in the south and the Mongolian People's Republic in the north, is covered with a network of ancient ruined towns, walled fortifications and ramparts. In 1946 the former Scientific Committee of the Mongolian People's Republic, today an Academy of Sciences, listed twenty-seven ruined towns in the Mongolian People's Republic alone. In addition there are twenty long walls, most of which have been ascribed to Jenghiz Khan, although in fact they go back a great deal further.

There is a similar picture in Inner Mongolia, where the ruins have not yet been listed but are none the less very numerous.

Right across the broad pastures of the steppe and along the Hsingan mountains stretch various walls and systems of fortifications, which go back, for the most part, to the time of the Wei (A.D. 220–29) and Chin (A.D. 265–420) dynasties. Lintung, Borogohoto and Tsaghan suburga in the eastern part of Inner Mongolia are old capitals of the Liao kingdom from the eleventh and twelfth centuries and have been explored by archaeologists.

Not many of the ruined towns in Mongolia date from the period of Mongol rule. Many are older, as, for example, Kara balgasaun or 'black town', which was the capital of the Uigur kingdom in the ninth century (A.D. 745–840) on the left bank of the river Orchon.

The ruined towns of Charuchain Kara balgasun, Chin tologoi and Bars choto date back to the time of the Kitans in the eleventh and twelfth centuries (916 to 1125). Other square, walled-in enclosures, such as the one near the present capital, are remains of fortified Hun camps.

But the Mongols frequently used the material from old ruins for fresh buildings. Within the old walled enclosures are ruins of medieval Buddhist monasteries, which were built with old bricks. One of these old ruined monasteries lies inside the mud walls of Charuchain Kara balgasun. The oldest Buddhist monastery in Northern Mongolia, Erdeni dshu, which was founded in 1586, was built with bricks from the neighbouring ruins of Jenghiz Khan's capital, Karakorum.

Very few of the old ruined towns of the medieval Mongol period have been excavated. Karakorum, the ancient capital of the Mongol Empire, has been under excavation since 1949 by Mongolian scholars and the Russian archaeologist Kiselev. Successive layers to a depth of several yards were found, corresponding to successive waves of settlers.

They were crammed with wrought-iron work and ceramics, mostly of Chinese origin. The foundation-walls of the great palace and throne-room, in which the Mongol Khans Ogotai and Mangu resided, were also uncovered. But the excavators found Buddhist frescoes, which show that, even before the Mongol palace was built on this site, a Buddhist temple had stood there.

In the thirteenth century Karakorum was one of the most important cities in the world, the seat of the Great Khan, to whom Popes and the French king, Louis IX, sent emissaries. Captives from Hungary, a master goldsmith from Lorraine, William, and his son, and a courtesan from Paris, Moslem traders and merchants, Uigur scholars, Nestorian-Christian monks lived side by side in Karakorum with Mongol soldiers and courtiers.

The Franciscan monks who came as emissaries to the Mongol court in the thirteenth century have left us colourful and enthusiastic descriptions of this fortified city in the heart of Mongolia. Father Wilhelm von Rubruck, who went to Karakorum as an emissary of Louis IX, later St Louis, from 1253 to 1255, paints a vivid picture of the Mongol Emperor's palace and of the wonderful things which Master William of Paris, the Lorraine goldsmith, had created there at the Khan's behest. He wrote:

'Mangu (Mangu Khan) has a large palace in Karakorum, which is not far from the city walls. This palace is surrounded by a brick wall, just as our monasteries are enclosed within walls. There too is a large castle, in which the Khan holds a great feast twice a year . . .'
In the same place are many buildings elongated in shape like barns,

in which his food supplies and treasures are stored. At the entrance to this great castle, where the carrying of skins of milk and other drinks presented an unattractive spectacle, William of Paris fashioned a large tree made of silver, at the roots of which lay four silver lions. Inside each lion is a pipe and from the mouths of all four comes white mare's milk. Inside the trunk of the tree are four pipes leading up to the crown, the ends of which are bent outwards, and round each of these a golden snake is coiled, its tail being round the trunk of the tree. From one of these pipes comes wine, from another Karakosmos, which is purified mare's milk, from the third bal, which is a drink made from honey, and from the fourth comes a wine made from rice which is called terracina.'

Rubruck was impressed by the size of the imperial palace and of the city. He wrote: 'This palace is built like a church: It has a nave and two aisles behind two rows of pillars and three doors facing south, and before the middle entrance stands the tree . . . As far as the city of Karakorum is concerned, you must know that, apart from the Khan's castle, it is not so imposing as the town of St Denis, and the monastery of St Denis is ten times larger than the castle. There are two quarters: one is the Saracen quarter, where the markets are held and where many traders come together on account of the court which is always held nearby, and also on account of the crowd of ambassadors, and the other is the quarter of the Chinese, who are all artisans. Outside this quarter stand the large houses belonging to the court-scribes. There are twelve temples dedicated to the idols of the various peoples, two mosques in which the law of Mohammed is taught, and a Christian church at the extreme end of the town. The city itself is surrounded by a mud wall, which has four gates. At the eastern gate millet is sold and other species of grain, which, however, are rarely imported here. At the western entrance sheep and goats are sold, at the southern entrance oxen and carts, and at the northern entrance horses.'

Much of this has been confirmed by the excavations so far carried out in Karakorum. A large number of brightly-coloured Chinese

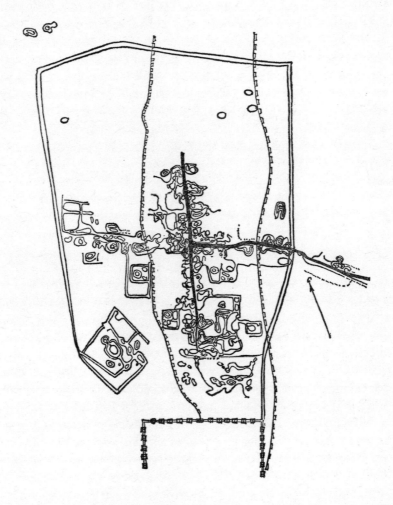

Ground plan of Karakorum

ceramics, brightly coloured majolica tiles from the ruined roofs, and iron-work of all kinds, arms, wheel-hubs, ploughshares and basins were found. Only one thing has not so far come to light in the course of these excavations: Mongolian manuscripts.

The Japanese excavations at Shang-tu, the summer residence of the Mongol Khan Kublai, which were carried out in 1939, also failed to reveal any books, documents or letters. On the other hand, the large cemetery on the edge of the old town of Shang-tu was left undisturbed. It was there that a discovery like the one on the Volga was most likely.

In all the excavations so far made, of course, the aim has been not to make a systematic search for old documents but to measure and photograph the ruins of the walls. It is hard to believe that some relics at least of the archives and the writings of that period are not buried in the sand. The experience gained at other places supports this.

THE TOWN OF MANY TEMPLES

In 1929 a member of Sven Hedin's Sino-Swedish Expedition, Mr Huang Wen-pi, who was excavating some twelve miles north of the lamaist monastery of Pailingmiao in Inner Mongolia, came upon the ruins of a walled town, which the Mongols called Olon süme, 'the ruins of many temples'. In the great walled enclosure, 1,000 by 600 yards, there were large heaps of stones and tiles. A large number of foundations in solid stone showed that at one time many imposing buildings, palaces and temples had stood there.

A little later, in 1932, the American expert on Mongolia, Owen Lattimore, visited the ruins. He found a great many stone pillars on which the cross of the Nestorian-Christians had been chiselled, and he came to the conclusion that this had been a large town which must at one time have been an important Nestorian-Christian centre. The local sagas and fairy-tales all referred to these ruins as 'bewitched'. A large part of the ruins consists of the foundation-walls of a great lamaist temple. In it stood a large black stone bearing a Mongolian inscription, part of which had been erased by

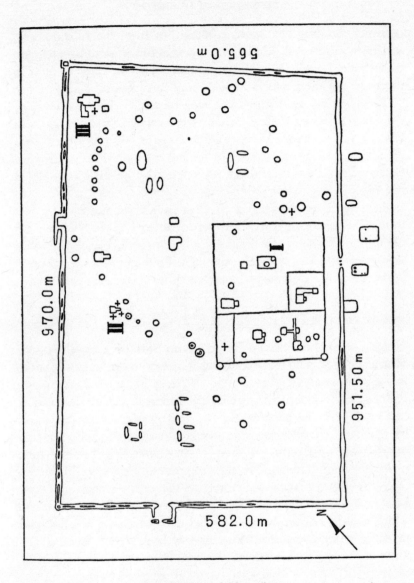

Ground plan of Olon süme

the ravages of time. It mentioned Altan Khan the Tumat, the great champion of Buddhism in the sixteenth century, who died in 1583.

At another point within the enclosure a group of ruins in white marble was found. It bore the names of Mongols in Chinese characters. From this and from the presence of the Nestorian crosses Lattimore rightly deduced that the town had enjoyed at least two periods of prosperity – one in the thirteenth century, another shortly before and shortly after the year 1600.

Two years after Lattimore, the Japanese archaeologist Namio Egami also went to Olon süme and saw the inscription on the marble. In fact there were two inscriptions: One from the year 1308 was in honour of a Chinese adviser to the king of the Onguts. The second inscription from the year 1347 gave the genealogy of the Ongut royal family as drawn up by a certain Alachus bis Batutemür.

Egami had a flash of inspiration. The papal legate Johannes of Montecorvino, who had been dispatched to the seat of the Mongol Emperor in 1291 as the first Archbishop of Peking, had referred in a report he sent to the Pope on 8th January 1305 to a king of the Onguts, one of the Nestorian Christian tribes to the north-west of Peking. 'A certain king of this part of the world,' Montecorvino wrote, 'named George . . . attached himself to me in the first year of my stay here and took the first vows, after he had been converted by me to the true Catholic faith . . . He brought a large part of his people with him to the true Catholic faith and built a church in truly kingly splendour . . .'

The names given in the Chinese inscription of 1347 at Olon süme were the same as those mentioned in Montecorvino's report. Were the ruins of Olon süme in fact the former capital of King George of the Onguts? If so, then there must be some trace left of the church referred to by Montecorvino.

REMAINS OF A GOTHIC CHAPEL IN MONGOLIA

In 1938 the Academy of Oriental Cultures in Tokyo organized an expedition led by Egami to explore Olon süme.

On this occasion the Japanese scholar actually discovered the remains of a building with cruciform foundations in the north-eastern part of the walled enclosure. The tiles discovered in the ruins, however, bore a Gothic-style leaf-pattern in high relief and were covered with dark blue glazing. The remains of a badly-damaged statue in European style were also found.

Egami had discovered the ruins of the Catholic church founded in 1292 by Archbishop Montecorvino. Yet another riddle of Central Asia's medieval history had been solved. Furthermore, the discovery also confirmed the accuracy of reports by the first Catholic monks in China in the thirteenth and fourteenth centuries.

So far as hand-written documents were concerned, Egami did not discover any of the twelfth or thirteenth century at Olon süme, such as had been found at Karakoto and Turfan. But he did find important pieces of manuscript from the sixteenth century, the second golden age of Olon süme.

Naturally the interest of the archaeologists centred round the exciting discovery of the Gothic church ruins. But between the ruins of the former palace and the ruins of the Gothic church is a hill about sixty feet across at the base, on which stand the remains of a pagoda.

Egami believes that the old, ruined lama temple in Olon süme was originally surrounded by 108 pagodas or stupas. In the ruins of the pagoda was a small cave, which Egami investigated one day out of sheer curiosity, In it he found a number of small clay models of the pagoda. Amongst them were several Mongolian and Tibetan manuscrips.

A family of mice had built a nest among the clay models, using scraps of paper from the manuscripts to line it. Egami's first haul was twenty fragments of prayers and manuals of astrology, together with a hand-written message from a princess to the abbot of a monastery.

When these fragments were later studied, they gave a valuable insight into the cultural life of a Mongol prince's court and a monastery in the early sixteenth century. So quite by chance a discovery was made, which threw a little light on one of the most obscure periods of Mongol history. For much less is known about the everyday life of the Mongols in the fifteenth and sixteenth centuries than is known about the period of Jenghiz Khan and his more immediate successors.

All we know about the Mongols of the fifteenth and sixteenth centuries has come mainly from contemporary Chinese accounts, and the Chinese were naturally prejudiced against the wild horsemen from beyond the Great Wall, who were continually overrunning the weak border-garrisons and then attacking and plundering the Chinese farm settlements. Sometimes they advanced almost as far as the capital Peking.

On one such occasion in 1449 they took the Chinese Emperor, Ying Tsung, prisoner and only released him many years later against a high ransom. So the Chinese of the Ming dynasty (1368–1644) had no reason to feel well-disposed towards the Mongols. This is reflected in their reports on their unruly northern neighbours, whom they referred to as 'barbarians'.

Hsiao Ta-heng, who was adviser to the Chinese Emperor on matters concerning the northern barbarians, wrote of them around 1594:

'The barbarians are by nature naïve and simple . . . If a barbarian can write . . . this entitles him to a higher position among the ordinary barbarians. That is why the barbarians have so much respect for the Bakshi . . . At present they employ wooden boards or hides to write on. Since they have been subjugated and pay tribute to China, we give them paper and brush but the paper is used only to write down reminiscences of the Emperor. Those who have learned to write also make use of wooden boards, which they prepare much as we prepare our lacquer boards, only they are much more uneven. They do not use the brush for writing but employ a reed instead . . .'

But very few written documents from that period had come to light, until Egami discovered a large number of fragments in a clearly definable area, the Tumat area, home of Altan Khan.

Archaeological Discoveries

Fate seemed to be against the excavations and discoveries at Olon süme. Although Namio Egami was able to return there in 1941 and again in 1944, any systematic archaeological exploration was out of the question.

The Second World War had broken out. At first Japan's position in Inner Mongolia was militarily secure but over the next few years it rapidly deteriorated till only the fortified places and the lines of communication were garrisoned. The open country was a no-man's-land, into which pro-Chinese Mongolian partisans and units of the 8th Communist Chinese Army penetrated more or less at will.

In such circumstances Egami's last visit to Olon süme in 1944 was very brief and the object of it was not so much to excavate as to investigate and explore the ruins which had already been excavated. But Egami paid one more visit to the mousehole in the large pagoda. All he was able to extract was scraps of paper and potsherds encrusted with clay. He took them back with him largely out of curiosity, and on his way home he also collected several sheets of charred manuscript from the monastery of Pailingmiao, which had been attacked and burnt down by partisans. Back in Tokyo he soon forgot about the clay-encrusted scraps of paper.

When the war ended, the relics found at Olon süme together with other objects excavated and collected in China had to be returned to the Chinese by Japan.

Nothing is known of their present whereabouts. One cannot even be certain that they ever reached China. It seems likely that the remains of Montecorvino's Gothic church together with the fragments of Mongolian manuscript have been lost for ever. All that survived was a small piece of blue-glazed tile with the Gothic leaf-pattern, which had somehow been overlooked when the relics were packed for dispatch to China and which Egami found later. He presented it to the Musée Guimet in Paris, that world-renowned storehouse of art treasures from Central Asia, in order that anyone should have access to it.

Archaeological Discoveries

Professor Egami told me of the sad fate of his discoveries at Olon süme in 1962, as we sat together in the Institute for Oriental Cultures in Tokyo. I asked Professor Egami about other manuscripts, for I had come to Japan to look for specimens of old Mongolian handwriting. Egami said he had nothing left, except microfilms of the fragments from Olon süme, but I was already familiar with them. There were, too, a few charred pieces of paper which he had rescued from the monastery of Pailingmiao and brought back in 1944. I naturally wanted to see them and was duly shown them.

There was nothing important amongst them which was not already included in comprehensive or complete manuscripts in other libraries. But finding nothing is part of the adventure of searching. There remained one small tattered roll of paper, wrapped round what looked like a matchbox, torn and worm-eaten. This was all that was left of a mouse's nest from the pagoda of Olon süme, which had been brought back merely as a souvenir and was otherwise quite worthless!

I was given permission to take the roll of clay to pieces and to detach the various scraps of paper. I spent hour after hour, day after day cleaning and rubbing, picking and scratching off the clay. I finally succeeded in detaching seventeen fragments of Mongolian manuscript. The mouse's nest at Olon süme proved to be an important find. Among the manuscripts it contained were a loan-agreement and fragments of Buddhist prayers. One of these fragments was part of a prayer against strife and witchcraft, which was in a form known to have been devised after 1587. This together with the names of grandsons of the Tumat prince Altan Khan given in the stone inscription found at Olon süme, whose life and spiritual activities were described in these fragments, around the late sixteenth and early seventeenth centuries. One piece of manuscript contained the remains of a hymn to Buddha, while another was a fragment of a didactic poem, which praised the worthy dignitary and Minister.

Most of the other fragments and, in particular, a large piece containing several lines proved to be parts of a Mongolian translation by the monk Chosgi odser in 1305 of the Buddhist manual of morals, Bodhicaryāvatāra.

One page of this manuscript had been among those previously discovered by Egami in 1938 at Olon süme. Other parts of the same work had now come to light. The individual scraps of manuscript fitted with fragments discovered in 1938, which until now had defied identification. When I had completed the laborious task of identification and collation, I found I had passages from the first, eighth and ninth chapters of this rare work.

The mice of Olon süme had rescued these important relics of medieval Mongolian literature. What they had failed to gnaw away was sufficient to give an insight into this sixteenth-century Mongolian community. And paper had been so scarce and so precious that princes, who were learning to write, had written their names clumsily between the lines.

There remains only one final question: how had all these various pieces of paper, on which loan-agreements and prayers, hymns and medical recipes were inscribed, come to be in the pagoda of Olon süme? Was the pagoda used as one of these secret and holy places, in which manuscripts which were no longer of use and loose pages from old books were preserved? Was this one of those graveyards of sacred scripts? Perhaps the industrious mice of Olon süme had collected the various sheets of paper from some archives, from a former monastery library, in order to line their nest. Or had important secular documents and sacred writings been brought to safety in the pagoda to preserve them against some threat and the monks had been unable to take them out again?

As long as further research and excavation in the ruins of Olon süme is forbidden, these questions must remain unanswered.

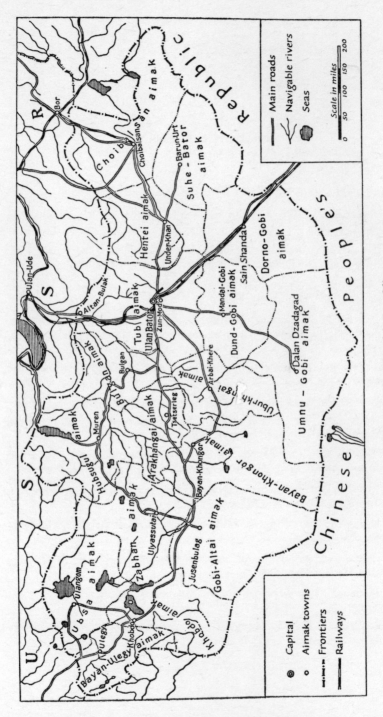

The Mongolian People's Republic

BIBLIOGRAPHY

VOICES FROM THE PAST

Roger von Varasdin, Carmen miserabile, Scriptores Rerum Hungaricarum I, 1937.

I. Baranov, Portrctnaja gallerija mongolskoj dinastii, Memoirs of the Club of Natural Science and Geography of the YMCA, Harbin 1941.

A. Mostaert, A Propos de quelques portraits d'empereurs Mongols, *Asia Maior* IV, Leipzig 1927.

W. Hung, The Transmission of the book known as the Secret History of the Mongols, *Harvard Journal of Asiatic Studies* 14, Cambridge (Mass.) 1951.

S. D. Dylykov, Edžen-choro. Filologija i isorija Mongol'skich narodov, Moscow, 1958.

B. L. Putnam Weale, Indiscreet Letters from Peking, London, 1906.

E. Haenisch, Die Schriftfrage im mongolischen Ostreich. Oriente Poliano, Rome 1957.

G. Doerfer, Zur Daticrung der Geheimen Geschichte der Mongolen, *Zeitschrift der Deutschen Morgenländischen Gesellshaft* 113, 1963.

O. Franke, Zur Frage der ursprunglichen Schriftform des Yuan-ch'ao pi-shih, *Studia Serica* X, Chengtu 1951.

E. Haenisch, Die Mongolei-Bilder aus alter und neuer Zeit, *Der Orient in deutscher Forschung.*

E. Haenisch, Untersuchungen über das Yüan-ch'ao pi-shih, die Geheime Geschichte der Mongolen, Leipzig 1931.

E. Haenisch, Die Geheime Geschichte der Mongolen, Leipzig 1941; Leipzig 1948.

C. Ž. Žamcarano, The Mongol Chronicles of the Seventeenth century, Moscow–Leningrad 1936; Wiesbaden 1955.

Bibliography

F. Bischoff, Eine buddhistische Wiedergabe christlicher Bräuche, *Monumenta Serica* XX, Nagoya 1961.

W. Heissig, Einige Bemerkungen über die Köke usudr, eine neuere mongolische Darstellung der Yüan-Zeit, *Monumenta Serica* VIII, Peking 1943.

Erdenitoghtachu, Indschanaschi, Köke Khota 1958.

Namžilcewen, Höh sudryn sudlalyn tobclol, Ulan Bator 1959.

FROM PEKING TO MOSCOW

R. A. Rupen, Mongolia in the Sino-Soviet Dispute, *The China Quarterly* 1963.

P. Pelliot and L. Hambis, Histoire des Campagnes de Gengis Khan, Leiden 1951

R. Grousset, L'Empire Mongol, Paris 1941.

B. J. Vladimircov, The Life of Chingis-Khan, London 1930.

H. Desmond Martin, The Rise of Chingis Khan and his Conquest of North China, Baltimore 1950.

R. H. van Gulik and Pi Hsi T'u K'ao, Erotic Colour Prints of the Ming Period, Tokyo 1951.

R. H. van Gulik, Sexual Life in China, Leiden 1961.

H. Schulte-Uffelage, Das Keng-Shen-Wai-Shih, eine Quelle zur späten Mongolenzeit Munich 1955, Berlin 1963.

W. Heissig, Mongolenreiche, in: *Propläen Weltgeschichte, Bd.* VI, Berlin 1964.

I. Ch. Ovdienko, Vnutrennaja Mongolija, Moscow 1954.

W. Heissig, Die Schwänke des – Verrükten – Šagdar (Festschrift für Erich Haenisch) Wiesbaden 1961.

REMAINS OF THE PAST

C. D. Barkmann, The Return of the Torghuts from Russia to China. *Journal of Oriental Studies* II, Hongkong 1955.

B. V. Dolbetov, Sud'ba kalmykov, bgežavšich c Volgi. Karašarskoe chanstwo, *Ulan ʒalat* II, Prague 1928.

O. Franke, Leibniz und China, Gottfried Wilhelm Leibniz, Hamburg 1946.

Bibliography

W. Heissig, Mongolisches Schrifttum im Lindenmuseum, *Tribus* VIII, Stuttgart 1959.

W. Heissig, Ein mongolisches Handbuch für die Herstellung von Schutzamuletten, *Tribus*, XI, Stuttgart 1962.

W. Heissig, Mongolische Handschriften, Blockdrucke, Landkarten. Wiesbaden 1961.

A. N. Pozdneev, Očerki byta buddijskich monastyrej, S. Petersburg 1837.

B. Ričnen, Üür-un tuyagha II, Peking 1953; Ulan Bator 1955.

O. Lattimore, Nationalism and Revolution in Mongolia, Leiden 1955.

J. F. Baddeley, Russia, Mongolia, China, London 1919.

N. Poppe, Renats Kalmuck Maps, *Imago Mundi* XII, 1955.

W. A. Berendson, The Oriental Studies of August Strindberg, *Central Asian Collectanea* 5, Washington 1960.

W. Heissig, Über mongolische Landkarten, *Monumenta Serica* IX, Peking 1944.

DANISH EXPEDITIONS IN MONGOLIA

K. Grønbech, Sprog og skrift i Mongoliet. Foreløbig beretning om det sproglige arbejde paa Det Kgl. Danske Geografisk Selskab Centralasiatiske Ekspedition 1938–39, *Geografisk Tidsskrift* 43, Copenhagen 1940.

K. Grønbech, Auszüge aus dem unveröffentlichten Expeditionstagebuch.

W. Heissig, Catalogue of Mongol Manuscripts, Xylographs and Books in the Royal Library Copenhagen (in preparation).

C. R. Bawden, On the Practice of Scapulimancy among the Mongols, *Central Asiatic Journal* IV, The Hague 1958.

C. R. Bawden, Astrologie und Divination bei den Mongolen: die schriftlichen Quellen, *Zeitschrift der Deutschen Morgenländischen Gesellschaft* 108, Wiesbaden 1958.

W. Heissig, Die mongolische Geschichtsschreibung im 18. und 19. Jh., *Saeculum* III, 1952.

W. Heissig, Die Familien- und Kirchengeschichtsschreibung der Mongolen, Wiesbaden 1959.

W. Heissig, Mongolische Literatur, Handbuch der Orientalistik, Bd. V, 1964.

Bibliography

THE TRAGEDY OF THE LAST GREAT KHAN

B. J. Vladimircov, Nadpisi na skalach chalchaskogo Tsoktu taidzi, Izvestija Akad. Nauk, 1926–1927.

W. Heissig, Zur geistigen Leistung der neubekehrten Mongolen des späten 16. und frühen 17. Jh., Ural-Altaische Jahrbücher 26, Wiesbaden 1954.

W. Heissig, Zur Entstehungsgeschichte der mongolischen Kandjur-Redaktion der Ligdan Khan-Zeit, Studia Altaica, Wiesbaden 1957.

W. Heissig, Beiträge zur Ubersetzungsgeschichte des mongolischen buddhistischen Kanons, *Abhandlungen der Akad. der Wissenschaften in Göttingen*, 1962.

THE EPIC OF GESER KHAN

W. Heissig, The Mongol Manuscripts and Xylographs of the Belgian Scheut-Mission, *Central Asian Journal* III, The Hague 1957.

W. Heissig, Helden-, Höllenfahrts- und Schelmengeschichten der Mongolen, Zürich 1962.

I. J. Schmidt, Die Thaten Bogda Gesser Chans, des Vertilgers der Wurzel der zehn Übel in den zehn Gegenden, S. Petersburg-Leipzig 1839.

B. Rinčen, Folklore Mongol III, Wiesbaden 1963.

LAMAIST MONKS DISPLACE THE SHAMANS

J. v. Hecken, Les Missions chez les Mongols aux Temps Modernes, Peiping 1949.

P. Fleming, The Siege at Peking, London 1959.

W. Heissig, Die Pekinger lamaistischen Blockdrucke in mongolischer Sprache, Wiesbaden 1954.

B. Laufer, Descriptive Account of the Collection of Chinese, Tibetan, Mongol, and Japanese Books in the Newberry Library, Chicago 1913.

B. Laufer, Skizze der mongolischen Literatur, *Keleti Szemle* VIII, Budapest 1907.

W. Heissig, Das mongolische Publikations- und Übersetzungswesen der Mandju-Zeit, *Sinologica* III, Basel 1953.

Š. Natsagdordsch, Halhyn tüüh, Ulan Bator 1963.

Bibliography

W. Heissig, Eine kleine mongolische Klosterbibliothek aus Tsachar, Jahrbuch d. Bernischen Hist. Museum, Bern 1961/62.

POLITICS IN NOTEBOOKS

O. Lattimore, The Mongols of Manchuria, London 1934.

W. Heissig, Ostmongolische Reise Darmstadt 1955.

A. N. Pozdneev, Mongolija i Mongoly, S. Petersburg 1896.

O. Lattimore, Nationalism and Revolution in Mongolia, Leiden 1955.

Dindob, Monggol-un tobči teüke, Ulan Bator 1934/35.

W. Heissig, A Description of the Mongolian Manuscripts in the University Library Oslo, *Acta Orientalia* XXIII.

Š. Natsagdordsch, Iz istorii aratskogo dviženija vo vnešnej Mongolii, Moscow 1958.

THE TWENTIETH CENTURY

R. A. Rupen, The Buriat Intelligentsia, *The Far Eastern Quarterly* XV, 1956.

R. A. Rupen, Cyben Žamcaranovič Žamcarano (1880?–1940), *Harvard Journal of Asiatic Studies* 19, Cambridge (Mass.) 1956.

E. M. Murzaev, Die mongolische Volksrepublik, Gotha 1954.

I. N. Ustjužaninov, Kul'tura mongol'skogo naroda, Mongol'skaja narodnaja respublika, Sbornik statej, Moscow 1952.

C. Ž. Žamcarano, Proizvedenija narodnoj slovesnosti burjat, Petrograd 1918.

C. D. Dylykov, Demokratičeskoe dvizenie Mongol'skogo Naroda v Kitae, Moscow 1953.

THEATRE IN THE YURT

Če. Damdinsürüng, Saran kökügen-u namtar, Corpus Scriptorum Mongolorum, Ulaanbaatar 1962.

Če. Damdinsürüng, Saran höhöönij duulalt žüžig, BNMAU *Sinzleh ubaany akademijin medee*, 1961/2.

Bibliography

ARCHAEOLOGICAL DISCOVERIES

E. Haenisch, Die geheime Geschichte der Mongolen aus einer mongolischen Niederschrift des Jahres 1240 von der Insel Kode'e im Keluren-FluB, Leipzig 1941.

A. v. LeCoq, Von Land und Leuten in Ost-Turkistan, Berlin 1928.

P. K. Kozlov, Mongolija i Amdo i mertvyj dorod Chara-choto, Moscow 1923.

F. W. Cleaves, An Early Mongolian Loan Contract from Qara Qoto, *Harvard Journal of Asiatic Studies* 18, Cambridge (Mass.) 1955.

Otto Franke, Geschichte des Chinesischen Reiches, IV, Berlin 1948.

E. Haenisch, Mongolica der Berliner Turfan-Sammlung. II. Mongolische Texte der Berliner Turfan-Sammlung in Faksimile, Berlin 1959.

V. S. Kiselev, Drevnije goroda Mongolii, *Sovjetskaja Archaeologija* 1957/2.

N. Poppe, Eine mongolische Fassung der Alexandersage, *Zeitschrift der Deutschen Morgenländischen Gesellschaft* 107, Wiesbaden 1957.

N. Poppe, Zolotoordynskaja rukopis' na bereste, *Sovetskoe Vostokovedenie* II, Moscow 1940.

O. Lattimore, A Ruined Nestorian City in Inner Mongolia, *The Geographical Journal* LXXXIV, 1934.

O. Lattimore, Mongol Journeys, London 1941.

N. Egami, Olon-Sume et la découverte de l'eglise catholique romaine de Jean de Montecorvino, *Journal Asiatique* CCXL, Paris 1952.

INDEX

INDEX